WORKBOOK

HARCOURT SCIENCE

Harcourt School Publishers

Orlando • Boston • Dallas • Chicago • San Diego

www.harcourtschool.com

Printed in the United States of America

ISBN 0-15-313182-9

27 28 29 30 1421 13 12 11 10 09

Contents

UNIT A Processes of Living Things

Chapter 1—From Single Cells to Body Systems	WB1–WB14
Chapter 2—Animal Growth and Reproduction	WB15–WB28
Chapter 3—Types of Plants and Their Adaptations	WB29–WB42
Chapter 4—Plant Processes	WB43–WB60

UNIT B Systems and Interactions in Nature

Chapter 1—Cycles in Nature	WB61–WB70
Chapter 2—Living Things Interact	WB71–WB88
Chapter 3—Biomes	WB89–WB98
Chapter 4—Protecting and Preserving Ecosytems	WB99–WB116

UNIT C Processes That Change the Earth

Chapter 1—Changes to Earth's Surface	WB117–WB130
Chapter 2—Renewable and Nonrenewable Resources	WB131–WB144
Chapter 3—Weather and Climate	WB145–WB158
Chapter 4—Exploring the Oceans	WB159–WB172

UNIT D

The Solar System and Beyond

Chapter 1—Earth, Moon, and Beyond WB173–WB182

Chapter 2—The Sun and Other Stars WB183–WB196

UNIT E

Building Blocks of Matter

Chapter 1—Matter and Its Properties WB197–WB210

Chapter 2—Atoms and Elements WB211–WB220

UNIT F

Energy and Motion

Chapter 1—Forces WB221–WB234

Chapter 2—Motion WB235–WB248

Chapter 3—Forms of Energy WB249–WB266

Chapter 4—How People Use Energy WB267–WB280

Name ___________________________

Reading in Science

Reading is very important in your becoming an independent learner–in being able to find, understand, and apply the information you need in the classroom and in your life. In science reading you are expected to find information, learn the meanings of scientific words, and put together ideas and observations. You can be helped in this reading and understanding by using the following suggestions.

To help you locate topics in *Harcourt Science* and most other science texts, use the:

- table of contents,
- titles of units, chapters, and lessons,
- headings and subheadings,
- index.

Look for and read these parts of a lesson in *Harcourt Science* to locate main ideas and other key information:

- Vocabulary Preview
- Investigate activity
- Process Skill Tip
- Find Out
- ✓ questions
- Picture captions
- Inside Story
- Summary
- Review
- Links
- Features

To help you recognize and read for specific kinds of information:

1. Recognize the text structure by looking for signal words
   - compare/contrast–*however, but, some, different, instead, on the other hand, like, unlike, both, neither*
   - sequence or how-to–*first, second, next, then, last, finally,* or the use of numbered steps
   - cause/effect–*since, because, as a result*

Name ____________________

2. Preview the material to see at a glance which material you already know something about and which contains new or unfamiliar topics.

3. First, read the questions at the end of a lesson or chapter. Then read the lesson or chapter to find the answers. Also use the **Find Out** statements to help you identify what you need to find out while reading.

4. Construct graphic organizers or use the graphic organizers provided in the workbook to help you remember key points as you read.

5. Read the Science **Process Skill Tip** in each investigation to help you understand the meaning of a process skill. Do the Process Skill Practice page in the workbook for more information.

6. Write a summary of the main ideas of a lesson. Put in your own words (paraphrase) what you read about. Then compare your summary to the lesson summary in the book.

7. Look for comparison words such as *like* or *similar to*. These words can help you to understand something new by comparing it to something you already know about.

8. Read the entire sentence and sometimes the sentences around highlighted vocabulary to tell you what these words mean.

9. Make an outline of what you read to record main points.

10. Ask questions as you read. Write facts in one column on a sheet of paper. Write your questions in the column next to the facts.

11. Reflect on what you read. Write notes not only about what you read, but also about what you think, and why.

12. Use the **Review** in the text and the **Concept Review** and **Vocabulary Review** in the workbook to help you prepare for the chapter test.

Chapter 1 • Graphic Organizer for Chapter Concepts

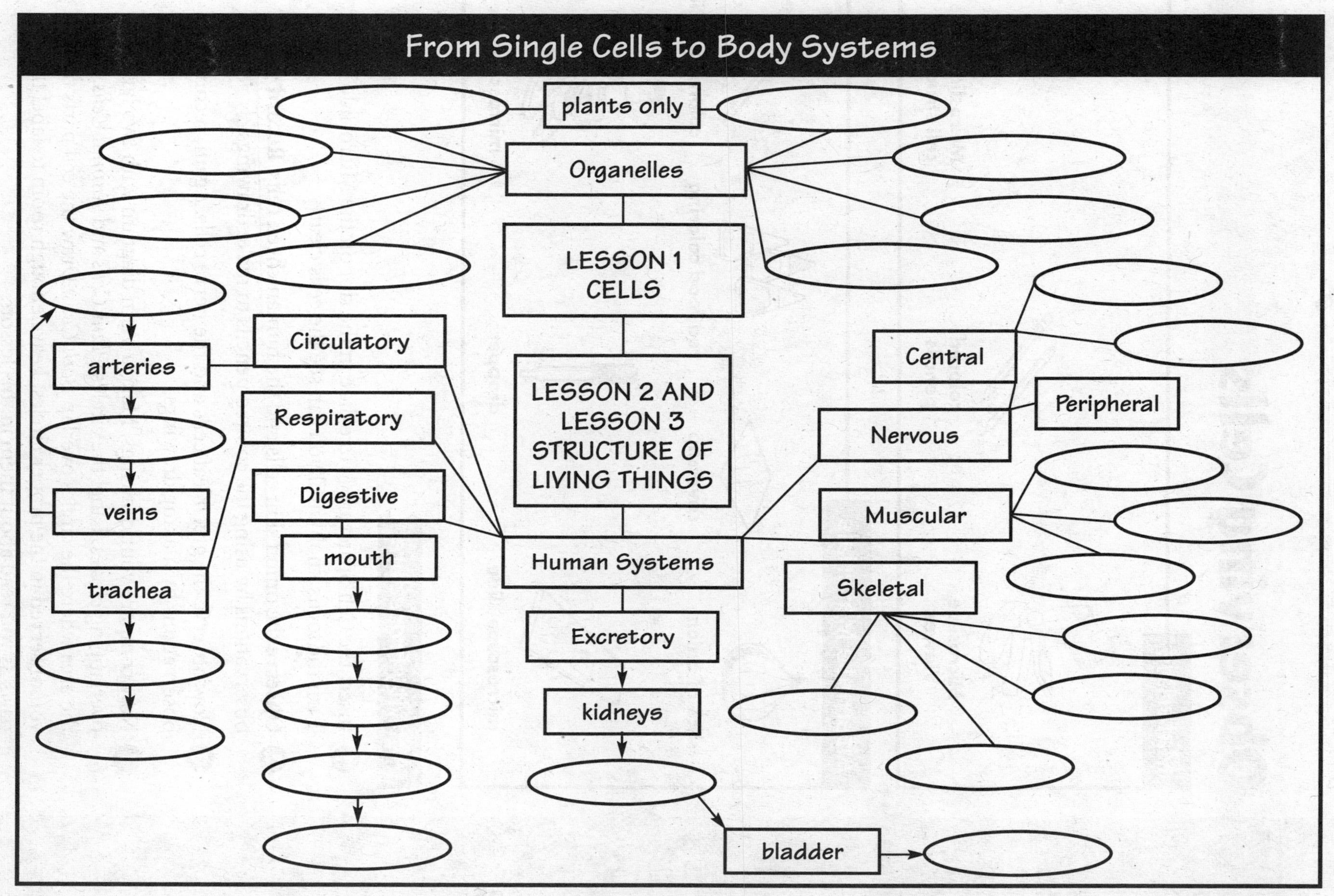

Name ______________________ Date ______________

Name ______________________

Date ______________________

Observing Cells

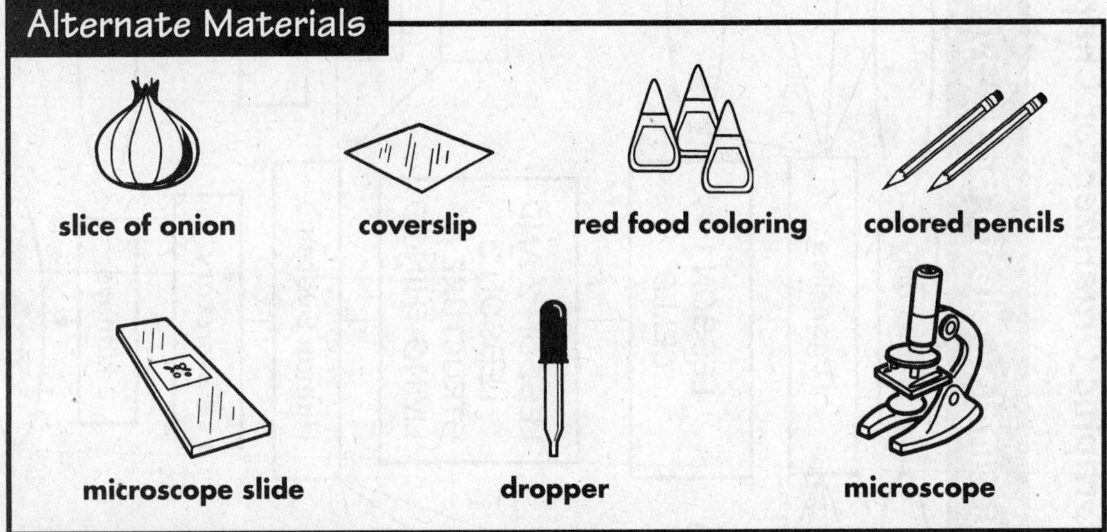

Activity Procedure

1. Insert the Cell Structure Microslide in the slot on the Microslide Viewer. Turn the focus knob until you can see the cells clearly.
2. **Observe** the onion skin cells and the human cheek cells. **Record** your observations by using the colored pencils to make drawings.
3. Now **observe** the green leaf cells and the nerve cells. Again, **record** your observations by making drawings.
4. Now **compare** your drawings. Make a Venn diagram with two large, overlapping circles. Label the circles *Plant Cells* and *Animal Cells.* Label the area where the circles overlap *Both Cells.* Draw the cell parts that you **observed** in the proper circles. Leave enough room to label the parts as you read about them in this lesson.

Name ______________________

Draw Conclusions

1. **Compare** the outer layers of plant and animal cells. ______________________

____

2. In the centers of most cells are structures that control the cells' activities. How many of these structures are there in each of the cells you **observed**?

____

3. **Scientists at Work** Scientists often **infer** characteristics of a group of objects by **observing** just a few of the objects. From your observations, what do you infer about the number of controlling structures in a cell? ______________________

____

Investigate Further Now that you have **observed** photomicrographs of cells, use the materials in the ***Alternate Materials*** list to observe living cells from onion skin. Then **compare** your observations with the drawings you made in this investigation. See page R5 for tips on using a microscope.

____

____

____

____

Name ______________________

Date ______________________

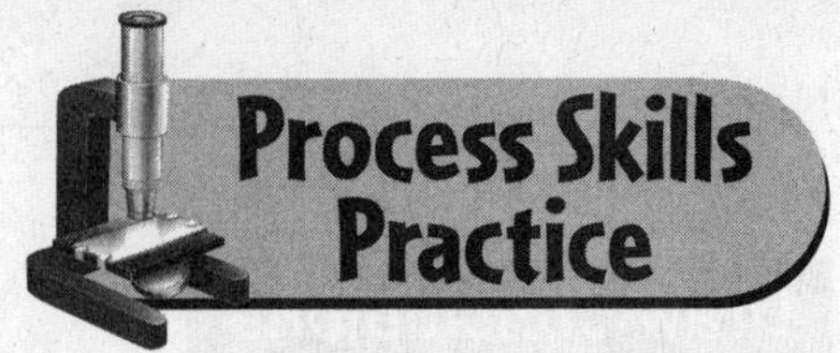

Observe and Infer

Observing is the most basic science skill. Making good observations will allow you to develop other important science skills, like inferring, comparing, classifying, and measuring. Inferring involves the use of logical reasoning to make conclusions based on observations. Inferences are explanations for events, are based on judgments, and are not always correct.

Think About Observing and Inferring

You looked at cells during the investigation for this lesson. Imagine you come to class and find that all the microscope slides have been removed from their holders and had their labels removed. Use your observations and your knowledge of cells to answer the following questions and make inferences.

1. Your teacher asks you and other students to help relabel the slides by separating the cell slides from the other slides. What do you need to look for to decide whether or not you are looking at a cell slide? ______________________

____

____

2. Next your teacher asks you to separate the plant cell slides from the animal cell slides. What do you need to look for to decide whether or not you are looking at a plant cell slide or an animal cell slide? ______________________

____

____

3. What would you look for to decide whether you were seeing that structure?

____

____

4. What inference could you make about why such a difference is found in plant and animal cells? ______________________

____

Use with page A5.

Name ______________________

Date ______________________

What Are Cells, and What Do They Do?

Lesson Concept

Living things are made of one or more cells, each able to support the functions of life. Plant cells differ from animal cells in that they have cell walls and chloroplasts.

Vocabulary

cell (A6)	**cell membrane** (A8)	**nucleus** (A8)
cytoplasm (A9)	**diffusion** (A10)	**osmosis** (A10)
tissue (A12)	**organ** (A12)	**system** (A12)

Match the name of each structure or process with its function.

_____ **1.** muscle tissue

_____ **2.** chromosomes

_____ **3.** passive transport

_____ **4.** diffusion

_____ **5.** nervous tissue

_____ **6.** active transport

_____ **7.** chloroplasts

_____ **8.** cell membrane

_____ **9.** nucleus

_____ **10.** vacuoles

A energy-free movement of materials through a cell membrane

B make food in plant cells

C store food, water, and waste materials for the cell

D can move an animal's skeleton by contracting and relaxing

E holds parts of the cell together and separates the cell from its surroundings

F the way most materials move in and out of cells

G threadlike structures that contain information about the characteristics of the organism

H carries electrical signals that affect muscle tissue

I controls the cell's activities

J use of a carrier and energy from a cell to transport materials through the cell

Name ______________________

Date ______________________

Cells and Tissues

Materials

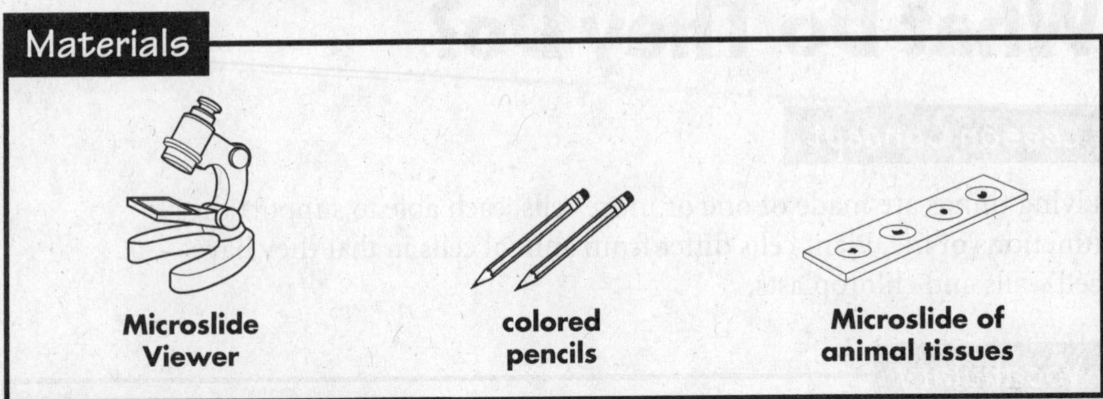

Alternate Materials

Activity Procedure

1. Insert the Animal Tissues Microslide in the slot of the Microslide Viewer. Turn the focus knob until you can see the cells and tissues clearly.
2. **Observe** the voluntary muscle cells. **Record** your observations by using the colored pencils to make a drawing. Label your drawing with the name of the tissue. Then describe the tissue. You may use the Microslide text folder to help you write your description.
3. Repeat Step 2 for the smooth muscle cells and the heart muscle.
4. **Compare** the three kinds of muscle tissue.

Name ______________________

Draw Conclusions

1. The muscle tissue cells all have a nucleus and mitochondria. How are the three kinds of muscle tissue alike? How are they different?

____

____

____

____

____

2. The dark-stained organelles you **observed** in the muscle tissues are mitochondria. Which kind of muscle tissue has the most mitochondria?

____

3. Scientists at Work When scientists **compare** objects, they often **infer** reasons for any differences. What do you infer about why one kind of muscle tissue has more mitochondria than the others? ______________________

____

____

Investigate Further Now that you have **observed** several kinds of tissues, use the materials in the ***Alternate Materials*** list to study other kinds of tissue. Observe the tissues under the microscope, and draw what you see. **Compare** these tissues with the muscle tissues you observed. See page R4 for tips on using a microscope.

____

____

____

____

____

Name ____________________

Date ____________________

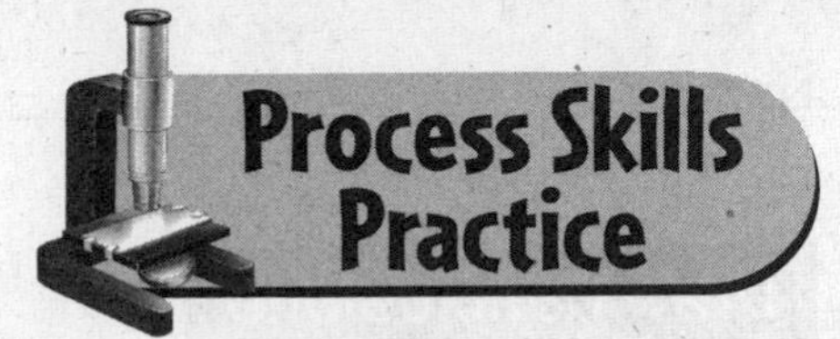

Compare and Infer

When you compare data, you arrange your information so that you can see similarities and differences. Inferring involves the use of logical reasoning to make conclusions based on observations.

Think About Comparing and Inferring

Rajean was doing a comparative study to test a new preservative. She made a nutrient solution for microorganisms from beef broth. Then she put 100 mL of the broth in three different beakers. She put 0.1 mL of the preservative in *Beaker A*, 0.01 mL in *Beaker B*, and 0.001 mL in *Beaker C*. The next day Rajean checked the beakers and found the broth discolored and cloudy in two of them. So, she used a microscope to check a sample from each of the three beakers. She recorded what she observed.

	Beaker A	Beaker B	Beaker C
Amount of preservative added to beaker	0.1 mL	0.01 mL	0.001 mL
Appearance of broth	Clear	Somewhat cloudy	Very cloudy
Microorganisms seen under microscope	None	Yeast cells	Yeast and bacteria

1. Compare the mixtures in each beaker. How are they different?

____

2. How are they alike? ____________________

____

3. After 24 hours, how do the beakers compare? ____________________

____

4. What can you infer about how effective the preservative is in keeping yeast from growing in the solution? ____________________

____

Use with page A15.

Name ______________________

Date ______________________

How Are Human Body Systems Organized?

Lesson Concept

Body cells are organized into tissues, organs, and systems that work together to keep the body alive. Four of the major systems are the circulatory, the respiratory, the digestive, and the excretory.

Vocabulary

capillaries (A17) **alveoli** (A18) **villi** (A19) **nephrons** (A20)

Match the name of each structure or process with its function.

______	**1.** circulatory system	**A**	blood vessels so small that blood cells have to move through them in single file
______	**2.** platelets	**B**	a long tube that leads to the stomach
______	**3.** alveoli	**C**	transports oxygen, nutrients, and wastes through the body in the blood
______	**4.** esophagus	**D**	tubes that empty wastes into the bladder from the kidneys
______	**5.** capillaries	**E**	vessels through which blood leaves the heart
______	**6.** ureters	**F**	moistens food and begins to break down starchy foods
______	**7.** trachea	**G**	pumps blood through blood vessels
______	**8.** arteries	**H**	cause blood to clot when a blood vessel is cut
______	**9.** heart	**I**	eliminates excess body heat
______	**10.** saliva	**J**	sometimes called the windpipe
______	**11.** pancreas	**K**	tiny air sacs in the lungs
______	**12.** sweating	**L**	produces a fluid that neutralizes stomach acid

Use with page A21.

Name ___________________________

Date ___________________________

How Muscles Cause Movement

Materials

tape measure

Activity Procedure

1. Place your left hand on top of your right arm, between the shoulder and elbow. Bend and straighten your right arm at the elbow. **Observe** the movement by feeling the muscles in your right arm.
2. The muscle on the front of the upper arm is called the *biceps*. The muscle on the back of the upper arm is called the *triceps*. **Compare** the biceps and the triceps as you bend and straighten your arm. **Infer** which muscle controls the bending movement and which controls the straightening movement.
3. Have a partner use the tape measure to **measure** the distance around your upper arm when it is straight and when it is bent. **Record** the measurements.
4. Repeat Steps 2 and 3, using your right hand and your left arm.
5. **Compare** the sets of measurements.

 Use with pages A22–A23.

Name ______________________

Draw Conclusions

1. What did you **infer** about the muscles controlling the bending and the straightening of your upper arm? ______________________

2. Why are two muscles needed to bend and straighten your arm? Why can't one muscle do it? ______________________

3. **Scientists at Work** Scientists often **hypothesize** about things they **observe.** Hypothesize about any differences between the measurements of your right arm and the measurements of your left arm. ______________________

Investigate Further Repeat the investigation with different pairs of muscles. Try bending your leg at the knee while **observing** the muscles in your thigh. See if these observations also support your hypothesis. ______________________

Name ______________________

Date ______________________

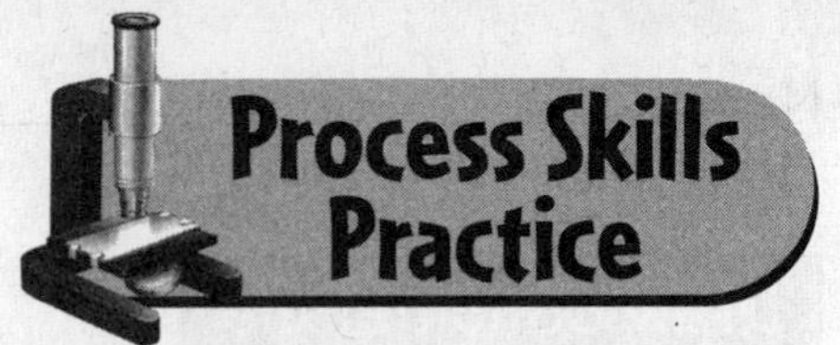

Hypothesize

When you hypothesize, you make an educated guess about the results of an experiment you plan to do. A hypothesis is based upon observation, prior knowledge, and prior experimental outcomes. A hypothesis is often altered based on the outcome of experiments that test it.

Think About Hypothesizing

A group of students decided to test the effect of sleep and repeated trials on reaction time. Their hypothesis was that reaction time would improve with more sleep and repeated trials. Each student in the test was asked to push a button as soon as he or she heard the sound of a bell. The amount of time between the sound of the bell and the pushing of the button was recorded as the reaction time.

The table below lists reaction times for three students on different days after receiving different amounts of sleep the night before. Each student underwent two trials on each day of testing.

Amount of Sleep	Reaction Time in Seconds					
	Student A		Student B		Student C	
	Trial 1	Trial 2	Trial 1	Trial 2	Trial 1	Trial 2
8 hours	0.20	0.16	0.15	0.12	0.25	0.19
6 hours	0.17	0.17	0.19	0.24	0.25	0.32
4 hours	0.30	0.45	0.35	0.47	0.40	0.45
2 hours	0.82	1.10	0.75	1.08	0.80	1.02

1. Was the hypothesis correct? ______________________

2. Use the data to form a hypothesis about the effect of sleeping less than eight hours a night on reaction time. ______________________

____

____

3. How would you test this hypothesis? ______________________

____

Use with page A23.

Name ______________________

Date ______________________

How Do Bones, Muscles, and Nerves Work Together?

Lesson Concept

Skeletal bones move because of the action of pairs of voluntary muscles. Smooth muscles line digestive organs and blood vessels. The walls of the heart are made of cardiac muscle. Nerves carry signals from sensory organs to the brain and from the brain to the muscles.

Vocabulary

bone marrow (A24)	**joints** (A24)	**tendons** (A25)
ligaments (A25)	**neuron** (A26)	**receptors** (A26)

Match the term in the left column with its description in the right column.

_____ **1.** bone marrow

_____ **2.** ligaments

_____ **3.** tendons

_____ **4.** smooth muscles

_____ **5.** cardiac muscles

_____ **6.** joints

_____ **7.** central nervous system

_____ **8.** receptors

_____ **9.** neurons

_____ **10.** dendrites

_____ **11.** axon

_____ **12.** synapse

A line digestive organs and blood vessels

B is made up of the brain and the spinal cord

C is the part of the neuron that carries signals and transmits them to other neurons

D are nerve cells that detect conditions in the body's environment

E attach bones to muscles

F branch out of the nerve cell and receive signals from other cells

G produces red and white blood cells

H make up the walls of the heart

I is a gap between the axon of one neuron and the dendrite of the next neuron

J attach bones to each other

K are the cells that nerves are made of

L are where the bones meet to attach to each other and to muscles

Name ____________________

Date ____________________

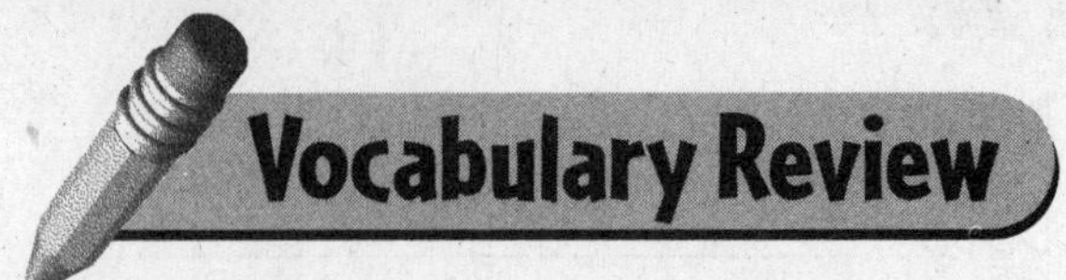

Recognize Vocabulary

Listed below are scrambled vocabulary terms from Chapter 1. Use the clues to unscramble the terms. Write the unscrambled terms on the lines provided.

1. SMOOSSI ____________________
   the movement of water and dissolved materials through cell membranes
2. LLRCASEIAPI ____________________
   blood vessels so small that blood cells move through them in single file
3. RUNNEO ____________________
   a specialized cell that can receive and transmit signals to other cells like it
4. LYMOCPSTA ____________________
   a jellylike substance containing chemicals that keep the cell functioning
5. GROAN ____________________
   tissues that work together form this
6. LCLE ____________________
   the basic unit of structure and function of all living things
7. JSTONI ____________________
   where bones meet and are attached to each other and to muscles
8. PREETOCRS ____________________
   nerve cells that detect conditions in the body's environment
9. IILVL ____________________
   tiny tubes sticking out from the walls of the small intestine
10. OMNOEAWBRR (2 words) ____________________
    connective tissue that produces red and white blood cells
11. FDNIUFIOS ____________________
    the way most materials move in and out of cells
12. MCLNEEMERLBA (2 words) ____________________
    a thin covering that encloses a cell
13. IGLESANTM ____________________
    bands of connective tissue that hold the skeleton together
14. VIOALEL ____________________
    tiny air sacs at the end of the smallest tubes in the lungs

Use with pages A1–A33.

Name ____________________ Date ____________________

Chapter 2 • *Graphic Organizer for Chapter Concepts*

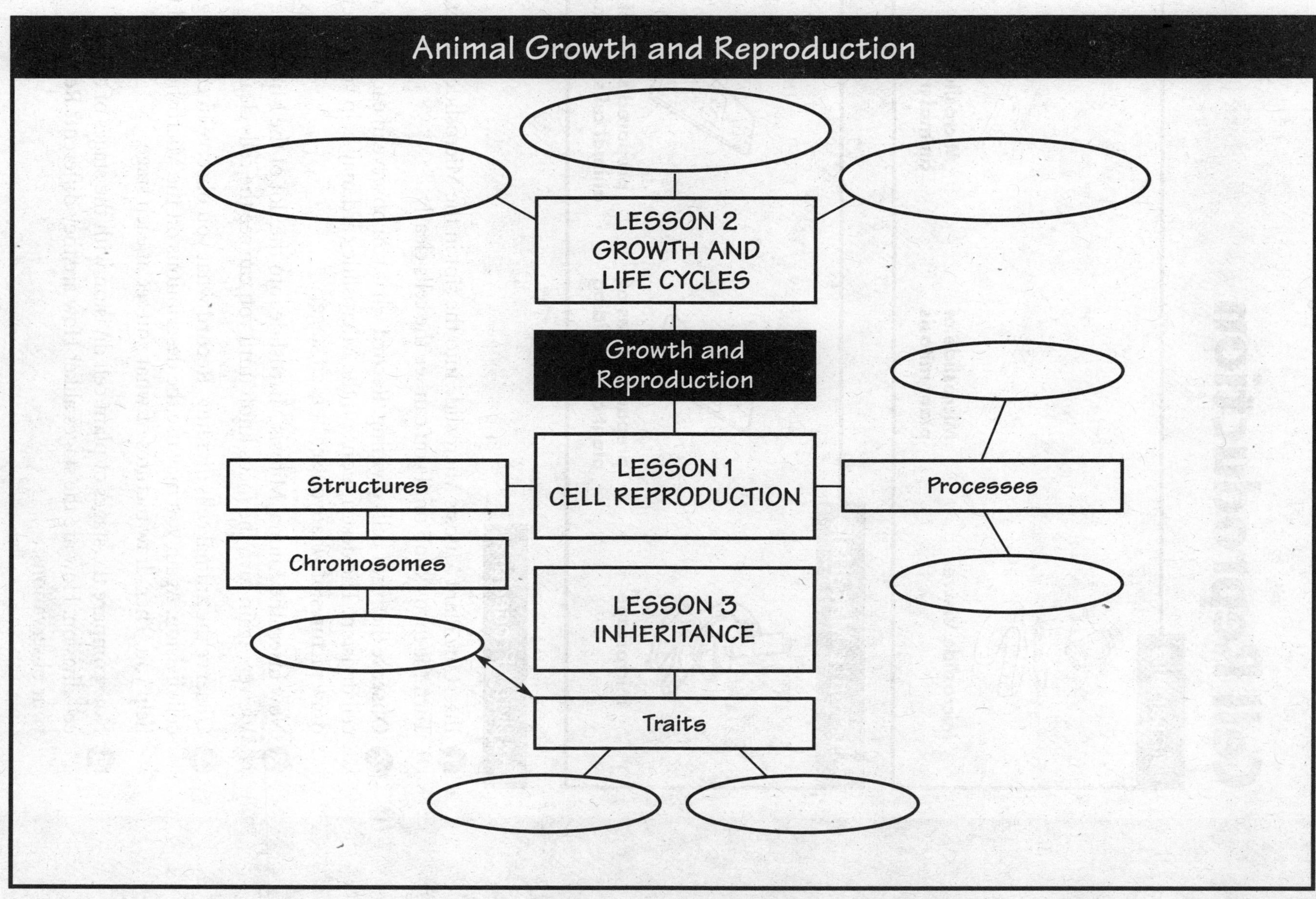

Name ______________________

Date ______________________

Cell Reproduction

Materials

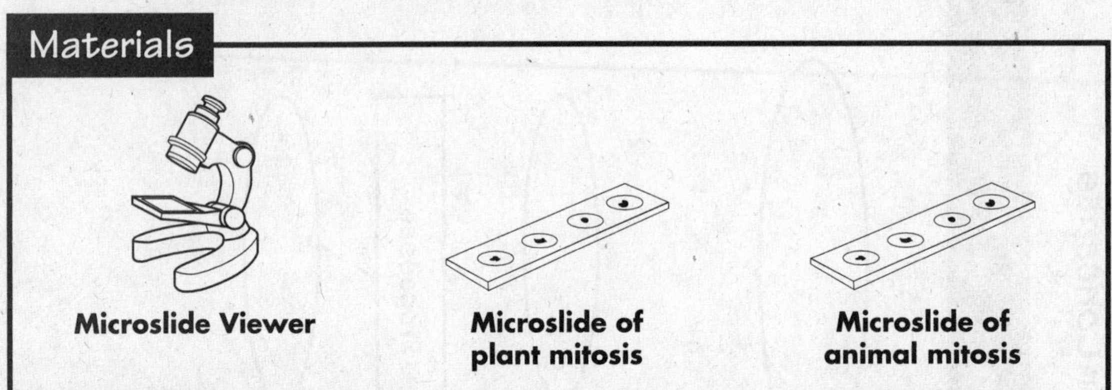

Microslide Viewer

Microslide of plant mitosis

Microslide of animal mitosis

Alternate Materials

microscope

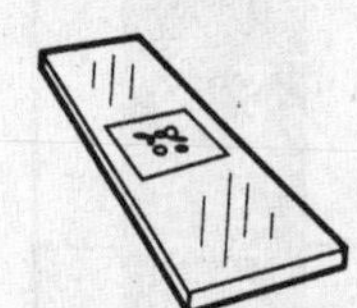

prepared slides of plant cells dividing

prepared slides of animal cells dividing

Activity Procedure

1. Insert the Plant Mitosis Microslide into the slot in the Microslide Viewer. Turn the focus knob until you can see the cells clearly.
2. **Observe** the plant cells dividing. **Record** what you observe in each stage of cell division. The descriptions on the Microslide card may help you. Then draw pictures of what you see at each stage.
3. Now insert the Animal Mitosis Microslide into the slot of the Microslide Viewer. Again turn the focus knob until you can see the cells clearly.
4. **Observe** the animal cells dividing. **Record** what you observe in each stage of cell division. Again you may use the descriptions on the Microslide card to help you. Then draw pictures of what you see at each stage.
5. Now **compare** the stages of plant cell division with the stages of animal cell division. How are the stages alike? How are they different? **Record** your observations.

Name ______________________

Draw Conclusions

1. What part of the cell changes as cell division occurs? What changes take place?

____

____

____

2. How many new cells does each dividing cell produce? ______________________

3. What similarities and differences did you **observe** between the dividing plant cells and the dividing animal cells? ______________________

____

____

____

4. **Scientists at Work** Scientists **observe** cells and ask questions based on their observations. What questions do you have about cell division, based on what you observed? ______________________

____

____

Investigate Further Now that you have **observed** photomicrographs of plant and animal cells dividing, use the materials on the ***Alternate Materials*** list to observe other cells dividing. See page R4 for tips on using a microscope.

____

____

____

Name ______________________

Date ______________________

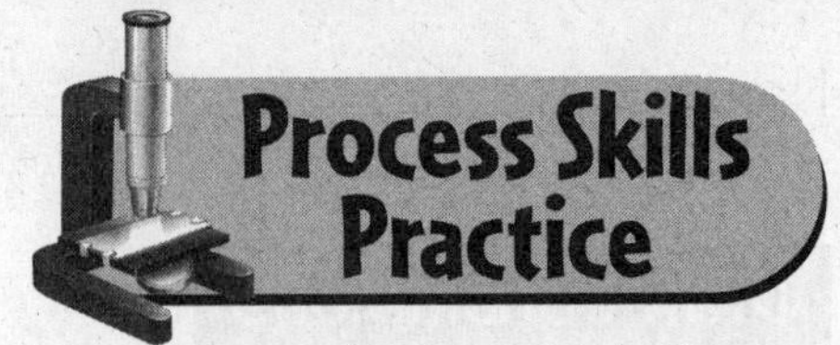

Observe

Observing is the most basic science skill. Making good observations will allow you to develop other important skills, such as comparing and classifying.

Think About Observing

Do all plant cells look alike? Do all animal cells look alike? Observe the drawings below, and compare them to what you know about cells. Then classify them by writing *plant* or *animal* beneath the drawing.

1. What observation can you make to determine which cells are plant cells?

____

2. Do you observe anything unusual about one of the plant cells and one of the animal cells? ______________________

____

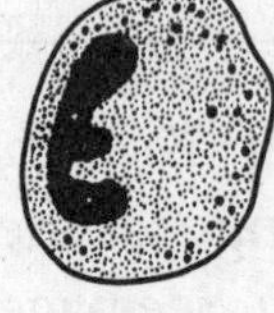

4. ______________________

3. ______________________

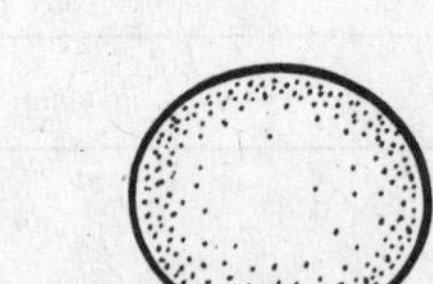

5. ______________________

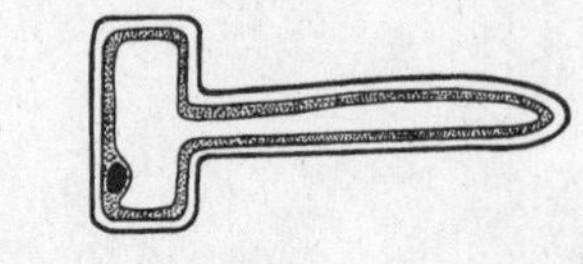

6. ______________________

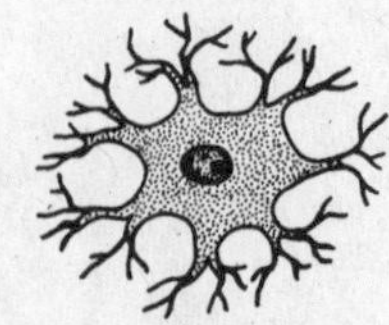

7. ______________________

Use with page A37.

Name ______________________

Date ______________________

Growth and Reproduction

Lesson Concept

Organisms grow when their cells divide. Body cells divide through mitosis. Reproductive cells divide through meiosis.

Vocabulary

chromosome (A39)	**mitosis** (A39)	**asexual reproduction** (A41)
sexual reproduction (A42)	**meiosis** (A42)	

Use the terms from the box to fill in the blanks in the paragraph that follows. Watch out! One term is used twice.

sexual reproduction	**regenerate**	**planaria**
mitosis	**meiosis**	**zygote**
asexual reproduction	**chromosomes**	**planarian**

Organisms grow when their cells divide in a process called ________________. To prepare for this process, a cell makes copies of its ________________. After this process, each of the new cells has an exact copy of the original cell's ________________. When a cut or scrape on your skin heals, it is because this process of cell division has allowed the damaged tissue to ________________. The freshwater flatworm, called a ________________, can regenerate most of its body through mitosis. Many simple one-celled organisms, like yeast or bacteria, can use this process of cell division to produce new organisms through ________________, in which a single parent produces offspring through mitosis. Most organisms, however, are reproduced from two parents in a process called ________________. In this process cells from two parents combine to form a ________________, which contains genetic material from each parent. Organisms produce reproductive cells through a process called ________________, which reduces the number of chromosomes in the reproductive cells, so they don't end up with twice as many as they need.

Name ______________________

Date ______________________

The Stages of a Mealworm's Life

Materials

mealworm culture

paper plate

hand lens

Activity Procedure

1. Your teacher will give you a mealworm from the mealworm culture.
2. Put the mealworm on the paper plate. Using the hand lens, **observe** the mealworm closely. Draw what you see.
3. Label these parts on your drawing: head, segment, antenna, outer shell, claw, mouth, and leg.
4. **Observe** the mealworm's movements. Does it move straight forward or from side to side? Does it move quickly or slowly? **Record** your observations.
5. Now your teacher will give you a beetle from the mealworm culture. Repeat Steps 2–4 with the beetle.
6. Finally, **observe** the mealworm culture. Try to find evidence of other stages of a mealworm's life, such as eggs and pupa cases. Draw pictures of what you find.
7. **Compare** your drawings of the eggs and pupa cases with your drawings of the mealworm and the beetle. Form a **hypothesis** about the order of these life stages. Then list the ways in which a mealworm changes as it grows.

 Use with pages A44–A45.

Name ___________________________

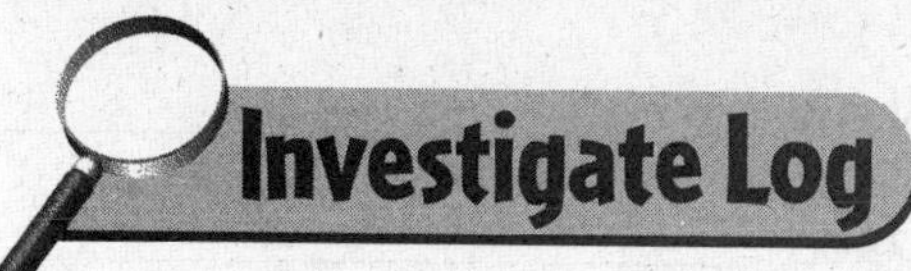

Draw Conclusions

1. How are the mealworm and the beetle similar? ___________________________

____

____

2. How is the beetle different from the mealworm? ___________________________

____

____

3. Scientists at Work Scientists often **observe** an organism and then **hypothesize** about their observations. What observations enabled you to form your hypothesis about the order of the life stages? ___________________________

____

____

Investigate Further Plan and conduct a simple investigation to test your hypothesis about the life stages of a mealworm. Decide what equipment or technology you will need to use to test your hypothesis. Then use the equipment or technology in your investigation. ___________________________

____

____

Name ______________________

Date ______________________

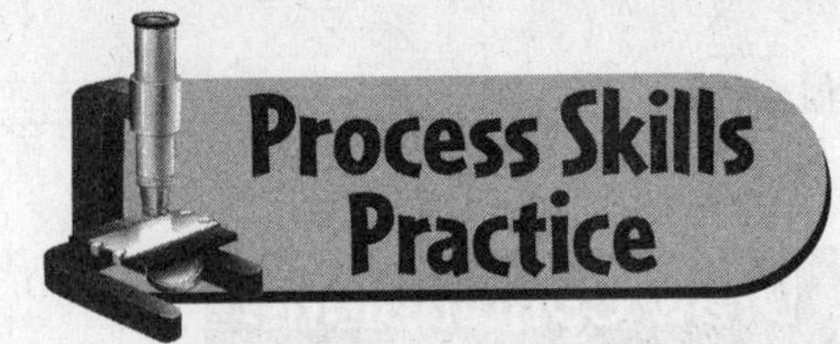

Hypothesize

To explain your observations you may form a hypothesis. A hypothesis is an explanation that you can test. Tests cannot prove a hypothesis. They can only support it. If test results don't support your hypothesis, then you need to form a new one.

Think About Hypothesizing

People used to believe that certain forms of life developed directly from nonliving things, such as dead animals or mud. This was known as spontaneous generation. The belief was a hypothesis based on observation. Eventually the hypothesis was subjected to scientific testing and found to be incorrect. See if you can think of ways to test the following hypotheses.

1. Many years ago maggots were believed to come from decaying meat. Suppose you are living in those days and you propose a new hypothesis that maggots hatch from fly eggs laid on the meat. How can you test your hypothesis?

____

____

____

____

2. Microorganisms were believed to arise spontaneously in water under certain conditions. For example, if you add hay to water and wait a few days, you will be able to use a microscope and find microorganisms in the water. What hypothesis could you form about this observation? How could you test it?

____

____

____

3. In 1745 an Englishman named John Needham wanted to show that microorganisms spring spontaneously from meat broth. It was known that boiling would kill any microorganisms in the broth. His hypothesis was that if microorganisms appeared in broth that had been boiled, then spontaneous generation would be proved. Do you agree with his hypothesis? Why or why not?

____

____

Use with page A45.

Name ______________________

Date ______________________

What Is a Life Cycle?

Lesson Concept

A life cycle is made of the stages that make up an organism's life. Some organisms grow through direct development, in which the only change is size. Others go through metamorphosis, which means they change shape and characteristics as they grow.

Vocabulary

life cycle (A46) **direct development** (A46) **metamorphosis** (A47)

Match the term on the left with the sentence on the right that describes it by writing the letter of the description in the blank next to the term.

Column A

_____ 1. molting

_____ 2. metamorphosis

_____ 3. larva

_____ 4. life cycle

_____ 5. complete metamorphosis

_____ 6. pupa

_____ 7. adult

_____ 8. cocoon

Column B

A A pupa may bury itself in the ground or it may make a protective covering around itself.

B When an organism reaches its final stage of development, it is able to reproduce.

C During the third stage of complete metamorphosis, insects neither eat nor move.

D Some insects have a life cycle that includes four distinct stages.

E Some insects that go through incomplete metamorphosis must shed their outer skeletons as they grow.

F Some organisms go through drastic changes in the shape or characteristics of their bodies.

G In complete metamorphosis, when an insect hatches from its egg, it enters the second stage of its development.

H Most organisms grow and mature through several distinct stages of life.

Name ____________________

Date ____________________

Inherited Characteristics

Materials

mirror

Activity Procedure

1. Use the chart below for this activity.
2. **Tongue Rolling** Use the mirror to **observe** what you are doing. Stick out your tongue, and try to roll its edges up toward the center. **Record** your results in the chart.
3. **Ear Lobes** Use the mirror to **observe** the shape of your ear lobes. Are they attached to your cheek, or do they hang free? **Record** your results in the chart.

Characteristic	Results (Circle one)		Class Totals
Tongue rolling	Yes	No	
Ear lobes	Attached	Free	
Folded hands	Left	Right	

4. **Folded Hands** Clasp your hands in front of you. **Observe** which of your thumbs falls naturally on top. **Record** your results in the chart.
5. Your teacher will now ask students to report the results of their observations. Tally the results in the chart as students report them. Total the number of students for each characteristic. Then **calculate** what fraction of the class has each characteristic.

Name ______________________________

Draw Conclusions

1. **Infer** whether a person could learn tongue rolling. Explain. ______________________________

____

____

2. What other inherited characteristics could you have **observed?**

____

____

3. **Scientists at Work** Scientists often **use numbers** to summarize the data they collect. Which trait in each pair occurred most often in your class?

____

____

Investigate Further Do your class results suggest how often these traits occur in other people? Choose one or two of these characteristics. **Predict** whether the results will be the same for another group. Then ask some of your friends, neighbors, and family members to participate in this activity, and **observe** the results. **Record** the results, and share them with your class. ______________________________

____

____

Name ______________________

Date ______________________

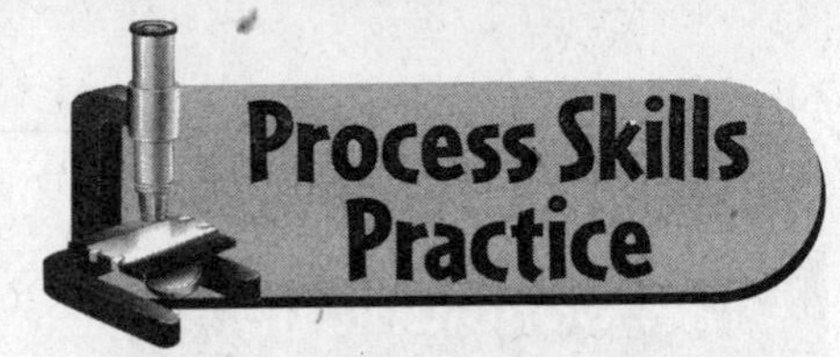

Use Numbers

When you use numbers, you summarize the data you collect. You can also use numbers to estimate, to count, and to figure out ratios or percentages.

Think About Using Numbers

Greg was experimenting with cross-breeding pea plants. He started with 100 plants. One of the things he wanted to study was seed color. When Greg crossed 50 plants having yellow seeds with 50 plants having green seeds, all the offspring had yellow seeds.

1. What percentage of this first generation had yellow seeds? ______________

2. Greg knew there would be two factors for seed color in each plant and that the factors would pair up. He represented this first generation with the following chart, using Y for what he began calling the yellow seed factor and G for the green seed factor. The parents with green seeds were GG and the parents with yellow seeds were YY. Looking at his chart, he realized that even though every offspring's seed was yellow, each offspring's seed also carried a factor for green.

	G	**G**
Y	YG	YG
Y	YG	YG

3. Next Greg planted all the yellow seeds from the offspring. When the plants grew up, he checked their seeds and found that 75 percent of them were yellow. The rest were green seeds. What percentage of this second generation of pea plants had green seeds? ______________________________

4. Greg represented this second generation with another chart. This time he knew that each parent plant had factors of both Y and G. Each square in the chart represents one-fourth the total number of seeds. What percent is represented by GG?

	Y	**G**
Y	YY	YG
G	YG	GG

____

5. What percent of the total number of seeds carried at least one Y factor?

____

Use with page A51.

Name ______________________

Date ______________________

Why Are Offspring Like Their Parents?

Lesson Concept

Many traits are inherited by offspring from their parents. These traits are determined genes. Gene combinations determine if traits are seen (dominant traits) or hidden (recessive traits).

Vocabulary

inherited trait (A52) **dominant trait** (A53)

recessive trait (A53) **gene** (A54)

Look at the traits shown for two generations in this family. Label the traits *D* for "dominant," *R* for "recessive," or *N* for "not inherited."

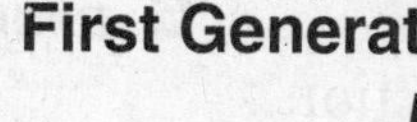

First Generation

Dad

Free earlobes
Short eyelashes
Plays tennis
Speaks English and French

Mom

Attached earlobes
Long eyelashes
Grows tomatoes
Speaks Spanish and English

Second Generation

Son

Free earlobes ______

Plays basketball ______

Speaks Spanish and English ______

Short eyelashes ______

Daughter

Free earlobes ______

Grows tomatoes ______

Speaks Spanish, French, and English ______

Long eyelashes ______

Daughter

Attached earlobes ______

Plays basketball ______

Speaks only English ______

Long eyelashes ______

Son

Free earlobes ______

Plays tennis and basketball ______

Speaks Spanish and English ______

Long eyelashes ______

Use with page A55.

Name ______________________

Date ______________________

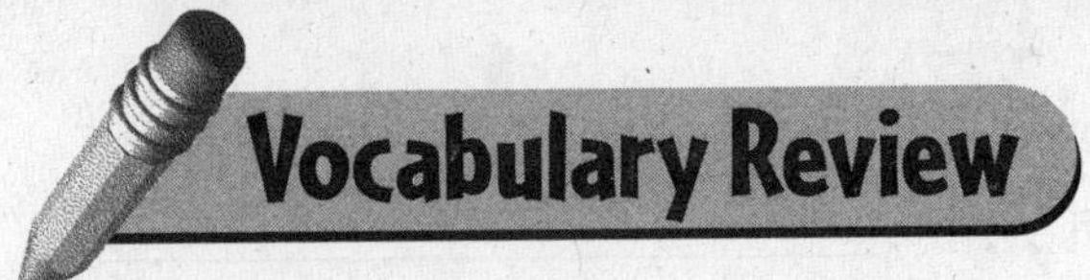

Recognize Vocabulary

Underline the vocabulary term that best completes each sentence.

1. Gametes, or reproductive cells, are formed during ____.
A meiosis **B** mitosis **C** metamorphosis **D** asexual reproduction

2. The DNA codes for a certain trait are found on a ____.
A inherited trait **B** dominant trait **C** recessive trait **D** gene

3. The code that tells each cell when to divide is contained in a threadlike ____.
A gene **B** life cycle **C** mitosis **D** chromosome

4. Worms change only in size as they grow to be adults, because they go through ____.
A direct development **B** mitosis **C** metamorphosis **D** asexual reproduction

5. When two parents each contribute a cell to form one cell, that's ____.
A asexual reproduction **B** sexual reproduction **C** meiosis **D** gene

6. Development and growth in an egg is the first stage of a bird's ____.
A metamorphosis **B** direct development **C** life cycle **D** asexual reproduction

7. Hair color is an example of a(n) ____.
A inherited trait **B** dominant trait **C** recessive trait **D** gene

8. The transformation of a caterpillar to a butterfly is an example of ____.
A direct development **B** mitosis **C** metamorphosis **D** asexual reproduction

9. If you scrape your skin, your body creates new skin cells through ____.
A meiosis **B** mitosis **C** metamorphosis **D** sexual reproduction

10. Yeast, a one-celled organism, reproduces by budding, a type of ____.
A asexual reproduction **B** sexual reproduction **C** meiosis **D** gene

11. Gregor Mendel found that in peas, tallness was a strong, or ____.
A inherited trait **B** dominant trait **C** recessive trait **D** gene

Use with pages A34–A61.

Name ______________________ Date ______________

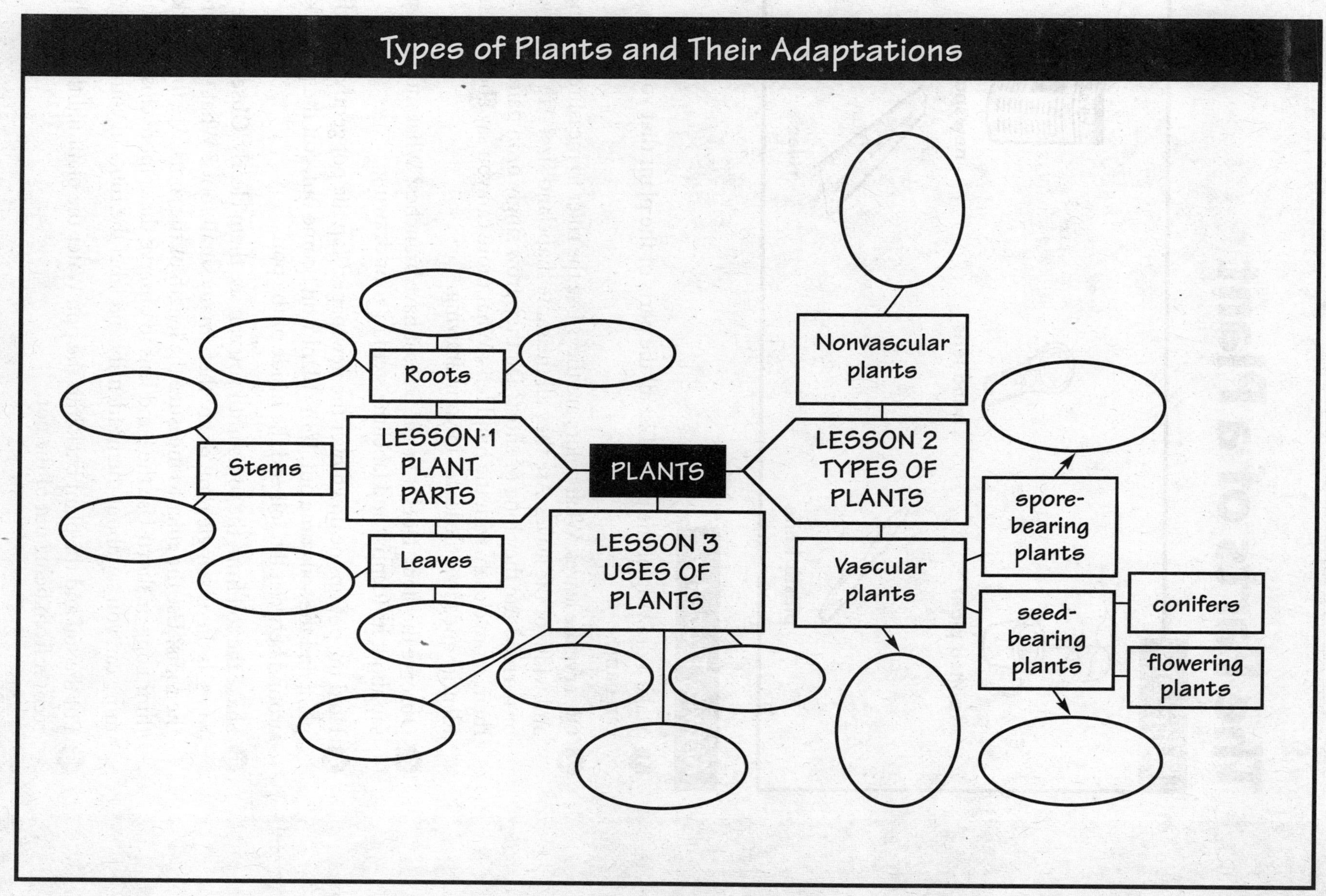

Chapter 3 • Graphic Organizer for Chapter Concepts
Types of Plants and Their Adaptations
PLANTS
LESSON 1 PLANT PARTS
Roots
Stems
Leaves
LESSON 2 TYPES OF PLANTS
Nonvascular plants
Vascular plants
spore-bearing plants
seed-bearing plants
conifers
flowering plants
LESSON 3 USES OF PLANTS

Name ______________________

Date ______________________

The Parts of a Plant

Materials

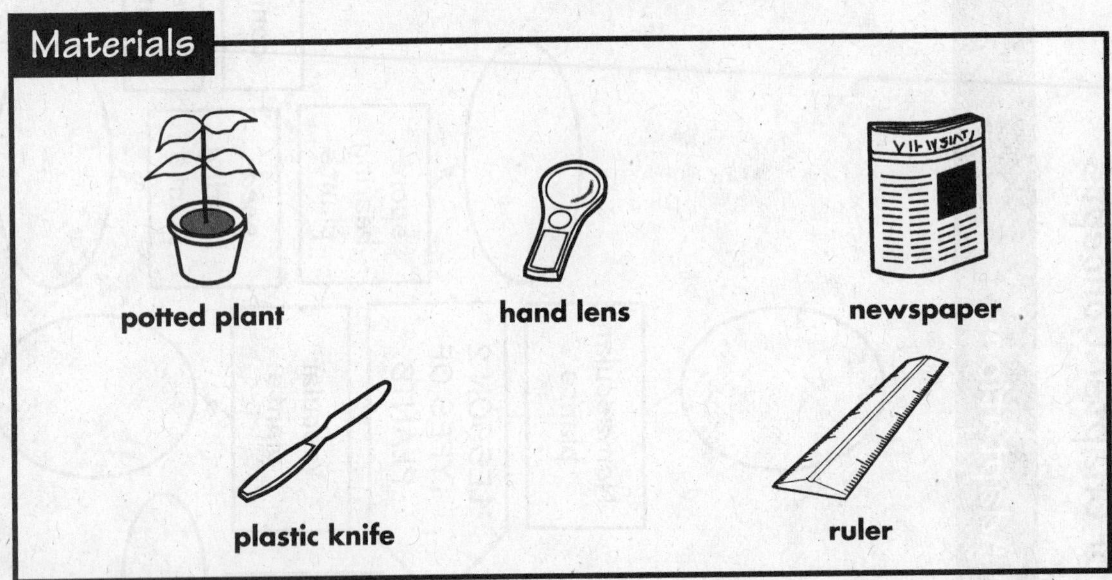

Activity Procedure

1. Make a drawing of the plant. List all the parts of the plant that you can name.
2. **Observe** the leaves. What colors are they? Use the ruler to measure the length and width of the leaves. Are they all the same shape and size? Are they wide or narrow? Are they long or short? Do they grow singly or in pairs? Observe them more closely with the hand lens. What more can you say about them? Identify and label the leaves in your drawing.
3. **Observe** the stem. Does it bend? Does it have branches? What more can you say about it? Identify and label the stem in your drawing.
4. Hold the pot upside down over the newspaper. Tap the pot gently until the plant and the soil come out. If the plant won't come out, run the plastic knife around between the soil and the inside of the pot.
5. Shake the soil from the roots until you can see them clearly. **Observe** the roots. Is there a single root, or are there many small roots? What shape are the roots? Use the ruler to **measure** the length of the roots. Are they thick or thin? Long or short? Use the hand lens to observe them more closely. What more can you say about them? Identify and label the roots in your drawing.
6. Put the soil and the plant back into the pot. Water the plant lightly to help it recover from being out of the pot.

Name ______________________

Draw Conclusions

1. What are the parts of the plant you **observed**? ______________________

2. **Compare** the plant parts you identified with the parts of a large tree. How are they the same? How are they different? ______________________

3. **Scientists at Work** Scientists learn by making observations. What did you **observe** about each part of the plant? ______________________

Investigate Further Observe a different type of plant. Then identify its parts. Does it have the same parts as the plant you observed in the activity? Do the parts look the same as the parts you observed in the activity? ______________________

Name ______________________

Date ______________________

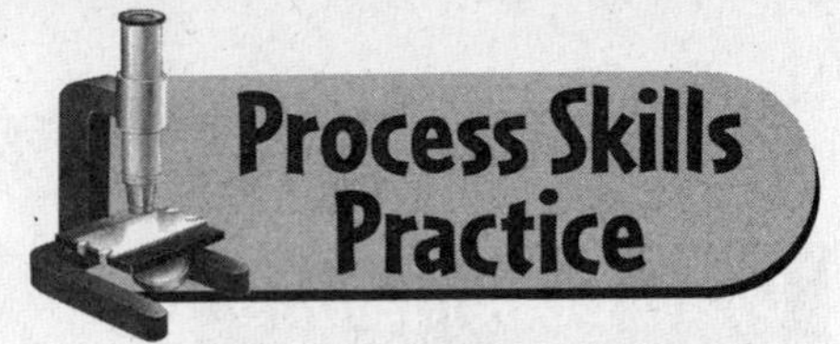

Observe

Observing involves using one or more of the senses to perceive properties of objects or events. Sometimes you need to use an instrument, such as a microscope, to extend your senses.

Think About Observing

Suppose you are walking beside a river on a summer afternoon. You observe several large slabs of concrete on the riverbank. When you look across the river, you observe more concrete slabs on the opposite bank. You are curious about them, but you decide to move on. After a short while, you come to a pipe that empties into the river. The water is foamy and cloudy near the pipe. It has no smell. You observe a lot of plants growing in the cloudy water and on the riverbank near the pipe.

1. What objects have you observed on your walk? ______________________

____

2. What senses have you used? ______________________
3. You observed something coming from the pipe. From your observations, do you think it was harmful to the plants? ______________________

____

____

4. How could you make a better observation about what was coming from the pipe? ______________________
5. If you decided to observe the foam more closely, what do you think you should be looking for? ______________________

____

6. If you decided to observe the concrete slabs more closely, would you need instruments to extend your senses? ______________________

____

Use with page A65.

Name ____________________

Date ____________________

What Are the Functions of Roots, Stems, and Leaves?

Lesson Concept

Each part of a plant has a different function. Roots anchor the plant and take in minerals and water. A stem supports the plant and moves materials between its parts. Leaves make food.

Vocabulary

xylem (A69) **phloem** (A69) **chlorophyll** (A70)

Match each term on the left with its description on the right.

	Column A		Column B
_____	**1.** fibrous roots	**A**	tiny holes in a leaf where carbon dioxide enters and oxygen exits
_____	**2.** phloem	**B**	a pigment that helps plants use light energy to make sugars
_____	**3.** stomata	**C**	a plant part that holds the plant up and carries food and water to other plant parts
_____	**4.** chlorophyll	**D**	tiny parts of roots that take in water and minerals from the soil
_____	**5.** xylem	**E**	a root that goes straight down so it can reach water deep underground
_____	**6.** taproot	**F**	a plant part that is the "food factory" of the plant
_____	**7.** stem	**G**	roots that form a thick and tangled mat just under the surface of the soil
_____	**8.** leaf	**H**	the parts in leaf cells where the food-making process takes place
_____	**9.** root hairs	**I**	tubes in plant stems that carry water and minerals
_____	**10.** chloroplasts	**J**	tubes in plant stems that carry food made in the leaves to other parts of the plant
_____	**11.** prop roots	**K**	roots that begin above ground so they can keep trees growing in loose, wet soil from being blown over by the wind

Use with page A71.

Name ____________________

Date ____________________

Simple Plants

Materials

Activity Procedure

1. **Observe** the moss and the liverwort. **Record** what you see.
2. Now **observe** the plants with a hand lens. Can you see different parts? Do any of the parts you see look like the parts of the potted plant you observed in Lesson 1?
3. **Observe** the plants by touching them with your fingers. Are they soft or firm? Are they dry or moist? What else can you tell by feeling them? Describe what they feel like.
4. Touch the plants with a pencil or other object while you **observe** them through the hand lens. Do the parts bend, or are they stiff? Do you see anything new if you push a part of the plant to one side? Describe what you see.
5. **Observe** the plants by smelling them. Do they have any kind of odor? Try to identify the odors. Describe what you smell.
6. Make drawings of the moss and liverwort, identify the parts you observed, and **infer** what each part does.

Name ______________________

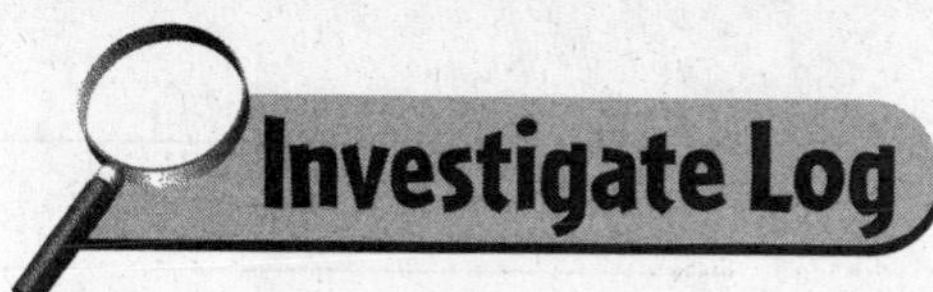

Draw Conclusions

1. What plant parts did you **observe** on the moss? What parts did you observe on the liverwort? ______________________

____

2. What do you **infer** each part of the plant does? ______________________

____

____

3. Scientists at Work Scientists use observations to **compare** things. Use the observations you made in this investigation to compare the moss and liverwort with the plant you observed in Lesson 1. ______________________

____

____

Investigate Further **Observe** a fern. How does it **compare** with the moss and the liverwort? ______________________

____

Name ______________________

Date ______________________

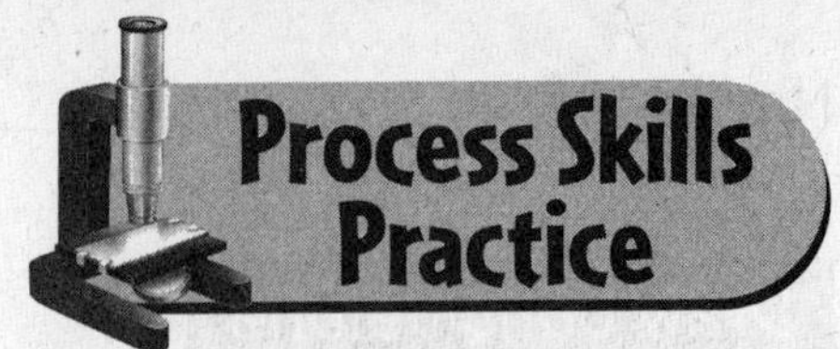

Compare

When you compare, you observe objects or events and try to find out how they are alike or different. You ask yourself questions while you are observing. Which plant is the smallest? Which plant has the most leaves? What does this plant have that the other does not have?

Think About Comparing

When you shop for fruits and vegetables, you see all different shapes and colors. You know from your experience that each of the items also has its own special taste and smell. All the shapes, the colors, the tastes, and the smells come from plants. Answer the questions about the following items: watermelon, cantaloupe, strawberries, carrots, apples, mushrooms, and lettuce.

1. Compare the mushrooms to the strawberries. Do they share any characteristics? How are they different? ______________________

____

____

____

____

2. How is the carrot different from all the other items? ______________________

3. Compare the lettuce to all the other items. Can you think of an important difference? ______________________

____

____

____

____

4. Choose the two items you think are most similar to one another. Explain your choice. ______________________

____

5. Choose the two items you think are most different from one another. Explain your choice. ______________________

____

Use with page A73.

Name ______________________

Date ______________________

What Are the Two Major Groups of Plants?

Lesson Concept

Vascular plants have xylem and phloem. Nonvascular plants do not have these tubes. Nonvascular plants and simple vascular plants reproduce with spores. Gymnosperms and angiosperms are seed-producing vascular plants. Plants go through several stages in their life cycles.

Vocabulary

nonvascular (A74)	**vascular** (A74)	**spore** (A75)
gymnosperm (A76)	**pollen** (A76)	**angiosperm** (A77)

Put each term on the list following into the Venn diagram below. Remember, in a Venn diagram, the areas where circles overlap are areas that include both categories shown in the circles. If a term belongs in or applies to both categories, put it in the area where the circles overlap. If it belongs in or applies to only one category, put it into the correct circle.

spore	**conifer**	**pollen**	**flower**
fruit	**mosses**	**ferns**	**apples**
xylem	**phloem**	**chloroplasts**	**life cycle**

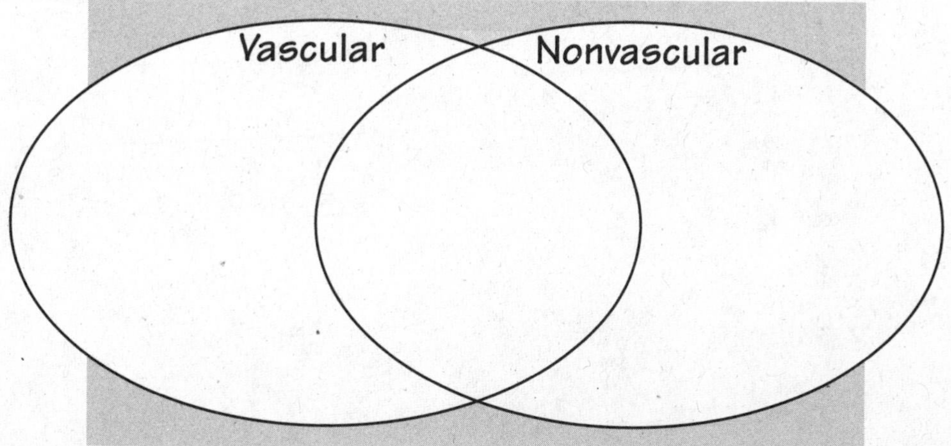

Name ______________________

Date ______________________

Popcorn

Materials

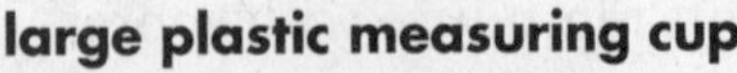

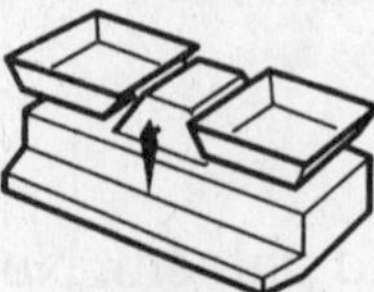

Activity Procedure

1. Cover the bottom of the measuring cup with unpopped popcorn seeds.
2. **Estimate** the volume of the unpopped seeds. Put the cup on the balance, and **measure** the mass of the unpopped seeds.
3. **Predict** what will happen to the mass and the volume when the seeds are popped.
4. Your teacher will help you pop the popcorn. Return the popped seeds to the measuring cup.
5. **Measure** the volume and mass of the cup of popped popcorn. Were your **predictions** correct?

Name ______________________

Draw Conclusions

1. How did the volume of the popcorn change? ______________________

____

2. How did the mass change? Explain. ______________________

____

____

3. Scientists at Work One reason why scientists **experiment** is to test predictions. If an experiment doesn't turn out the way they predicted, it may mean that their predictions were wrong. Or it may mean that they did not consider everything that could affect the experiment. Did you predict the volume and mass of the popped popcorn correctly? Explain.

____

____

____

Investigate Further Water turns into a gas when it is heated. What do you **predict** will happen when that gas cools? **Experiment** to test your prediction.

____

____

____

Name ______________________

Date ______________________

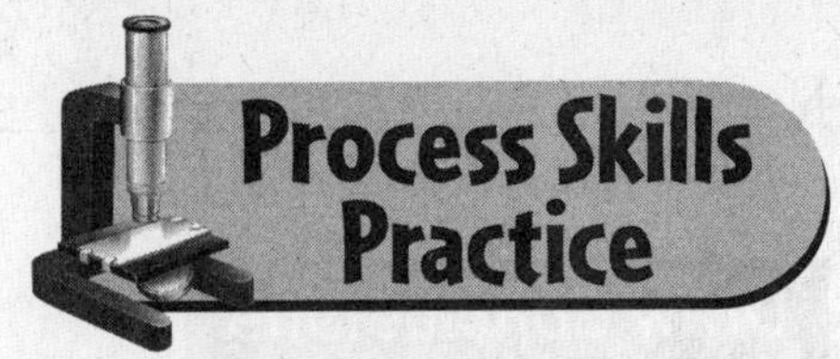

Experiment

When you experiment, you gather data to test a hypothesis. A well-designed experiment will allow you to test for certain variables while controlling others so you will know which factors affect the outcome.

Think About Experimenting

Juan and Ahmal were planning an experiment to see which of four different fertilizers would grow the biggest and healthiest plants. Juan gathered four pots from the garage, labeled them *Pot A* through *Pot D*, and filled them with dirt from his backyard. He put various seeds into each pot. He labeled the fertilizers *A* through *D* and put a teaspoon of *Fertilizer A* into *Pot A*, *Fertilizer B* in *Pot B*, and so on until each pot had a spoonful of different fertilizer. Ahmal watched him do this. Then he reminded Juan that he had not controlled his experiment. Juan agreed. They started over again.

1. What are some variables Juan should control? ______________________

____

____

2. Juan and Ahmal also need a control sample. How do they make one?

____

____

3. As he was filling the pots with potting soil he had bought at the hardware store, Juan thought of another problem. What if, without meaning to, they paid more attention to one of the plants, because they had already formed a hypothesis that *Fertilizer A* worked better than the others? How could they avoid this? ______________________

____

____

4. What do you think would be the best way to gather data from this experiment?

____

____

Use with page A81.

Name ______________________

Date ______________________

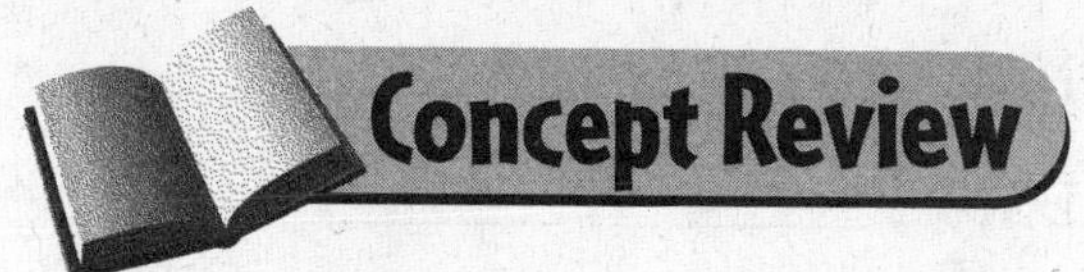

How Do People Use Plants?

Lesson Concept

People eat the leaves, the stems, the roots, the seeds, the fruits, and the flowers of various plants. When they are sick, people often use medicines made from plants. In fact, many things people use every day come from plants.

Vocabulary

grain (A82) **fiber** (A84)

Read the statements below. Put a *T* in front of the true statements and an *F* in front of the false statements. If the statement is false, write a correction in the space provided after it.

_____ **1.** People use plants more for food than for any other purpose.

____

____

_____ **2.** Fruits form the largest part of the Food Guide Pyramid.

____

____

_____ **3.** Quinine, which is made from the bark of a tree, is used to treat measles. ______________________________

____

_____ **4.** Grains are the seeds of certain types of grasses. ____________

____

_____ **5.** Digitalis, which is made from the leaves of the maple tree, is a heart medicine. ______________________________

____

_____ **6.** A fiber is any material that can be separated into thread.

____

____

Name ____________________

Date ____________________

Recognize Vocabulary

Read the clues to decide which vocabulary term to use to fill in the word puzzle.

Across

1. tubes that carry food in plants
2. plants that lack tubes for carrying food and water
3. a reproductive cell that grows into a new plant
4. plants that have tubes for carrying food and water
5. a plant with seeds covered by fruit
6. plant structures that contain male reproductive cells
7. tubes that carry water and minerals in plants

Down

8. a plant whose seeds are not protected by fruit
9. a pigment that helps plants produce sugar from light energy

Use with pages A62–A91.

Name ______________________ Date ______________

Chapter 4 • Graphic Organizer for Chapter Concepts

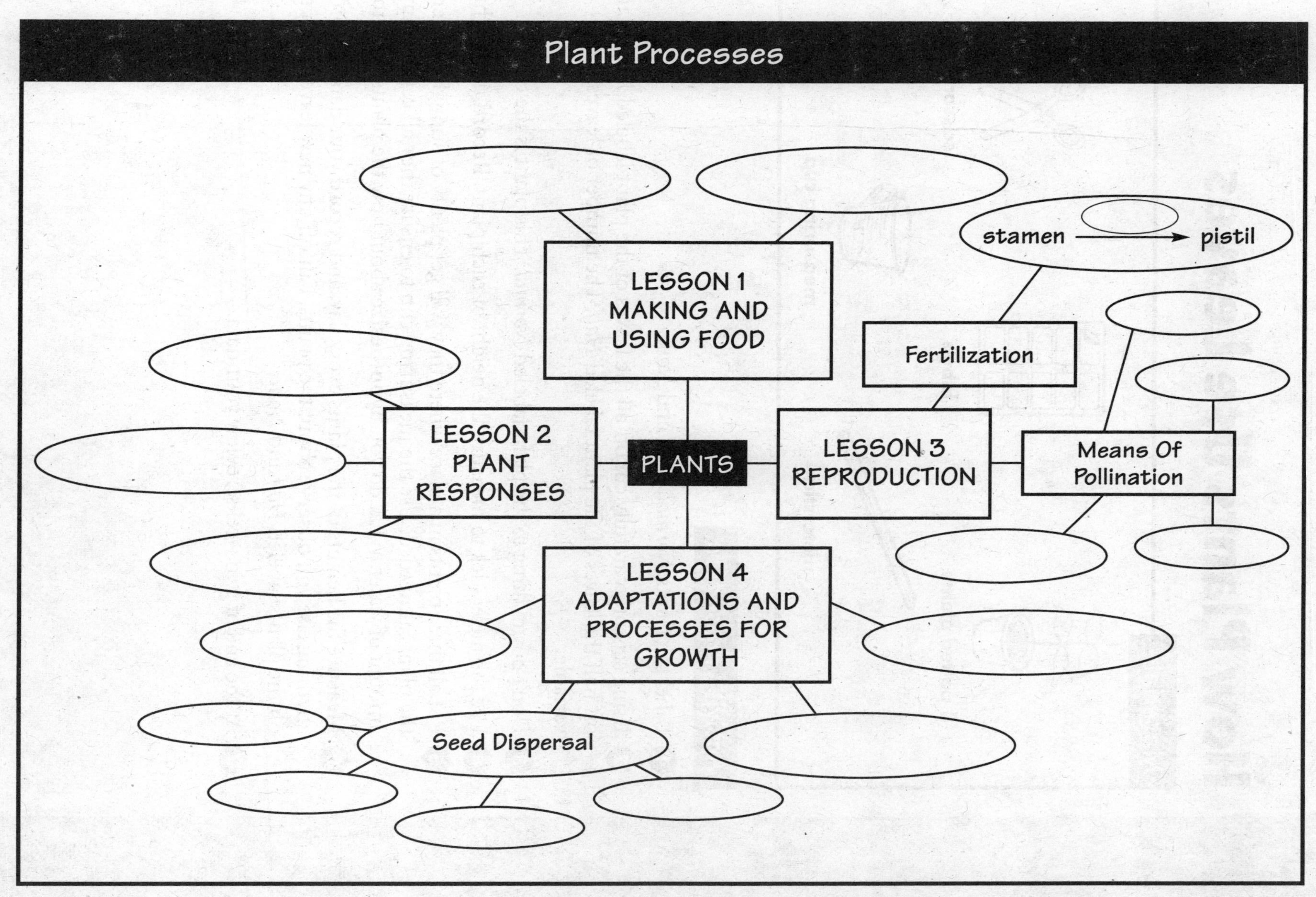

Name ______________________

Date ______________________

How Plants Use Leaves

Materials

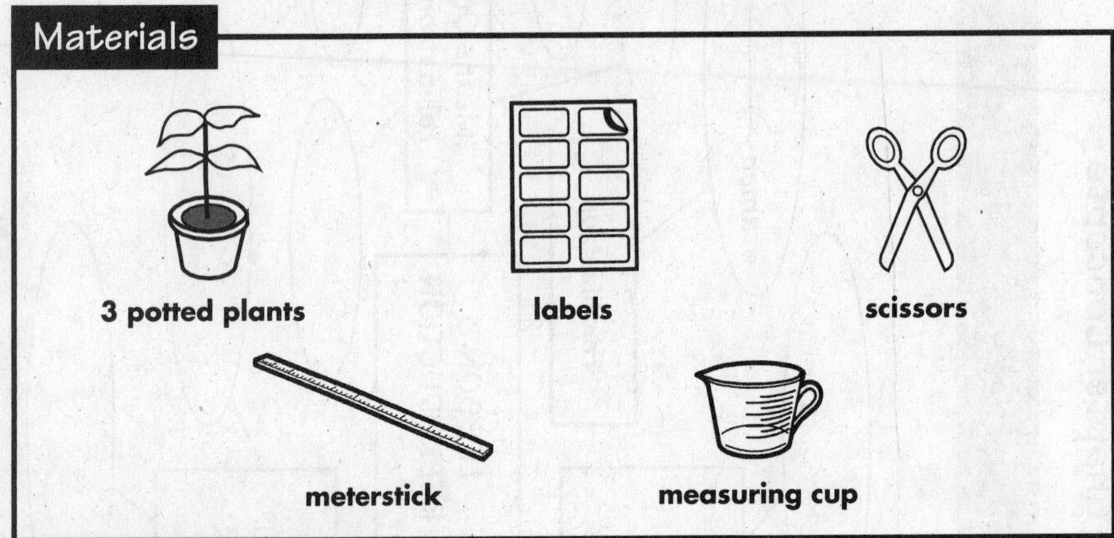

Activity Procedure

1. Label the plants *Normal*, *Half*, and *None*.
2. Using scissors, carefully cut off all the leaves of the plant labeled *None*. Cut off half the leaves of the plant labeled *Half*. The number of leaves is the variable.
3. Don't do anything to the plant labeled *Normal*. This plant is the control.
4. Use the meterstick to **measure** the height of each plant. **Record** the heights.
5. Put all three plants in a place where they will get plenty of sunlight. Water the plants as needed. Use the measuring cup to ensure they all get the same amount of water. What do you **hypothesize** about how the plants will grow?
6. **Measure** the heights of the plants every day, and **record** your data. Record anything else you **observe** about the plants. Cut off any new leaves that grow on the plants labeled *Half* and *None*.
7. At the end of two weeks, review your data.

Name ______________________

Draw Conclusions

1. Which plant grew the most in height? Which plant grew the least? Does the data support your **hypothesis**? What can you conclude about the importance of leaves? ______________________

____

____

2. Why was making sure the three plants received the same amount of sunlight important in this investigation? ______________________

____

____

3. Scientists at Work Scientists always **control variables** when they **experiment.** Why was watering all the plants with the same amount of water important in your investigation? ______________________

____

____

Investigate Further Does adding plant food really improve plant growth, as advertisements would have you believe? **Plan and conduct a simple investigation** to find out. Be sure you have a way to **control variables** in your investigation.

____

____

____

____

Name ______________________

Date ______________________

Process Skills Practice

Control Variables

When you control variables, you are better able to draw valid conclusions about the data you collect in an experiment. The first step is to identify which conditions in an experiment may change the experiment's outcome. Then you control all but one of those conditions.

Think About Controlling Variables

Mary has a large pond stocked with several kinds of fish. She has been feeding the fish the same food for years, and her fish have always been healthy. Now she has found another brand of food that is less expensive. She is concerned, however, that the new brand will not be as good for her fish as the more expensive brand. To experiment, she takes water from the pond and puts the same amount into two identical aquarium tanks. She puts a few fish in each tank, making sure that each tank has the same number, kind, and size of fish. She sprinkles the old brand of fish food in one tank and the new brand in the other tank. After one week Mary sees that the fish in both tanks are still healthy. After another week all the fish are still healthy, but some of the fish eating the new brand of food have actually grown larger.

1. What are the variables in Mary's experiment? ______________________

____

____

2. Which of the variables did Mary deliberately change? ______________________

3. Mary forgot to control one other important variable. Which one was it?

____

4. How do you think having two uncontrolled variables will affect the experiment? ______________________

____

5. Other than the type of food, can you think of another variable that may explain why the fish got bigger in one tank? ______________________

____

____

____

Use with page A95.

Name ____________________

Date ____________________

How Do Plants Make Food?

Lesson Concept

Plants make food in their leaves by photosynthesis, the process in which chlorophyll uses light energy to combine water and carbon dioxide to form glucose and oxygen. Plants use most of this food and store the rest. The extra food is passed to animals that eat the plants. Plants and animals use food energy, which is released by cellular respiration.

Vocabulary

photosynthesis (A96) **epidermis** (A97) **palisade layer** (A97)
cellular respiration (A100)

Match each term on the left with its description on the right.

Column A	Column B
______ **1.** upper epidermis	**A** a process by which plants make food
______ **2.** glucose	**B** a substance in chloroplasts that changes light energy into chemical energy
______ **3.** cellular respiration	**C** the system of xylem and phloem tubes in leaves
______ **4.** palisade layer	**D** a layer of cells that lies below the palisade layer and has many air spaces
______ **5.** photosynthesis	**E** structures that contain chlorophyll, which gives plants their green color
______ **6.** guard cells	**F** a type of sugar made in leaves
______ **7.** chlorophyll	**G** the waxy covering of the epidermis
______ **8.** chloroplasts	**H** a layer of cells that have many chloroplasts and that lie directly below the upper epidermis
______ **9.** spongy layer	**I** a process by which plants release the energy in food to carry on life processes
______ **10.** cuticle	**J** the single layer of protective cells on the upper surface of a leaf
______ **11.** veins	**K** cells that form the edges of the stomata

Use with page A101.

Name ______________________

Date ______________________

How Plants Get the Light They Need

Materials

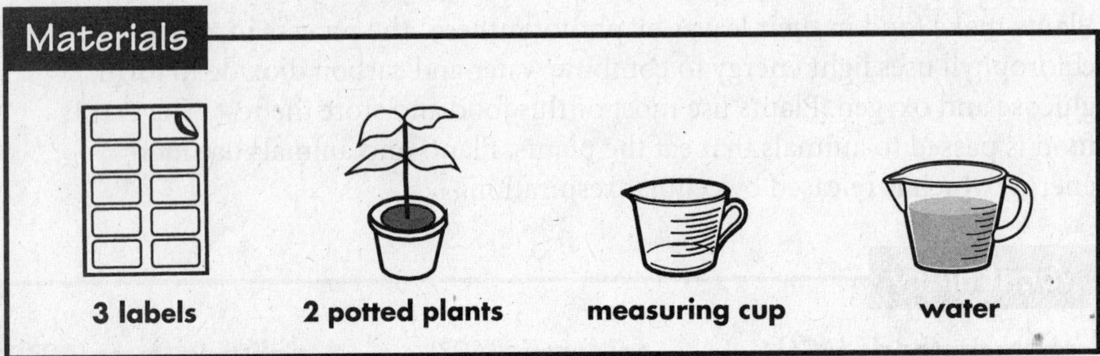

Activity Procedure

1. Write *Odd days* on one of the labels. Put the label on one side of a pot. Write *Even days* on a second label. Put this label on the other side of the same pot. Write *Don't move* on the third label, and put it on the other pot.
2. Place both potted plants in a sunny area. If you don't have a sunny area, put them under and to one side of a light source, such as a lamp. Make sure both plants are on the same side of and at the same distance from the lamp.
3. Use the measuring cup to give both plants the same amount of water at the same time each day. **Observe** the plants every day, and **record** your observations.
4. Turn the plant labeled *Odd days/Even days* one-half turn every day. If you start the **experiment** on an even-numbered day, place the pot so you can see the *Even days* label. If you start on an odd-numbered day, place the pot so that you can see the *Odd days* label. Do not turn the plant labeled *Don't move.*
5. After ten days write a summary of your **observations** about how the plants have grown. Draw pictures showing how the plants looked at the beginning and at the end of the **experiment**.

Name ______________________

Draw Conclusions

1. What did you **observe** about the growth of the plants during the investigation?

____

2. **Compare** the two plants. What variable were the plants responding to?

____

3. **Scientists at Work** Scientists often **compare** organisms to help them understand how organisms respond to their environments. In this investigation, how did comparing the way the plants grew help you **draw conclusions** about the way plants respond to light? ______________________

____

____

Investigate Further **Hypothesize** about all plants needing the same amount of sunlight. Try putting two different plants in a very sunny window. Give both plants the same amount of water. **Observe**, and **record** your observations of the plants for two weeks. ______________________

____

____

Name ____________________

Date ____________________

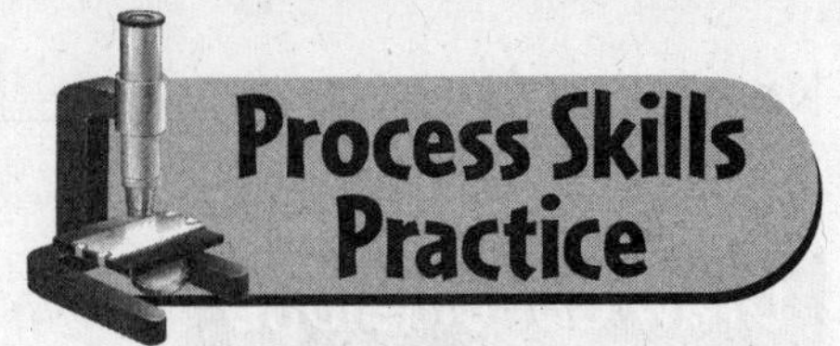

Draw Conclusions

When you draw conclusions, you use many other process skills, such as processing data collected from literature research.

Think About Drawing Conclusions

Jason was buying grass seed for his mother's lawn. His mother wanted the grass to grow well under the maple trees, in the direct sun at the south side of the house, and in the moist shaded area at the bottom of the backyard slope. Jason went to the garden center and looked at the different types of grass seed. Each bag of seed had a description of what the grass would look like and where it would grow best. He took the following notes:

Jackson Brand: dark green, thick "carpet," grows well in shade, keep out of full sun, turns green in mid-March, goes dormant (brown) at first frost

Black Beard Grass: dark green, average thickness, grows best in moist, shaded areas, stays green all year

Wicked Weed Grass: medium green, medium thickness, needs full sun, turns green in mid-March, goes dormant at first frost

1. Fill in the chart to help in drawing conclusions.

	Jackson Brand	Black Beard	Wicked Weed
Color			
Thickness			
Needs sun or shade			
When it turns green			
When it goes dormant			

2. What conclusions can you draw from the data in the chart? ____________________

____

____

Use with page A103.

Name ______________________

Date ______________________

How Do Plants Respond to Light and Gravity?

Lesson Concept

Tropisms cause plants to respond to certain stimuli, such as light and gravity. Some plants respond to touch.

Vocabulary

tropism (A104) **phototropism** (A104) **gravitropism** (A105)

Write a *T* in front of the true statements and an *F* in front of the false statements. If the statement is false, write a correction to it in the space provided.

______ **1.** A plant's response to a stimulus is called a tropism. ______________________

____

______ **2.** Gravitropism is an adaptation that causes some plants to live longer than others. ______________________

____

______ **3.** Some plants have parts that can move in response to being touched.

____

______ **4.** If a seed lands upside down, its roots will grow upward and may never touch the soil. ______________________

____

______ **5.** Phototropism is a plant's response to light. ______________________

______ **6.** A stimulus is anything that causes an organism to respond.

____

______ **7.** A plant bends toward the light, because the cells on the side of the plant facing the light are shorter. ______________________

____

Use with page A107.

Name ____________________

Date ____________________

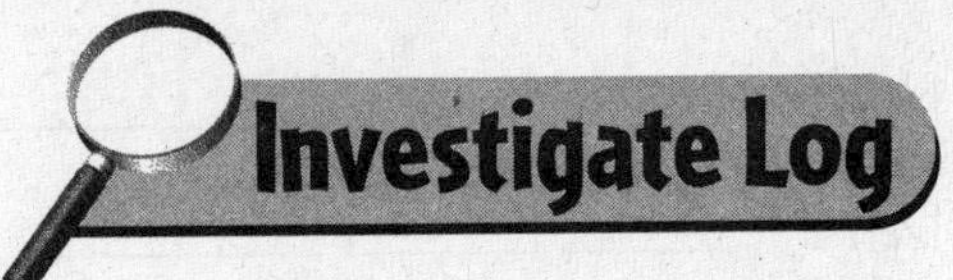

Flower Parts

Materials

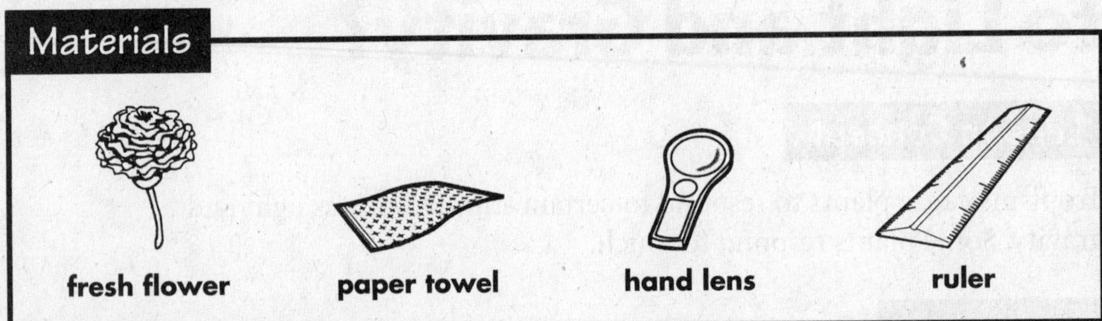

Activity Procedure

1. Place a fresh flower on a paper towel.
2. **Observe** the outside of the flower. Notice the green, leaflike parts around the petals. These are called *sepals* (SEE•puhls). How many sepals does the flower have? What shape are the sepals? **Record** your observations.
3. Now **observe** the flower's petals. How many petals does the flower have? What shape are they? What color are they? Do the petals have any patterns, or are they one color? What do the petals feel like? **Record** your observations.
4. **Observe** the flower with your eyes closed. Does it have an odor? How would you describe the odor? What part of the flower do you think the odor is coming from? **Record** your observations about the flower's odor.
5. Using the hand lens, **observe** the inside of the flower. What parts do you see? What are the shapes of these parts? **Measure** these parts. **Record** your observations about the inside of the flower.
6. Now make a drawing of the inside of the flower. As you draw each part, try to **infer** what it does.

Name ______________________

Draw Conclusions

1. Colorful markings and strong odors often attract birds and insects to flowers. How might the location of the markings and odors attract birds and insects to the flower? ______________________

2. In the very center of a flower is the female reproductive part. Stalks surrounding the center contain male reproductive parts. **Infer** how it might help the plant to have the male parts around the female part.

3. **Scientists at Work** When scientists **infer** a part's function, they sometimes base their inferences on **observing** the part's location. Based on the sepals' location, what could you infer about the function of sepals? ______________________

Investigate Further **Observe** the parts of another kind of flower. How does that flower **compare** to the one you observed in this investigation? Does it have the same number of sepals? Are the petals arranged the same way? Do the flower's inner parts look the same? What other questions could you answer by observing the flower? ______________________

Name ____________________

Date ____________________

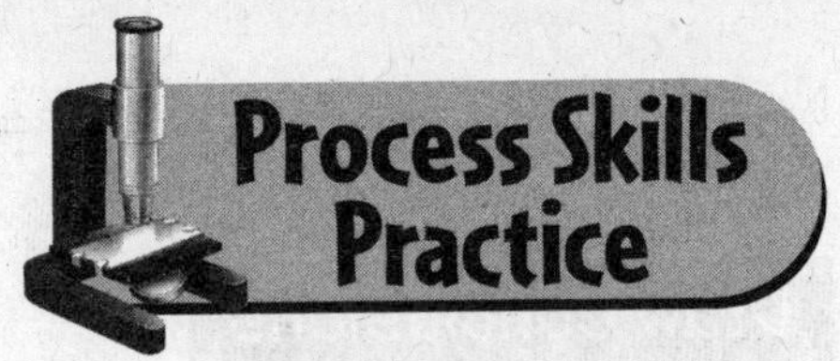

Infer

When you infer, you explain an event by using observation, previous information or experience, and your own judgment. Inferences supported by observation and reasoning are always valid, but they may not always be correct.

Think About Inferring

Tami saw an article in the newspaper about the poor apple harvest in her area. Farmers were blaming the poor harvest on the heavy rains that had fallen earlier that year. One farmer interviewed for the article said, "There was so much rain in the spring that the bees couldn't get out. Those that did go out of their hives were knocked to the ground and drowned." Tami was confused. She asked herself, "What do bees have to do with a poor apple harvest?"

1. What event was Tami trying to explain? ____________________

2. What observations can she use? ____________________

____

3. What previous knowledge or experience could Tami use to help her understand why the apple harvest was poor? ____________________

____

____

4. Tami tries an inference: perhaps the bees add honey to the apples to make them sweeter. What are some reasons this inference might be wrong? ____________________

____

____

5. Can you think of one inference Tami could make based on her observations that would be valid? ____________________

____

Harcourt

Use with page A109.

Name ______________________

Date ______________________

How Do Plants Reproduce?

Lesson Concept

Most flowers have both male and female reproductive parts. Pollen, which has sperm cells, is produced by the stamens. The pistil has the eggs. Pollen is transferred from the stamens to the pistil. After fertilization, the eggs develop into seeds.

Vocabulary

fertilization (A110) **stamens** (A110) **pistil** (A110) **ovary** (A111)

Answer each of the questions below by writing *yes* or *no* in the space on the left. Then, on the lines beneath the question, explain your answer.

______ **1.** Do most flowers have only female reproductive parts? ______________________

______ **2.** Do the stamens have eggs? ______________________

______ **3.** Is pollen transferred from the pistil to the stamens? ______________________

______ **4.** Is the pistil the flower's female reproductive part? ______________________

______ **5.** Do animals carry eggs from one flower to another? ______________________

______ **6.** Do some plants depend on the wind to transfer pollen? ______________________

______ **7.** Do gymnosperms have flowers? ______________________

______ **8.** Are fertilization and pollination the same thing? ______________________

Use with page A113.

Name ______________________

Date ______________________

The Parts of a Seed

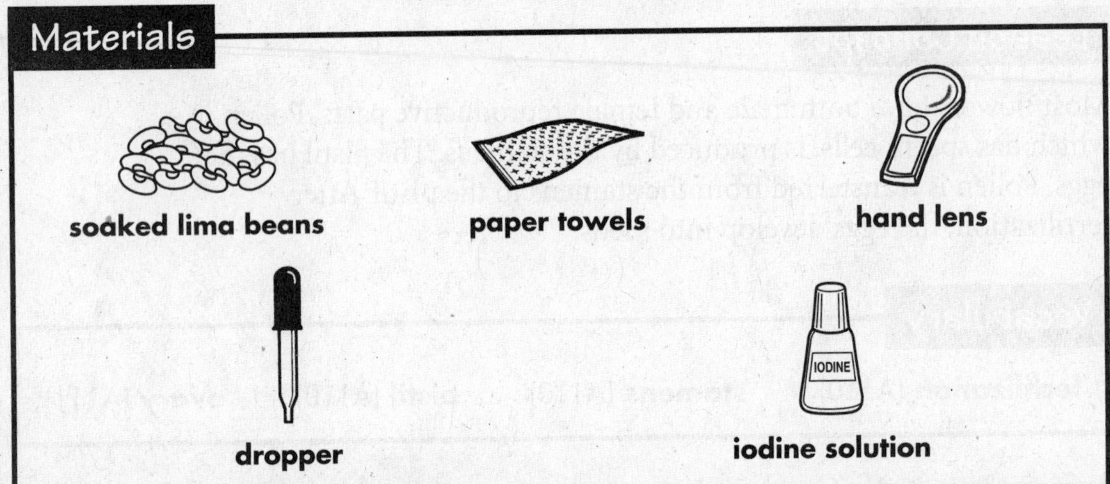

Materials
soaked lima beans
paper towels
hand lens
dropper
IODINE
iodine solution

CAUTION

Activity Procedure

1. Put a soaked lima bean on a paper towel. **Observe** the seed with the hand lens. **Record** your observations by drawing a picture of what you see.
2. Carefully peel away the outer covering of the bean. This covering is called the *seed coat.*
3. Gently open the bean by splitting it in half. Use the hand lens to **observe** the parts inside the bean. **Record** your observations by drawing a picture of what you see.
4. Using the point of a pencil, carefully remove the part of the bean that looks like a tiny plant. This is called the *embryo.* Look through the hand lens to identify the parts of the embryo that look like leaves, a stem, and a root.
5. CAUTION **Iodine can stain your hands and clothes.** Carefully, put a drop or two of the iodine solution on the other parts of the bean. These parts are called the *cotyledons.* **Observe** what happens. **Record** your observations.
6. Label the seed coat, embryo, and cotyledons on your drawing from Step 3. On the embryo, label the parts that look like leaves, a stem, and a root.

 Use with pages A114–A115.

Name ______________________

Draw Conclusions

1. What words would you use to describe the seed coat of the bean? What do you **infer** is its function? ______________________

____

____

2. Iodine turns black in the presence of starch, a kind of food that plants store. Because of this, what do you **infer** is the function of the cotyledons?

____

____

3. **Scientists at Work** Scientists **observe** many plant parts. They often **communicate** to other scientists inferences they have made about the functions of certain parts. They use descriptions, data tables, graphs, and drawings. How would you communicate to a classmate your inferences about the function of cotyledons? ______________________

____

____

____

Investigate Further **Observe** other seeds that can be easily opened, such as green peas, squash seeds, or watermelon seeds. Examine the seed coats, and then gently split the seeds open. **Compare** them to the bean seed you studied in this investigation. Draw pictures, and label the parts of the seeds you observe.

____

____

____

Name ______________________________

Date ______________________________

Process Skills Practice

Communicate

When you communicate, you give information. In science you communicate by showing results from an activity in an organized way, such as by using a chart. Then you and other people can interpret the results.

Think About Communicating

Richard was working in his basement laboratory every night. He was trying to invent a new kind of glue that would stick to almost everything but would not be poisonous. He decided to use only things that you can eat. He mixed flour with water. It was a good glue, but Richard was sure he could do better. So he mixed corn starch with milk and grape jelly. That was good, too, but he wanted to see if he could do even better. After several weeks in his laboratory, he had still not invented the glue he was looking for. He called his friend Jefferson, who was working on the same problem in his own basement laboratory. Jefferson asked him which formula he had been working on. Richard realized then that he couldn't say exactly.

1. What information should Richard have recorded while he was working in his laboratory? ______________________________

2. Why should Richard have kept better records? ______________________________

3. What would be a good method for keeping track of what Richard had tried? ______________________________

4. How could Richard be sure he had communicated his information well? ______________________________

5. Can you think of any other way effective communication might have made Richard's experimentation easier? ______________________________

Use with page A115.

Name ____________________

Date ____________________

How Do Plants Grow?

Lesson Concept

Seeds contain embryo plants and stored food. Under the right conditions, seeds germinate. Seedlings are young plants that grow from the embryos. Some plants may reproduce asexually through vegetative propagation. Farmers and scientists use cross-pollination and grafting as other means of plant reproduction.

Vocabulary

embryo (A116) **cotyledons** (A116) **germinate** (A118)
seedling (A118) **vegetative propagation** (A119) **grafting** (A120)
tissue culture (A120)

The following boxes make up a flowchart showing how a plant grows. Below the boxes you will find captions describing each part of the growth process. Put the letter of the correct caption in each box of the flowchart.

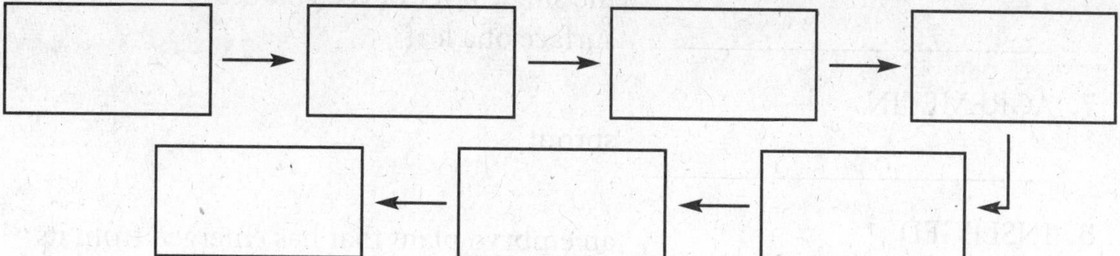

A As the root gets longer and thicker, a stem begins to emerge.

B Landing on moist, warm, fertile soil will allow the seed to take in moisture, to swell, and to germinate.

C The seed contains an embryo and stored food.

D The first part to emerge from the seed is the root.

E The seedling cannot yet make its own food but uses food stored in its cotyledons to grow.

F The seedling now has a well-developed root system, and its first leaves are producing food.

G The seed is dispersed by animals, wind, or water.

Use with page A121.

Name ______________________

Date ______________________

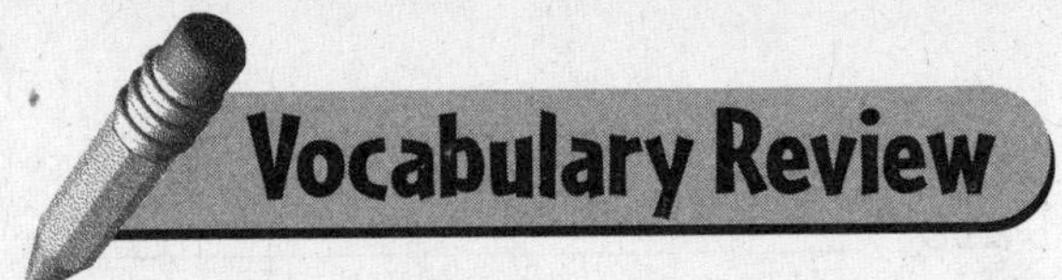

Recognize Vocabulary

Listed below are scrambled vocabulary terms from Chapter 4. Use the clues to unscramble the terms. Write the unscrambled terms on the lines provided.

1. PIPOOSTORMTH ______________________ a plant's response to light
2. PRECLURELINARSATOIL (2 words) ______________________ the process by which plants release energy in food to carry on life processes
3. FRANGITG ______________________ a form of artificial reproduction that involves attaching branches from one plant to the branches of another plant
4. CEDOSTLOYN ______________________ structures inside a seed that store food
5. ZELNITARITIOF ______________________ the joining of a male reproductive cell with a female reproductive cell
6. EMISPIDER ______________________ the single layer of cells on the surface of a leaf
7. AGREMETIN ______________________ sprout
8. INSLEGED ______________________ an embryo plant that has emerged from its seed and that is using energy from its cotyledons to grow
9. EMANSTS ______________________ the parts of a flower that produce pollen
10. HISPETHONSOYTS ______________________ the process by which plants make food
11. EVAPORATIONGIVETEPAGT (2 words) ______________________ the ability of some plants to reproduce without seeds

Use with pages A92–A127.

Name ______________________ Date ______________

Chapter 1 • *Graphic Organizer for Chapter Concepts*

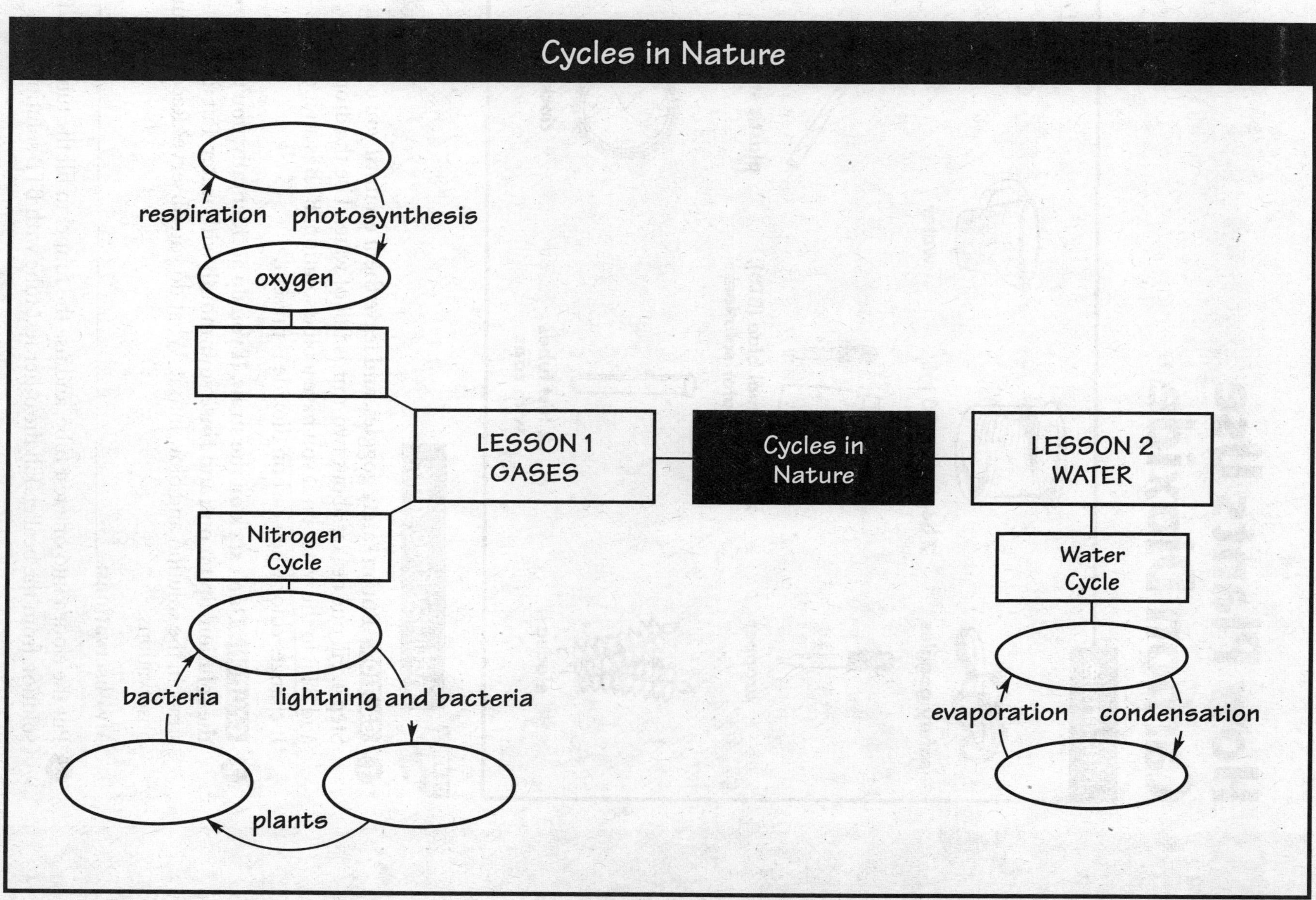

Name ______________________

Date ______________________

How Plants Use Carbon Dioxide

Materials

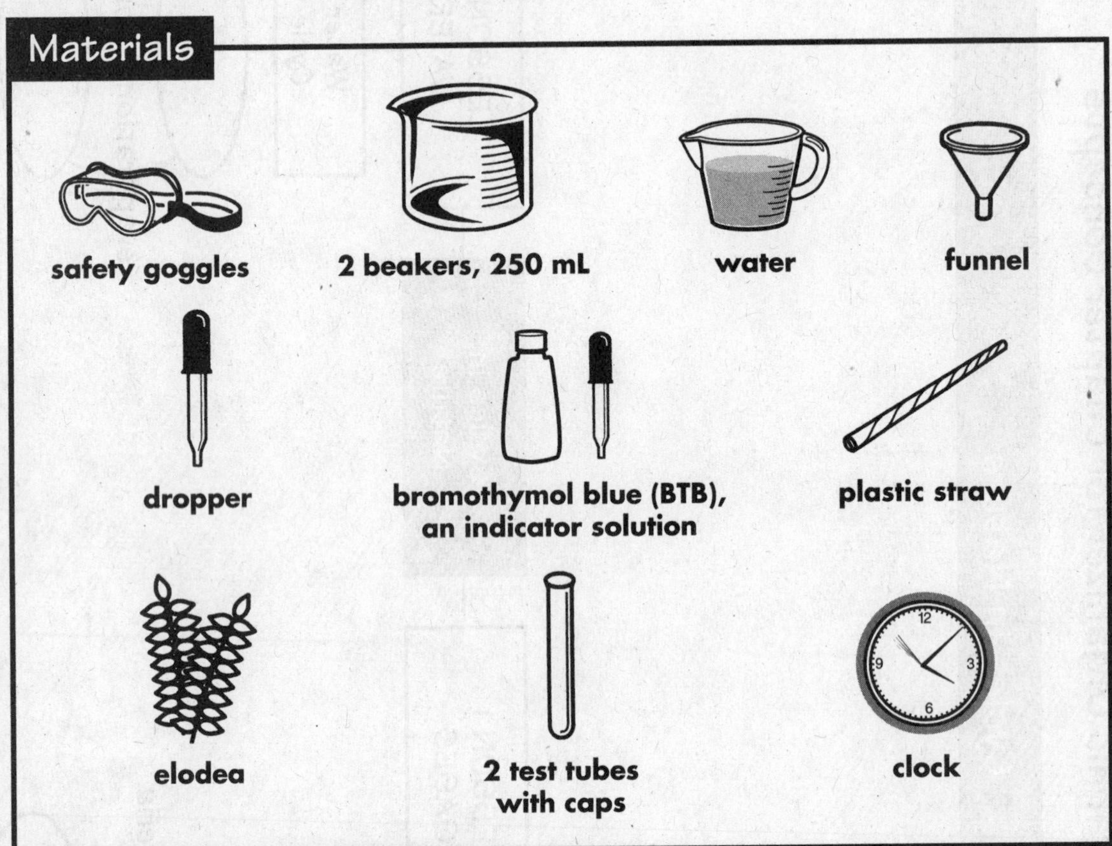

Activity Procedure

1. **CAUTION Put on safety goggles, and leave them on until you complete Step 4.** Fill one beaker about two-thirds full of water. Use the dropper to add BTB to the water until you have a blue solution. BTB is an indicator. It changes color when carbon dioxide is present.

2. **CAUTION Don't suck on the straw. If you do accidentally, don't swallow the solution. Spit it out, and rinse your mouth with water.** Put the plastic straw in the solution and blow into it. What do you **observe**? **Record** your observations.

   My observations: ______________________

3. Put the elodea into one test tube, and use the funnel to fill the tube with BTB solution from the beaker. Fill the other test tube with BTB solution only.

Name ______________________

Investigate Log

4. Seal the test tubes with caps. Carefully turn the test tubes upside down, and place them in the empty beaker.

5. Put the beaker containing the two test tubes in a sunny window for 1 hour. **Predict** what changes will occur in the test tubes. After 1 hour, **observe** both test tubes and **record** your observations.

My prediction: ______________________

____

My observations: ______________________

____

Draw Conclusions

1. What changes did you **observe** in the BTB solution when you blew into it through the straw? Explain. ______________________

____

2. What changes did you **observe** in the test tube of BTB after the elodea plant had been in it for 1 hour? ______________________

3. **Compare** the color of the BTB solution in the test tube that had the elodea with the color of the BTB in the test tube that did not have the elodea. Describe any differences. ______________________

____

4. **Scientists at Work** Scientists **observe** changes that happen during experiments. Then they **infer** what caused the changes. What can you infer about any changes that took place in the test tubes? ______________________

____

Investigate Further What is the importance of sunlight in this investigation? **Hypothesize** about the importance of sunlight. Then **plan and conduct a simple investigation** to test your hypothesis.

My hypothesis: ______________________

____

My investigation design: ______________________

____

My results: ______________________

____

Name ___________________________

Date ___________________________

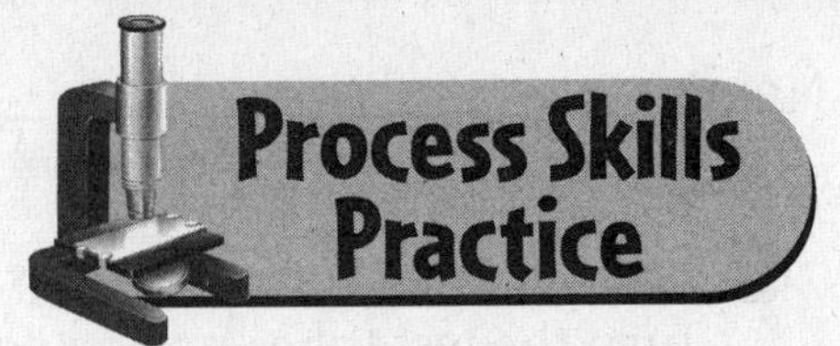

Observe

Observing is a basic science skill. Making good observations will allow you to develop other important science skills, like inferring, comparing, classifying, and measuring.

Think About Observing

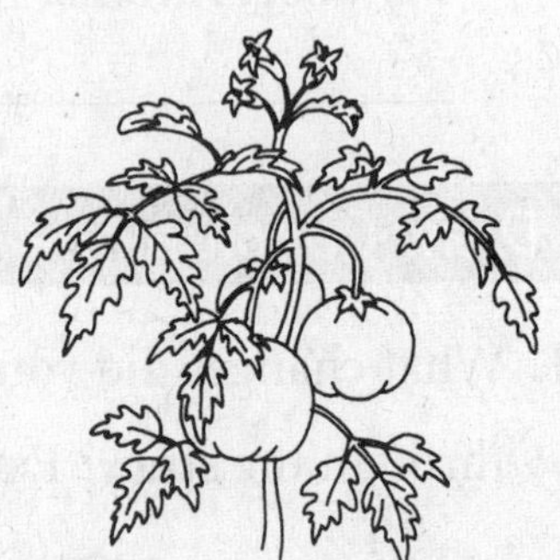

Cecelia likes to grow tomatoes. She wanted to see if adding certain things to the soil would improve her tomato harvest. She treated different parts of her garden with kitchen-scrap compost, leaf-litter compost, and nitrogen fertilizer. Some parts of the garden were not treated. For five years she treated the soil and recorded the number of tomatoes produced by the plants in each area of her garden.

	Untreated Soil	Kitchen-Scrap Compost	Leaf-Litter Compost	Nitrogen Fertilizer
Year 1	130	145	140	165
Year 2	125	155	155	155
Year 3	110	160	165	155
Year 4	95	155	170	145
Year 5	70	165	180	150

1. Which treatment produced the best results over time? ___________

2. Cecelia thought she should make a bar graph of her results. Do you think it would be easier to read her data this way? ___________

____

3. What inference could you make about how Cecelia could improve the yield of plants grown in the untreated area of her garden? ___________

____

Use with page B5.

Name ______________________

Date ______________________

How Does Nature Reuse Materials?

Lesson Concept

Many of the materials organisms need are cycled through nature.

Vocabulary

nitrogen cycle (B7) **carbon dioxide–oxygen cycle** (B8)

Choose the correct caption from the table below each diagram, and write the appropriate letter below each picture.

______ ______ ______

A	Animal wastes and decaying organisms return nitrates and ammonia to the soil.
B	Animals get nitrogen by eating plants and other animals.
C	Plants make proteins from nitrogen in the soil.

______ ______ ______

A	Plants use carbon dioxide and release oxygen during photosynthesis.
B	Plants and animals use oxygen and release carbon dioxide during respiration.
C	Bacteria and fungi use as food some carbon from the tissues of dead animals. The rest is released as carbon dioxide.

Use with page B11.

Name ____________________

Date ____________________

Water, Water Everywhere

Materials

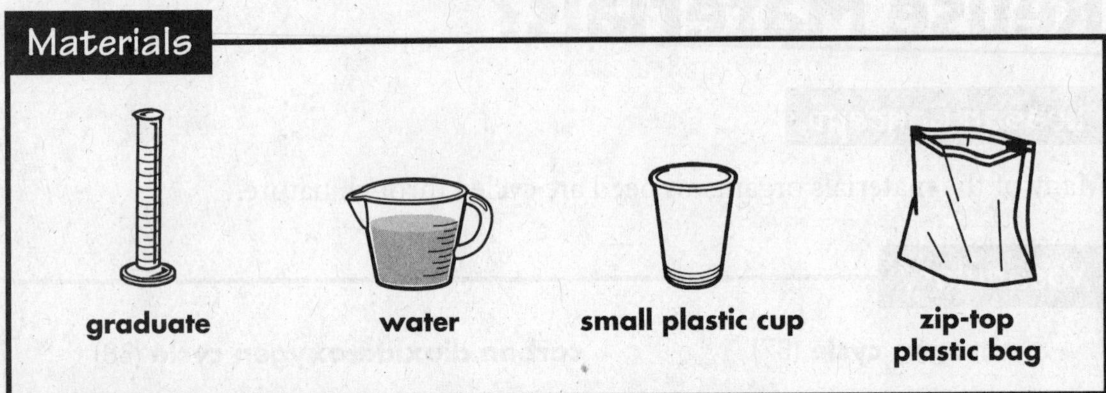

Activity Procedure

1. Using the graduate, **measure** and pour 100 mL of water into the cup.
2. Open the plastic bag, and carefully put the cup inside. Then seal the bag. Be careful not to spill any water from the cup.
3. Place the sealed bag near a sunny window. **Predict** what will happen to the water in the cup.

   My prediction: ____________________
4. Leave the bag near a window for 3–4 days. **Observe** the cup and the bag each day. **Record** what you see.

   My observation: ____________________

   ____
5. Remove the cup from the bag. **Measure** the amount of water in the cup by pouring it back into the graduate. **Calculate** any difference in the amount of water you poured into the cup and the amount of water you removed from the cup.

   My measurement: ____________________

   My calculation: ____________________

Name ___________________________

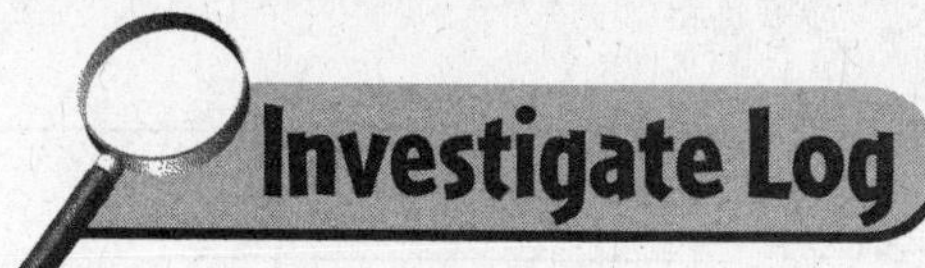

Draw Conclusions

1. What did you **observe** during the time the cup was inside the bag?

____

2. Where do you infer the water in the bag came from? Explain.

____

____

3. Scientists at Work Scientists often **infer** the cause of something they **observe.** What can you infer about the amount of water in the bag? ______________

____

Investigate Further How could you find out if the amount of water in the bag is the same as the amount of water missing from the cup? Decide what equipment you would need to use. Then **plan and conduct a simple investigation** that would help you answer the question.

My hypothesis: ______________________________

____

My investigation plan: _________________________

____

____

My results: _________________________________

Name ______________________

Date ______________________

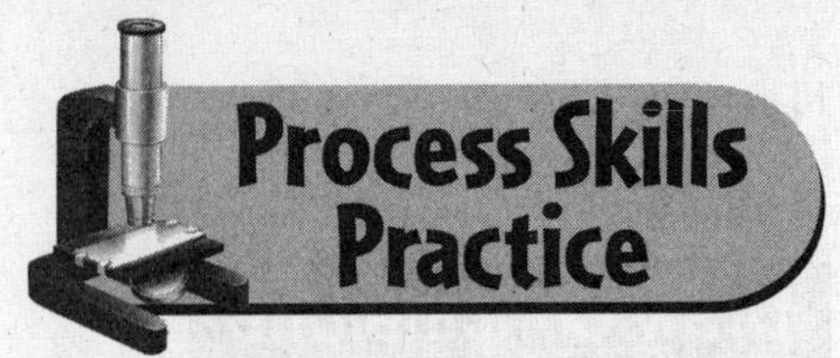

Infer

When you infer, you draw conclusions to explain events. Your inferences may not always be correct.

Think About Inferring

1. Dion lives in a town with a lake nearby. People use the lake to swim, fish, and go boating. Dion reads in the newspaper that the rainfall in the area has been less than normal for the summer. When he went to the lake, he noticed that the water level in the lake was lower than usual for the time of year. What could Dion infer caused the water level in the lake to be below normal?

____

____

2. Since there had been little rain in Dion's town, people were told not to water their lawns. Many plants in Dion's yard and garden turned brown and died. But the big trees were still green and leafy. What could Dion infer caused some plants to die and the trees to survive? ______________________

____

____

3. Last year Dion's uncle Jeb had a house built outside Dion's town. Jeb built a deep well to pull water up into his house. This year Jeb was not able to get any water from his well. What could Jeb infer caused him to not get water from his well this year? ______________________

____

4. Jeb found out that he needs to dig his well deeper to get water. The county engineer explained to Jeb that many people built houses and drilled wells near Jeb. This caused the groundwater level to drop several feet when everyone started using their wells. The county engineer also told Jeb that his groundwater comes from an underground river. The lack of rain during the summer would not affect the groundwater level. Knowing this, tell whether your inference was correct in Question 3. ______________________

5. What does Question 4 show you about making inferences? ______________________

____

____

Use with page B13.

Name ______________________ Date ______________

Chapter 2 • Graphic Organizer for Chapter Concepts

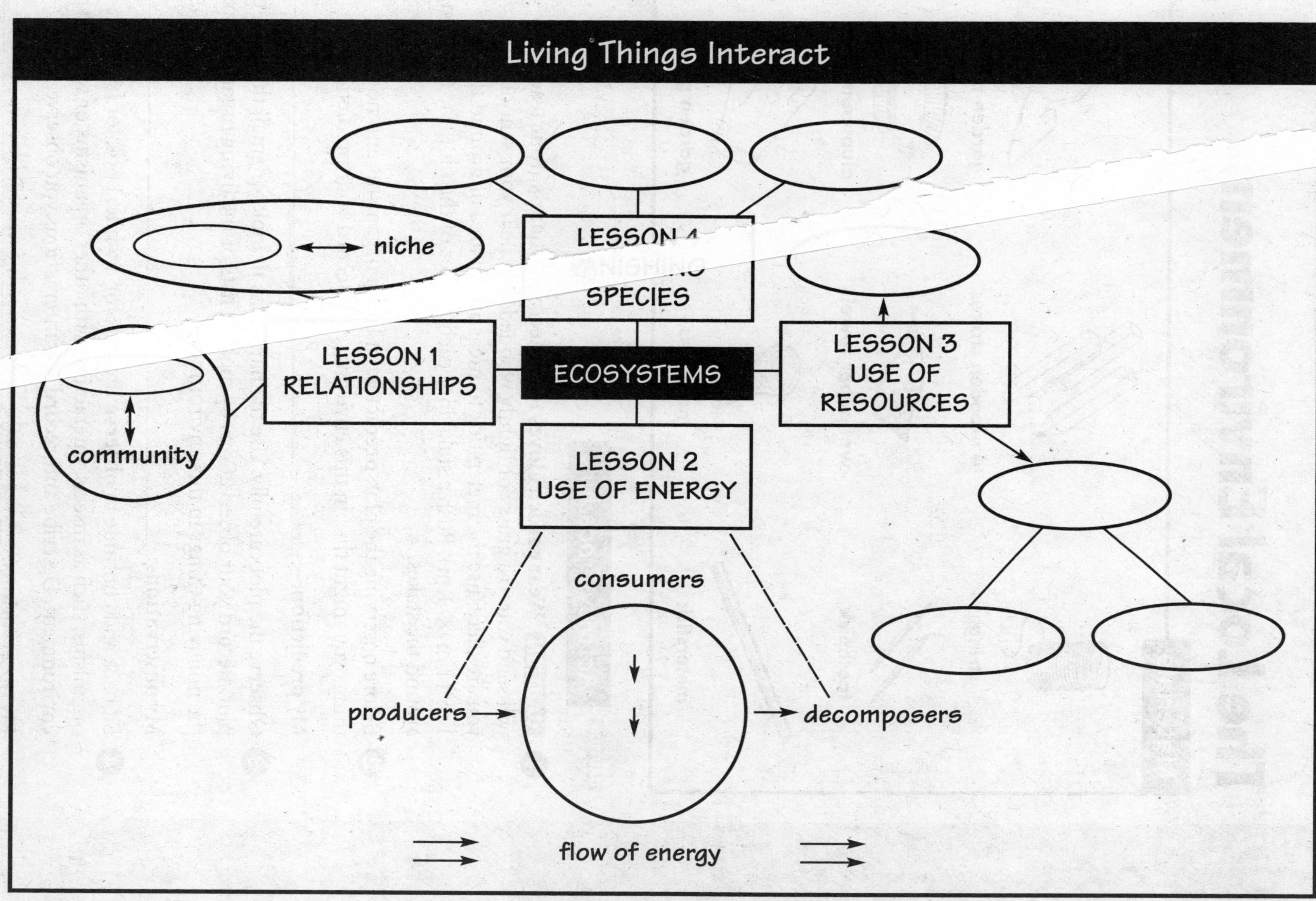

Harcourt

Name ______________________

Date ______________________

The Local Environment

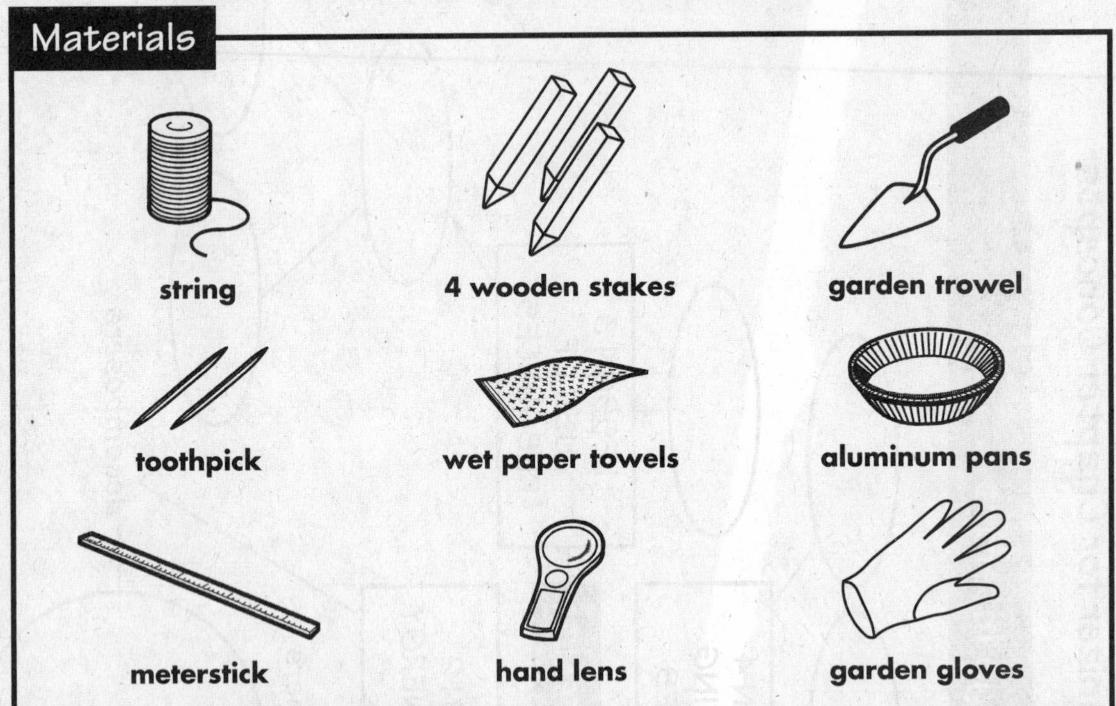

CAUTION Activity Procedure

1. **CAUTION** **Wear garden gloves to protect your hands.** Your teacher will send you to a grassy or lightly wooded area near your school. Once you are there, use the meterstick to **measure** an area of ground that is 1 m^2 ($1 \text{ m} \times 1 \text{ m}$). Push a stake into each corner of the plot. Tie the string around the stakes.

2. Before observing the plot, **predict** what living organisms and nonliving things you might find in this environment. **Record** your prediction.

   My prediction: ______________________

3. **Observe** the plot carefully. Use the hand lens to look for small things in the plot. **Record** your observations by making lists of the living organisms and the nonliving things in this environment.

   My observations: ______________________

4. Sit back and continue to **observe** the plot for a while. Look for living organisms, such as insects, interacting with other organisms or with the environment. Describe and **record** any interactions you observe.

   My observations: ______________________

Name ______________________

Investigate Log

5. Put wet paper towels in the aluminum pan, and use the garden trowel to scoop some soil onto them. Use a toothpick to sift through the soil. Be careful not to injure any living organisms with the toothpick.

6. **Record** what you **observe**, especially any interactions. Then return the soil to the plot of ground.

My observations: ______________________

Draw Conclusions

1. How did what you **predicted** compare with what you **observed**?

____

____

____

2. What did you **observe** that showed living organisms interacting with one another or with the environment? ______________________

____

____

____

3. **Scientists at Work** Scientists often use prior knowledge to **predict** what they might find or what might happen. What prior knowledge did you use to predict what you would find in the plot of ground? ______________________

____

____

____

Investigate Further Sometimes you can **infer** what interactions are occurring in an environment by **observing** what's in that environment. Choose an environment near your home or school. Observe what kinds of organisms live there, and infer how they interact with one another and with the environment.

____

____

____

____

Name ______________________

Date ______________________

Process Skills Practice

Predict

Scientists use what they already know to predict what they may find or what may happen. Careful observation helps them make a prediction rather than a guess.

Think About Predicting

Below is information about two different regions. Make predictions about the data by answering the questions that follow.

	Region I Temperate Grasslands	Region II Tropical Rain Forest
Soil conditions	porous soil, rich in organic matter	fragile soil
Vegetation	grasses and shrubs	tall, broad-leafed trees; multilevel canopy; sparse understory
Climate	short hot summers, long cold winters	tropical, hot throughout the year with rainy season
Annual rainfall	25–75 cm (10–30 in.)	200–400 cm (80–160 in.)

1. In which region would you be more likely to find animals that graze on grasses? ______________________

2. In which region would you be more likely to find animals adapted to traveling along treetops? ______________________

3. Which region would you predict could recover more quickly after a fire? Explain your answer. ______________________

____

____

____

4. Predict which region would have the greater diversity of animals. Explain.

____

____

Use with page B27.

Name ________________________

Date ________________________

What Are Ecosystems?

Lesson Concept

An ecosystem consists of communities of living things and the environment in which they live.

Vocabulary

individual (B28)	**population** (B28)	**community** (B28)
ecosystem (B28)	**habitat** (B29)	**niche** (B29)

Use the vocabulary terms above as well as the terms listed below to complete the sentences about ecosystems.

temperature	**survival**	**density**	**rainfall**
soil conditions	**plants**	**limiting factor**	

1. A single organism in an environment is called an ________________.
2. A population has a role, or ________________, in its environment.
3. The sizes of animal populations are determined by the kinds and numbers of ________________ in an ecosystem.
4. Individuals of the same species make up a ________________.
5. Populations of different organisms live together in a ________________.
6. The ________________, ________________, and ________________ of an environment determine the types of plants that grow there.
7. In a healthy ecosystem, each population contributes to the ________________ of the other populations.
8. The amount of food is a ________________ that affects population ________________, or the number of individuals of a species in an ecosystem.
9. Communities and the environment make up an ________________.
10. A ________________ is a place where a population lives in an ecosystem.

Use with page B31.

Name ______________________

Date ______________________

What Eats What In Ecosystems

Materials

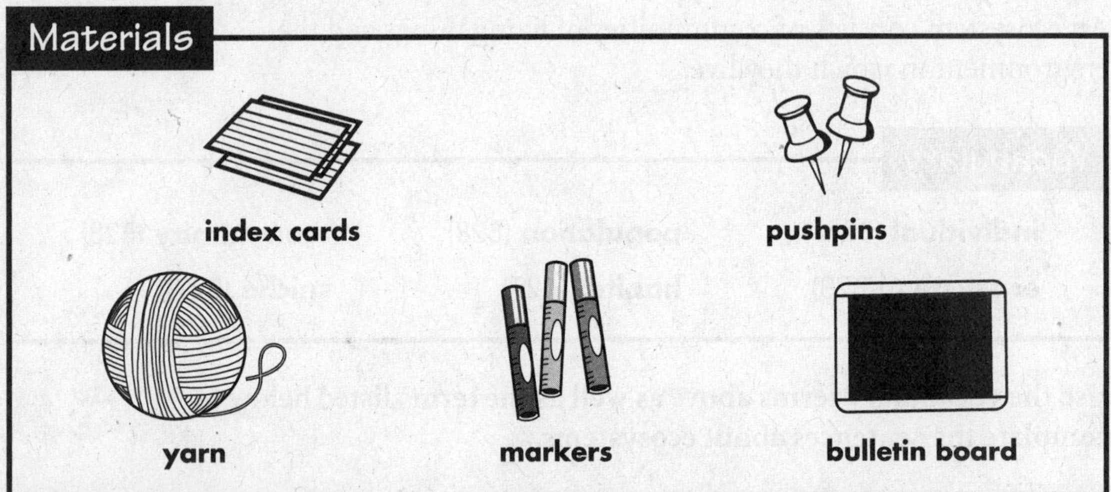

Activity Procedure

1. Your teacher will assign you an organism from a prairie ecosystem. Use an encyclopedia to find out what your organism eats. Then **classify** your organism into one of the following groups:
   - plants
   - meat-eating animals
   - plant-eating animals
   - animals that eat both plants and meat
   - animals that eat dead organisms
2. Use markers to draw your organism or write its name on an index card.
3. Your teacher will now assign you to a class team. Each team will have at least one organism from each group listed above. With your teammates, **order** your team's cards to show what eats what in a prairie ecosystem.
4. When your team's cards are in order, pin them in a line on the bulletin board. Connect the cards with yarn to show what eats what—both within your team's group of organisms and between those of other teams.

Name ______________________

Draw Conclusions

1. When your team put its cards in **order**, what kind of organism was first?

____

2. How would you **classify** the organism that came right after the first organism?

____

3. **Scientists at Work** When scientists **classify** things that happen in a particular order, it helps them understand how something works. Look again at your team's cards on the bulletin board. Could you classify or order them in any other way to explain what eats what in an ecosystem? ______________

____

Investigate Further Find out what eats what in another ecosystem. If possible, use a computer to help you with your research. Then make a drawing to show the flow of energy in that ecosystem. Share your drawing with the class.

Name ______________________

Date ______________________

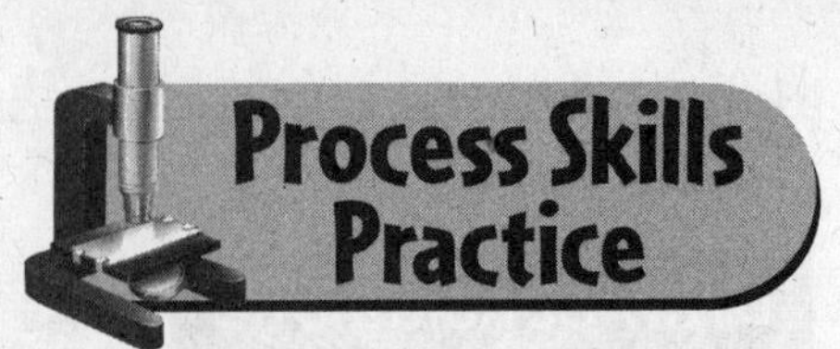

Classify and Order

When you classify things, you put them into groups based on their similarities. When you order these groups, you can see relationships between the different groups.

Think About Classifying and Ordering

1. Read the descriptions of four groups of organisms. Then use the numbers of the groups to classify the living things in the chart shown below.

Group 1 eats foodmakers
Group 2 eats decaying things
Group 3 eats animals
Group 4 makes its own food

Living Things	Group
Plant-eating mice	
Grasses	
Bacteria that break down animal wastes and dead organisms	
Grass-eating voles	
Worms that eat decaying grasses and berries and waste products of animals	
Owls that eat weasels, mice, and voles	
Shrubs that produce berries	
Weasels that eat mice and voles	

2. Order by what eats what from the living things listed. Start with the organism that doesn't eat anything. Use each of these living things only once.

owl—grass—vole—waste-eating bacteria ______________________

____

3. Can you see another relationship between these groups other than what eats what? ______________________

____

____

Use with page B33.

Name ______________________

Date ______________________

How Does Energy Flow Through an Ecosystem?

Lesson Concept

Energy starts to flow through an ecosystem when an organism uses the sun's energy to make food. Energy continues to flow when one organism eats another organism.

Vocabulary

producers (B34)	**consumers** (B34)	**food chain** (B35)
decomposer (B35)	**food web** (B36)	**energy pyramid** (B38)

Below is an energy pyramid and a list of organisms. Write the names of the organisms where they belong on the energy pyramid.

Grass **Lion**
Vulture **Antelope**

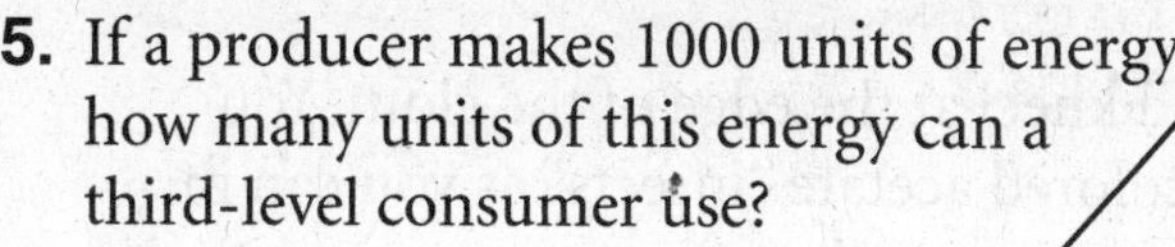

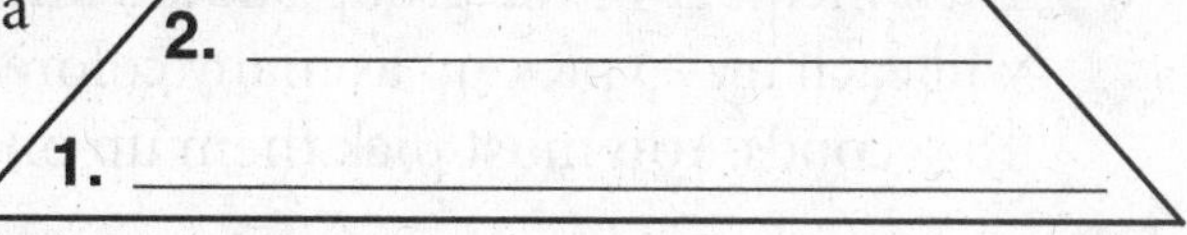

4. ______________

3. ______________

2. ______________

1. ______________

5. If a producer makes 1000 units of energy, how many units of this energy can a third-level consumer use?

____

6. What does it mean to say that an organism is a producer? ______________________

____

7. First-level consumers are called ______________________, while second- and third-level consumers are called ______________________.

8. Is the energy pyramid more like a food chain or a food web? Explain.

____

____

____

9. What kind of organism connects both ends of a food chain? ______________________

Use with page B39.

Name ______________________

Date ______________________

Body Color

Materials

colored acetate sheets: red, blue, green, yellow

hole punch

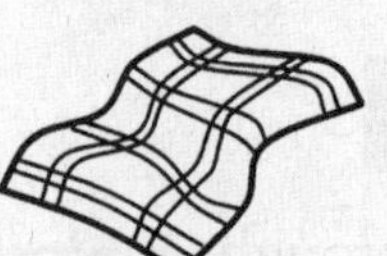

large green cloth

clock with second hand

Activity Procedure

1. Use the table on the next page. Use the hole punch to make 50 pieces from each of the acetate sheets. These colored acetate pieces will stand for insects that a bird is hunting.
2. **Predict** which color would be the easiest to find in grass. Predict which would be the hardest to find. **Record** your predictions.

   My predictions: ______________________
3. Spread the cloth on the floor. Your teacher will randomly scatter the acetate "insects" over the cloth.
4. Each member of the group should kneel at the edge of the cloth. You will each try to pick up as many colored acetate "insects" as you can in 15 seconds. You must pick them up one at a time.
5. Total the number of acetate pieces of each color your group collected. **Record** the data in the table.
6. Put aside the "insects" you collected. Repeat Step 4 two more times. After each 15-second "hunt," **record** the number of acetate pieces of each color your group collected. After the third hunt, total each column.

Name ______________________

	Number of Insects Found			
	Red	Blue	Green	Yellow
Hunt 1				
Hunt 2				
Hunt 3				
Totals				

Draw Conclusions

1. Look at the data you **recorded** for each hunt. What color of acetate was collected least? ______________________

   Were the results of each hunt the same, or were they different? Explain.
   ____

2. **Compare** the results with what you **predicted.** Do the results match your prediction? Explain. ______________________

3. **Scientists at Work** Scientists often **gather data** before they **infer** a relationship between things. Based on the data you gathered, what can you infer about the survival chances of brown-colored insects in areas where grasses and leaves turn brown in the fall? ______________________

Investigate Further Many insects have a body shape that allows them to blend in with their background. **Hypothesize** about what body shape might help an insect hide in a dead tree. Then **plan and conduct a simple investigation** to test your hypothesis.

My hypothesis: ______________________

My plan: ______________________

My results: ______________________

Name ___________________________

Date ___________________________

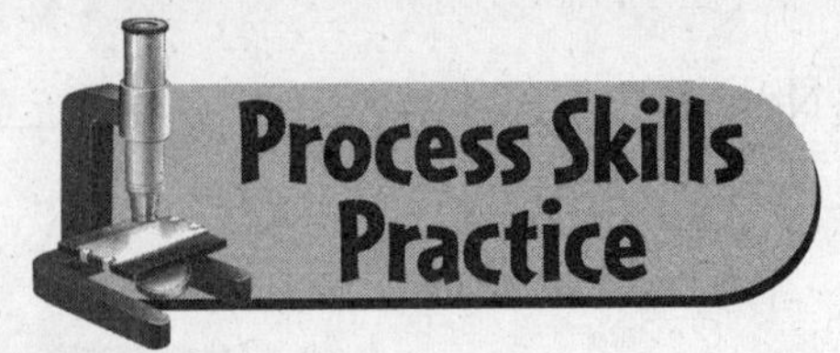

Gather Data and Infer

One way to gather data is to observe objects or events. You can use the data to make inferences. You may need to gather more data to decide if your inference is correct.

Think About Gathering Data and Inferring

Abdul learned that periwinkles, small shelled organisms similar to snails, cling to rocks near the ocean shoreline. He spent a day at the shoreline gathering data about periwinkles on one cliff. He observed four types of periwinkles that were clinging to different levels of the cliff. He made a table to show the number of each type at each level.

Cliff Level	Periwinkle Type			
	Large Pink	Medium Blue	Small Pink	Large Gray
Splash zone (above or at high-tide level)	0	2	8	0
Upper shore (under water 6–12 hr a day)	1	5	3	3
Middle shore (under water 12–18 hr a day)	4	3	0	7
Lower shore (under water 18–24 hr a day)	7	1	0	1

1. What can Abdul infer about the lower shore? ___________________________

____

2. What inference can Abdul make about the splash zone? ___________________________

____

3. What can Abdul infer about the different sizes of periwinkles on the cliff?

____

____

4. What other data could Abdul gather to support inferences he made?

____

Use with page B41.

Name ______________________

Date ______________________

How Do Organisms Compete and Survive in an Ecosystem?

Lesson Concept

Organisms have various ways to compete for limited resources in ecosystems.

Vocabulary

competition (B42)
instinct (B46)
symbiosis (B45)
learned behavior (B46)

Fill in the chart below about how these organisms survive in their ecosystems.

Canada Goose	Cheetah	Raccoon
Resource It Must Share or For Which It Must Compete		
Adaptation That Helps It Compete		
Instinct		
Behavior It Might Learn		

Use with page B47.

Name ______________________

Date ______________________

Vanishing Habitats

Materials

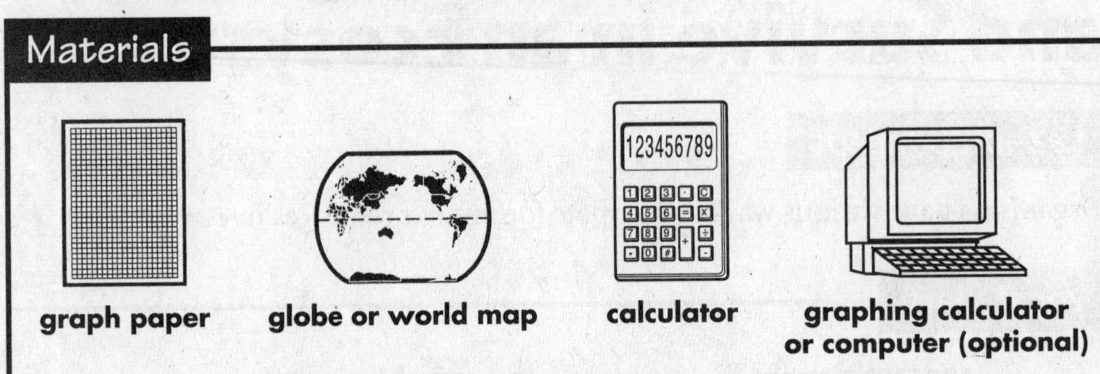

Rain Forest Area and Human Population In Ecuador				
Year	**1961**	**1971**	**1981**	**1991**
Rain forest (square km)	173,000	153,000	No data	112,000
Population (in millions)	5.162	7.035	No data	10.782

Activity Procedure

1. Locate Ecuador, a country in South America, on the globe or world map.
2. Study the table above. It shows the size of Ecuador's rain forests and the size of its human population between 1961 and 1991.
3. **Calculate** and **record** the changes in rain forest area for each period shown (1961–1971 and 1971–1991). Then calculate and record the changes in the population size for the same periods.
4. Using graph paper and a pencil, a graphing calculator, or a computer, make a double-bar graph that shows changes in forest area and population size for these periods.

Name ______________________

Investigate Log

Draw Conclusions

1. **Compare** the two sets of data in the double-bar graph. What relationship, if any, do you **observe** between the growth of the human population and the amount of rain forest in Ecuador? ______________________

____

2. Based on the **data collected**, what can you **infer** about the size of Ecuador's human population and the area of its rain forests in 1981? ______________________

____

____

3. According to the data, what do you **predict** the size of the rain forests in Ecuador will be in 2001 if the human population increases at the same rate as it has in the past? ______________________

4. **Scientists at Work** Scientists often **interpret data** to help them **infer** what may happen. If the size of the rain-forest habitat keeps getting smaller, what can you infer about the populations of animals that live there? ______________________

____

Investigate Further Research the changes in the size of the human population over several decades in your area. Then make a graph of the changes. **Infer** how these changes in the human population might have affected animal populations in your area.

Name ____________________

Date ____________________

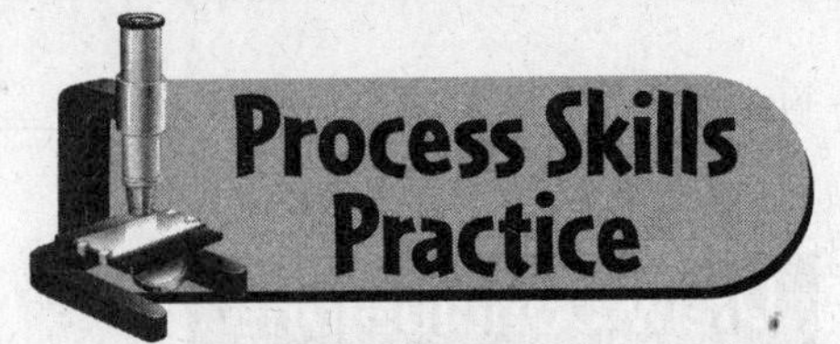

Interpret Data

Interpreting data involves using other skills, such as predicting and hypothesizing, to explain patterns or relationships in data. Interpretations may change when additional data is obtained.

Think About Interpreting Data

The table shows the number of individuals of different populations in two similar regions. Both regions were forests in 1995. Both became the sites of housing developments in 1999. On one site a network of forest areas was left between house lots. On the other site all the trees were removed, houses were built, and each lot was individually landscaped.

Forest Areas Left			Newly Landscaped		
	1995	**2000**		**1995**	**2000**
Owl	8	4	Owl	9	1
Bobcat	5	0	Bobcat	4	0
Fox	11	7	Fox	11	4
Beaver	7	2	Beaver	7	0
Rabbit	28	35	Rabbit	24	40
Deer	6	9	Deer	7	12
Skunk	4	7	Skunk	4	9

1. Which populations decreased at both sites? ____________________

2. Which populations increased at both sites? ____________________

3. How do you explain the different impacts of the housing developments on the populations that increased and the populations that decreased?

____

____

4. How would you use this data for planning another housing development?

____

____

____

Use with page B49.

Name ______________________ Date ______________

Chapter 3 • Graphic Organiz… …r Chapter Concepts

Biomes

L…SON 1 …AND BIOMES	LESSON 2 WATER BIOMES
T… 1. ____ 2. ____ 3. ____ 4. ____ 5. ____ 6. ____	Types 1. ____ 2. ____ 3. ____ 4. ____

Name ______________________

Date ______________________

Biomes and Climates

Materials

map of North American climate zones

map of North American biomes

markers or colored pencils

Activity Procedure

1. On the map of North American climate zones, color the different climates as shown in the table below.

North American Climate Zones

Area	Climate	Color
1	More than 250 cm rain; warm all year	green
2	75–250 cm rain or snow; warm summer, cold winter	purple
3	20–60 cm rain or snow; cool summer, cold winter	blue
4	10–40 cm rain or snow; warm summer, cold winter	orange
5	Less than 10 cm rain; hot summer, cool winter	yellow
6	250 cm snow (25 cm rain); cold all year	brown

2. On the map of North American biomes, color the biomes as shown in the chart on the next page.

Name ______________________

North American Biomes		
Area	**Biome**	**Color**
A	Tropical rain forest	green
B	Deciduous forest	purple
C	Taiga	blue
D	Grassland	orange
E	Desert	yellow
F	Tundra	brown

3 **Compare** the green areas on the two maps. How does the area with a warm, wet climate compare to the area of tropical rain forest? Compare other biomes and climate zones that are colored alike.

Draw Conclusions

1. How do areas on the climate map **compare** to areas shown in the same color on the biome map? ______________________

____

2. **Observe** the maps. If an area is too wet to be a desert but too dry to be a forest, what biome would you expect to find there? ______________________

3. **Order** the biomes from wettest to driest. ______________________

____

4. **Scientists at Work** When scientists **compare** sets of data, they can **draw conclusions** about relationships between the data sets. Conifers are dominant plants of the taiga. Broad-leaved trees are the dominant plants of the deciduous forest. What conclusions can you draw about the water needs of conifers compared to those of broad-leaved trees? ______________________

____

____

Investigate Further Use a computer to make a chart showing the climates of the six biomes and a map combining climate zones and biomes.

Name ______________________________

Date ______________________________

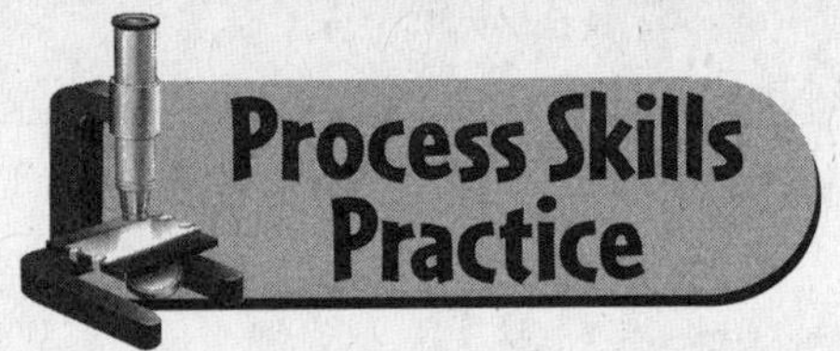

Compare

When you compare, you identify ways objects or events are similar or different.

Think About Comparing

Jessica made a chart to compare three different biomes in the United States.

	Desert	Deciduous Forest	Grassland
Climate	hot and dry summers, warm and dry winters	warm summers, cold winters, plenty of rain	hot summers with little rain; warm, wet springs and falls; cold winters
Vegetation	slow-growing plants that conserve water, like cacti and thorny shrubs	mostly trees and shrubs that shed leaves in fall, some grasses and flowers	mostly fast-growing grasses, some flowers, a few shrubs and trees
Animal adaptations	move to warmer or cooler locations during temperature changes, conserve water	hide in vegetation, fur is shed in spring and thickens before winter	can burrow or move fast, fur is shed in spring and thickens before winter, some can travel far

1. Which two regions have similar vegetation? Explain. ______________________________

____

____

2. Jessica notices that grassland and forest animals have different ways of escaping danger. Why would animals need to run fast on grassland but hide in a forest?

____

____

3. Jessica knows that the fur of grassland animals grows thicker in winter. How do you think the thickness of fur on grassland animals that moved to a warmer place in the winter compares to the fur of animals that didn't move? Explain.

____

____

Use with page B63.

Name ______________________

Date ______________________

Concept Review

What Are Land Biomes?

Lesson Concept

A biome is a large-scale ecosystem. There are many kinds of biomes, each with a different climate and organisms that have adaptations to live in it.

Vocabulary

biome (B64) **climate zone** (B64)

Read the descriptions of the biomes below, and name each type of biome.

You'll find several layers of plants here. In the fall, people come to see the pretty leaves.

1. ______________________

Grains that feed people and animals grow here.

2. ______________________

It can be very hot during the day and very cold at night.

3. ______________________

The trees are green year-round here. It is cold and has many mosquitoes.

4. ______________________

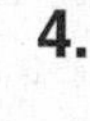

When it's dark up here, everything is white.

5. ______________________

Half of Earth's varieties of plant life are found here.

6. ______________________

Name ____________________

Date ____________________

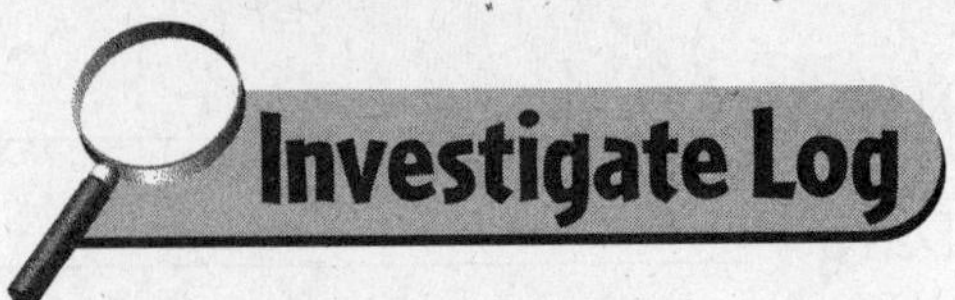

Life in a Pond Community

Materials

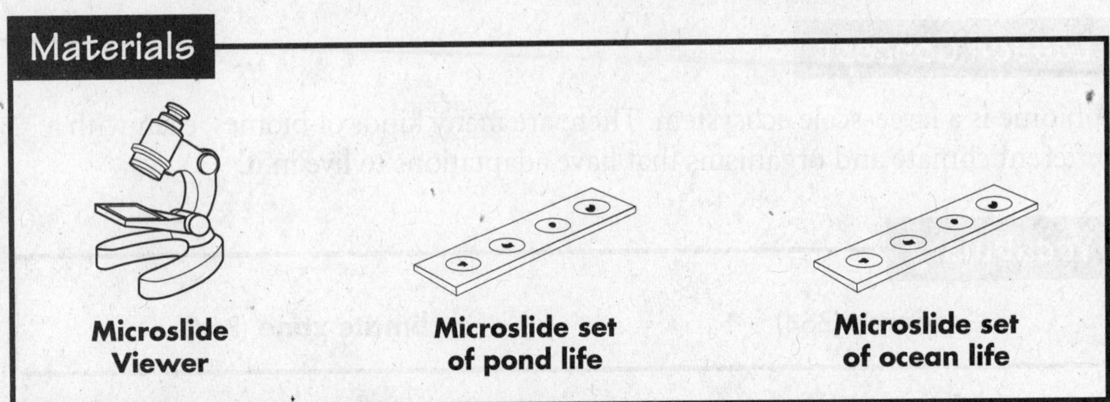

Alternate Materials

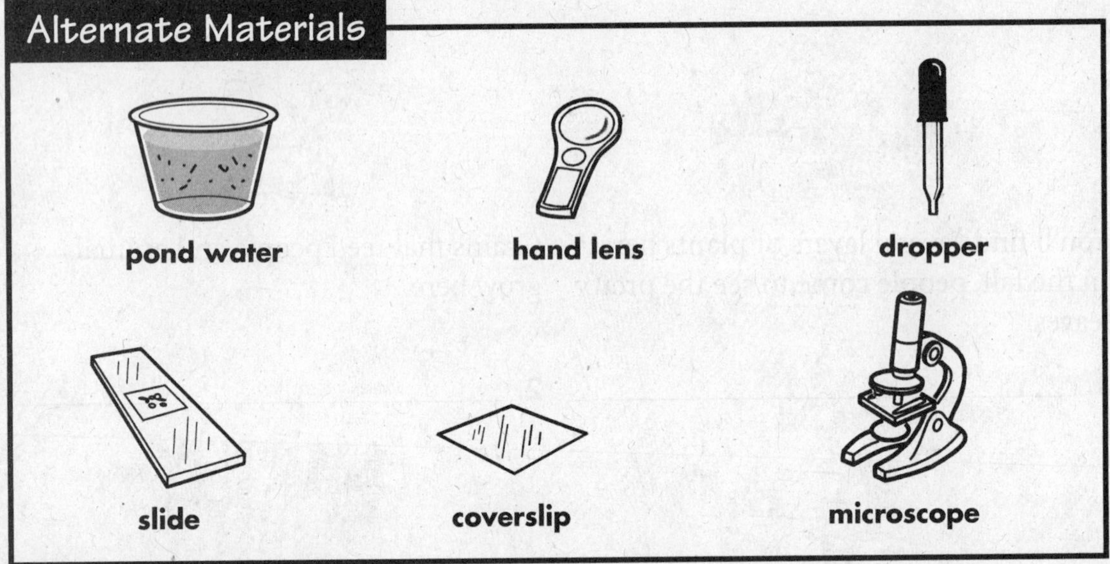

Activity Procedure

Note: If microscopes are available, your teacher may provide an alternate procedure that you will follow to make a slide and observe a drop of pond water.

1. Put the "Pond Life" Microslide in the Microslide Viewer. **Observe** the first photograph, which shows the fish and plants found in a pond. **Record** your observations by making a drawing and writing a short description of these organisms. You may use the information on the Microslide card to help you with your description.
2. The other photographs in the set show microscopic life in a pond. **Observe** each of the organisms. Then **record** your observations by making a drawing and writing a short description of each organism.

Name ______________________________

Investigate Log

3. **Classify** each of the organisms as producer or consumer. **Record** this information on your drawings and in your descriptions.

4. Now put the "Marine Biology" Microslide in the Microslide Viewer. **Observe** each of the organisms, but don't read the information on the Microslide card yet. **Predict** which of the organisms are producers and which are consumers.

   My prediction: ______________________________

5. Now read the information on the Microslide card to see if your predictions were correct.

Draw Conclusions

1. **Compare** the two sets of organisms. Which pond organism was similar to the coral polyp? Which marine organisms were similar to the algae?

   ____

2. In what way were all the producers alike? ______________________________

   ____

3. **Scientists at Work** Scientists often **infer** relationships between organisms after they **observe** them in their natural habitats. Think about your observations of pond life and ocean life. What organisms in a pond community have the same position in a pond food chain as zooplankton has in an ocean food chain?

   ____

Investigate Further Now that you have observed photographs of pond organisms, use the materials in the ***Alternate Materials*** list to **observe** a drop of water from a pond or other water ecosystem. Then **classify** as producers or consumers the organisms you observe. See page R5 for tips on using a microscope.

Name ______________________

Date ______________________

Process Skills Practice

Infer

Inferring involves using logical reasoning to draw conclusions from observations.

Think About Inferring

Vladimir and his family just moved into their new home in Arkansas. He wrote a letter to his cousin Victor. In the letter he described the pond behind his home.

> *June 18*
>
> *Dear Victor,*
>
> *I love our new home! When you visit, we can go swimming in the pond behind our house. Today would be great for swimming. It's a hot, sunny day. It's 2:00 in the afternoon, and the thermometer says it's 82° Fahrenheit.*
>
> *I'm looking out at the pond. I can see plants with roots in pond mud. They have long, thin stems and large, flat leaves floating on the pond's surface. Along the shore are clumps of tall grasslike plants with blades about a meter high. Lots of small bugs with long jointed legs walk on the surface of the water, more easily than I walk on the sidewalk. In the middle of the pond, six turtles are sitting on a log in a sunny spot. A female duck with five ducklings behind her is swimming by the turtles. I can hear buzzing and whirring from all the insects nearby.*
>
> *I can't wait for your visit. Don't forget to bring your swim trunks!*
>
> *Your cousin,*
>
> *Vladimir*

1. Victor knows that plants need to get sunlight to survive. What could Victor infer about the pond plants Vladimir observed? ______________________

____

____

2. Vladimir mentioned that many insects were walking on the pond's surface. Should Victor infer that the pond's surface where the insects were walking was calm or wavy? Explain. ______________________

____

3. Victor is coming to see Vladimir in five weeks. What could Victor infer about what the pond will be like at that time? ______________________

____

____

Use with page B75.

Name ____________________

Date ____________________

What Are Water Ecosystems?

Lesson Concept

Water ecosystems occur in fresh, salt, and brackish water.

Vocabulary

intertidal zone (B77) **near-shore zone** (B77)

open-ocean zone (B77) **estuary** (B80)

Use the terms below to label the parts of the picture.

fresh water **open-ocean zone** **intertidal zone**

near-shore zone **estuary**

6. Where do near-shore zones get their nutrients and in what form are these nutrients? ____________________

____

____

7. Name three important roles of estuaries. ____________________

____

____

____

Name ______________________

Date ______________________

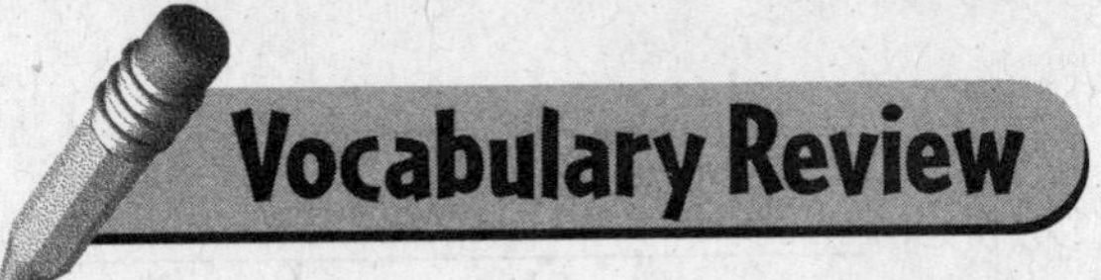

Recognize Vocabulary

biome	**climate zone**	**intertidal zone**
near-shore zone	**open-ocean zone**	**estuary**

Use the clues below to fill in the puzzle with the vocabulary terms.

Across

3. a saltwater ecosystem with calm waters; most nutrients provided by rivers

4. a place with similar yearly patterns of temperature, rainfall, and amount of sunlight

6. a large-scale ecosystem

Down

1. a saltwater ecosystem where breaking waves provide oxygen and nutrients

2. a saltwater ecosystem with very deep water

5. where a freshwater river empties into the ocean

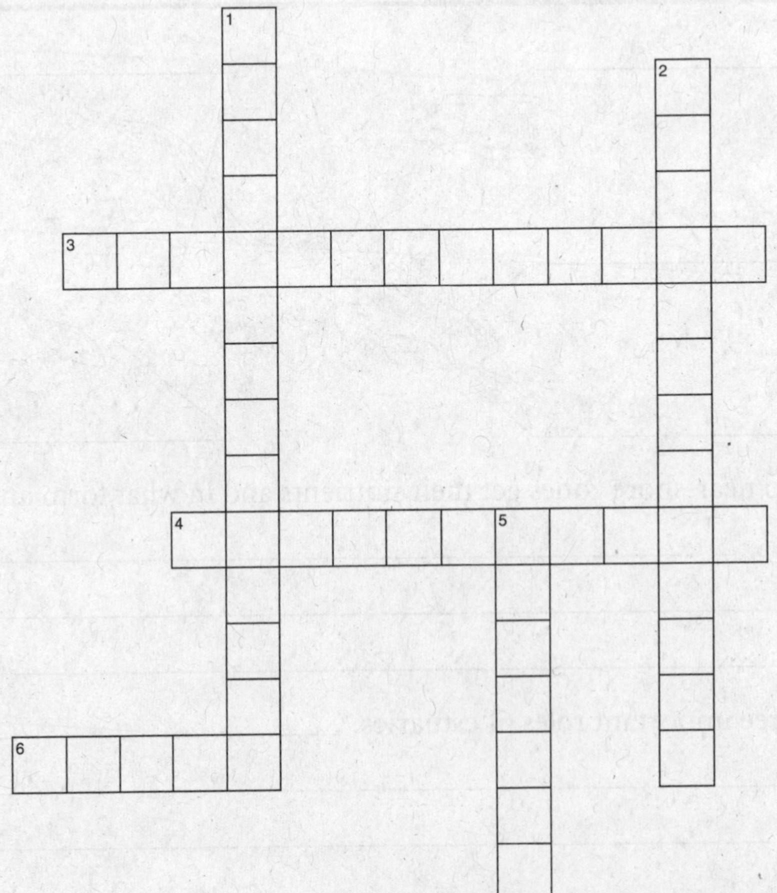

Use with pages B62–B81.

Name ______________________ Date ______________

Chapter 4 • Graphic Organizer for Chapter Concepts

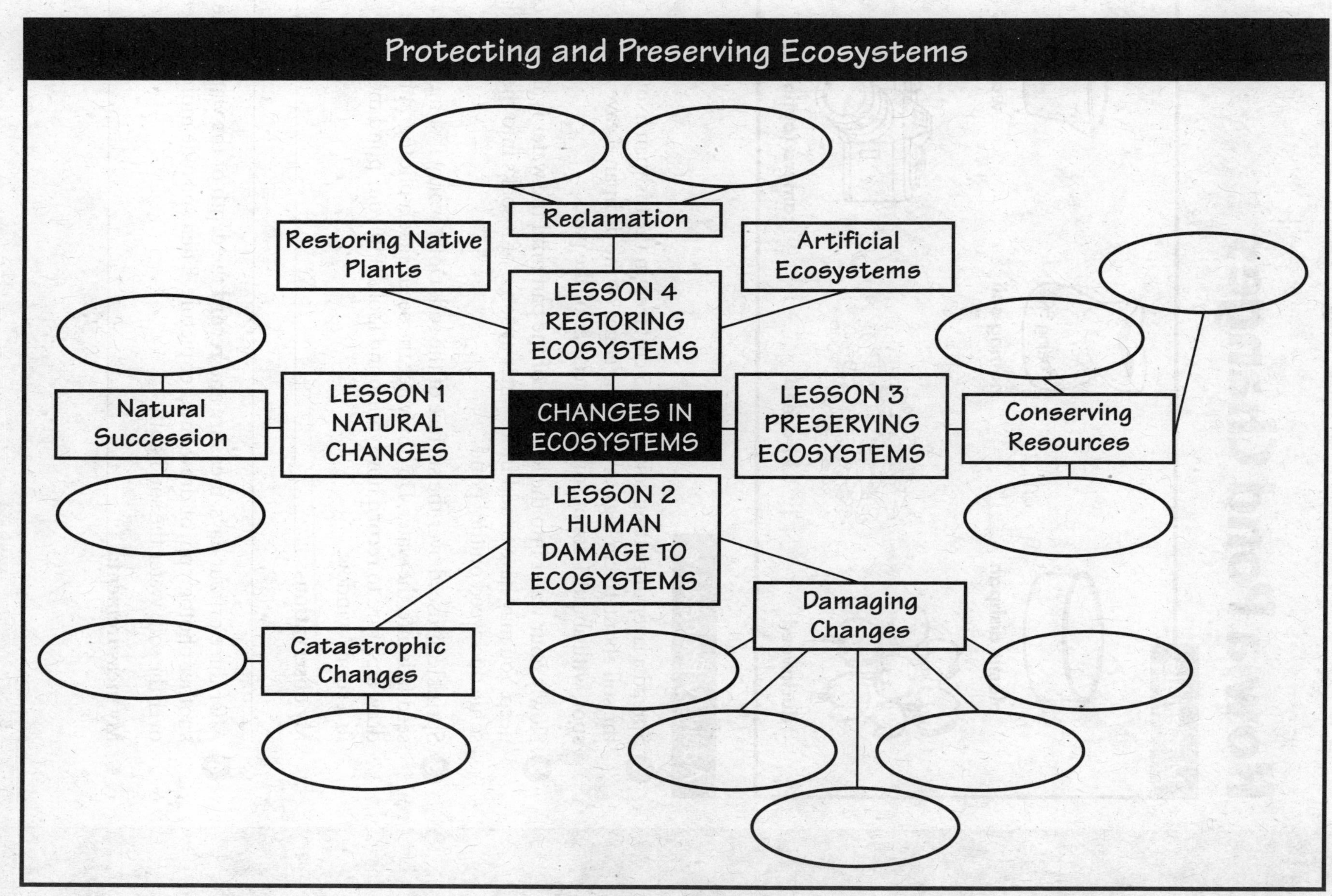

Name ______________________

Date ______________________

How a Pond Changes

Materials

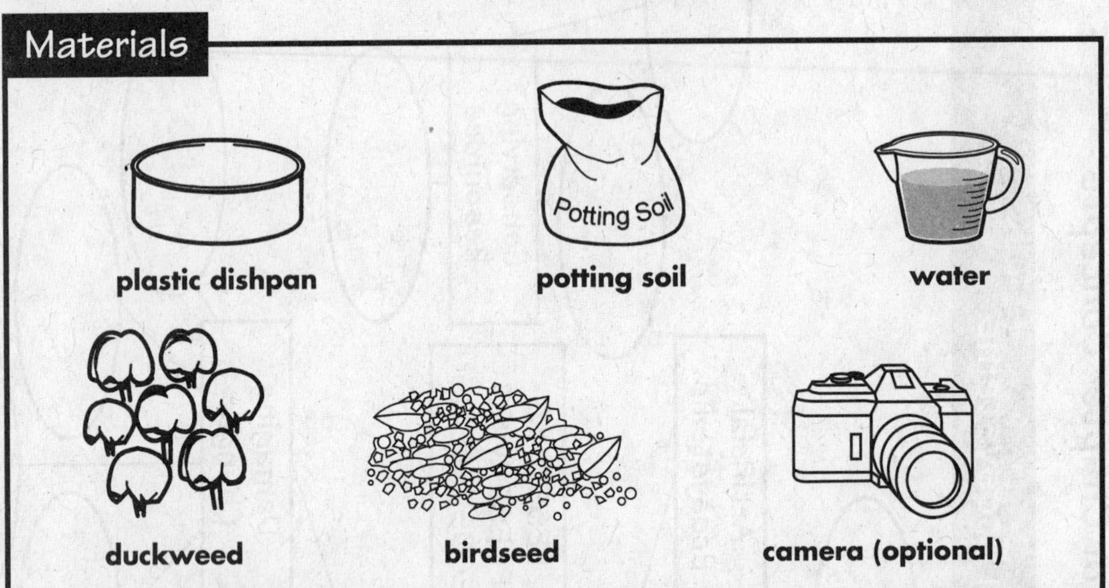

Activity Procedure

1. Spread a layer of potting soil about 5 cm deep in the dishpan. Now bank the soil about 10 cm high around the edges of the dishpan. Leave a low spot, with about 1 cm of soil, in the center of the pan.
2. Slowly pour water into the low area of the pan until the water is about 4 cm deep. You may have to add more water as some of it soaks into the soil. Place some duckweed on the "pond."
3. Sprinkle birdseed over the surface of the soil. Don't worry if some of the seed falls into the water. Do not water the seed. Take a photograph or draw a picture to **record** how your pond looks. Put your pond model in a sunny window.

   My observations: ______________________

   ____

4. After three or four days, **measure** and **record** the depth of the water. Take another photograph, or draw another picture. Then sprinkle more birdseed over the soil. Water the soil lightly.

   My measurement: ______________________

Name ________________________

Investigate Log

5 After three or four more days, **observe** how your pond has changed. **Measure** and **record** the depth of the water. **Compare** your observations with the photographs you took or the pictures you drew.

My measurement: ________________________

My comparisons: ________________________

____

____

Draw Conclusions

1. Describe any changes in the pond during the week. How did the depth of the water change? ________________________

____

____

2. **Compare** the changes in your model with those in a real pond. How are they the same? ________________________

____

____

____

How are they different? ________________________

____

3. **Scientists at Work** By **observing** the changes that occur while **they use models**, scientists can **infer** changes that might occur in nature. From what you observed in your model, what do you infer might happen to a real pond over time? ________________________

____

____

Investigate Further An actual pond ecosystem has a greater diversity of plants and animals than your model. **Make another model** that includes a greater variety of living things.

Name ____________________

Date ____________________

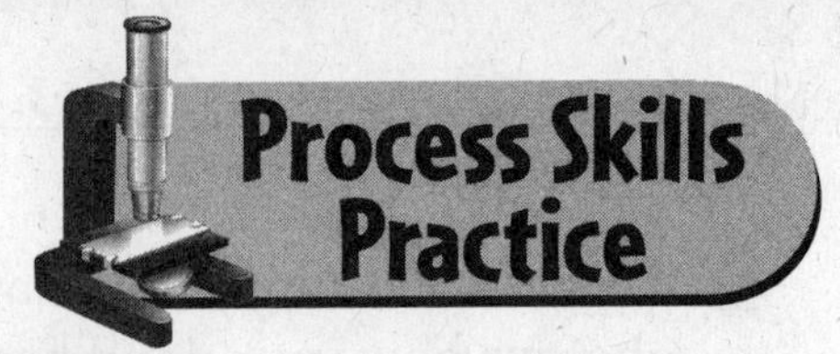

Use Models and Infer

When objects are very big or very small, or when processes take a long time or do not happen often, a mental or physical model can help you understand the process. You can use observations of models to make inferences.

Think About Using Models and Inferring

While planting a vegetable garden in his backyard, Mr. Koumjian decided to make a model of a region that has undergone a natural disaster. He did this by turning over the soil in one corner of the garden and leaving it unplanted. He wondered what would happen to this patch of soil if he didn't do anything to it. The garden was surrounded by a grass lawn. There were berry bushes and honeysuckle vines in another part of the yard, along with two apple trees and two pear trees.

1. Is Mr. Koumjian's garden patch a good model for an area left after a fire? Why or why not? ____________________

2. Is Mr. Koumjian's garden patch a good model for an area left after a flood? Why or why not? ____________________

3. Is Mr. Koumjian's garden patch a good model for an area left after a volcanic eruption? Why or why not? ____________________

4. How long will Mr. Koumjian have to observe his model to see the changes that occur in an area after a natural disaster? ____________________

5. Why do you think Mr. Koumjian chose to make this model instead of going to a place where there had been a natural disaster? ____________________

Use with page B91.

Name ______________________

Date ______________________

How Do Ecosystems Change Naturally?

Lesson Concept

Slow changes occur naturally in ecosystems every day. Quick changes, like fires, also occur naturally.

Vocabulary

succession (B92) **pioneer plants** (B92) **climax community** (B93)

Use the vocabulary terms above to complete the captions.

A Alder and willow trees can take root now. These trees have relatively slender trunks and grow quickly. They also add acids to the soil.

B Now the soil is deep enough to support the tall, sturdy hemlock and spruce trees. These trees are the ______________________. If left undisturbed, this forest could stay almost the same for thousands of years.

C Grasses and flowering plants begin to take root. The thick root structure of these plants anchors the soil as it deepens. These plants also attract insects, birds, worms, and small mammals that add wastes to the soil.

D In the early stages of ______________________, lichens form a thin layer of soil, which allows moss, a ______________________, to grow. Bits of organic matter and bird droppings become trapped in dense moss and add more nutrients to the deepening soil.

Write the letter of the caption above that goes with each picture below.

1. __________ **2.** __________ **3.** __________ **4.** __________

Name ______________________

Date ______________________

How Chemical Fertilizer Affects a Pond

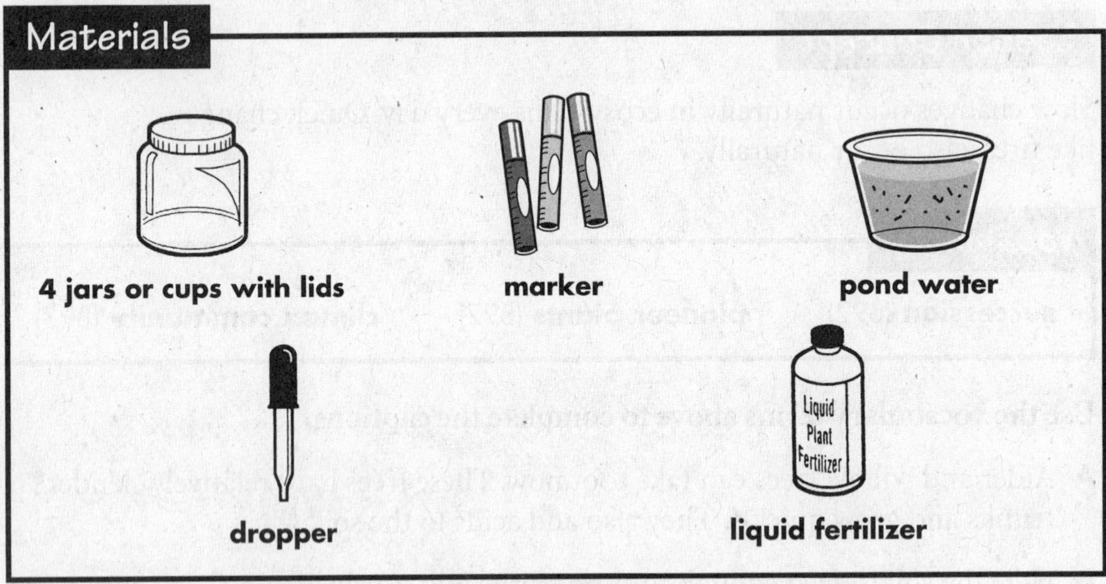

Activity Procedure

1. Use the marker to label the jars 1, 2, 3, and 4.
2. Fill the jars with pond water.
3. Put 10 drops of liquid fertilizer in Jar 1, 20 drops in Jar 2, and 40 drops in Jar 3. Don't put any fertilizer in Jar 4.
4. Put the lids on the jars. Then place the jars in a sunny window.
5. **Observe** the jars every day for two weeks. **Record** your observations.

   My observations: ______________________

Name ______________________

Draw Conclusions

1. What differences did you **observe** among the jars? Which jar had the most plant growth? Which had the least plant growth? How could you tell?

____

____

2. As organisms die and decay, they use up the oxygen in the water. Which jar do you **infer** will eventually have the least oxygen? ______________________

____

3. When water ecosystems are contaminated by fertilizer, fish and other animal populations begin to die off. Why do you think this happens?

____

____

4. **Scientists at Work** When scientists **identify and control variables**, they can **observe** the effects of one variable at a time. What variable were you observing the effect of in this investigation? ______________________

What variables did you control? ______________________

____

____

Investigate Further Some fertilizers contain additional chemicals that are supposed to kill weeds. **Predict** the effects of using these chemicals on a lawn. Then **plan and conduct a simple investigation** to test your prediction.

My plan: ______________________

____

____

My observations: ______________________

____

____

My results: ______________________

____

____

____

Name ______________________

Date ______________________

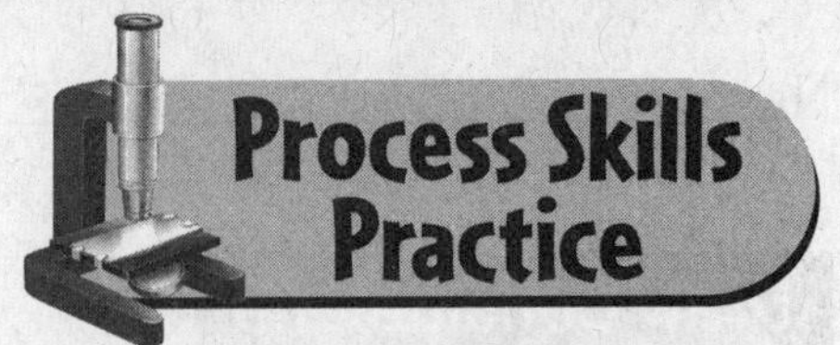

Identify and Control Variables

When you identify variables in an experiment, you pick out the factors that can be changed in a situation. You control variables in an experiment by changing one of the variables and keeping all the others the same.

Think About Identifying and Controlling Variables

Read the descriptions of each of the experiments below. Then, on the line below the description, identify the variables that affect the outcome of the experiment.

1. Fill each of three 1-quart glass jars with 2 inches of clay, 2 inches of sand, and 2 inches of potting soil. Put four earthworms in one jar, four ants in another jar, and no animals in the third jar. Observe the jars every day for a week. Make notes about the ways the contents of the jars change or stay the same. What is the variable in this experiment and what could you learn by controlling it?

____

____

2. Fill two aluminum baking pans of the same size with a layer of potting soil 3 inches deep. Plant grass seed in one of the pans. Place both pans in a sunny location, and water both pans with the same amount of water every two days. After the grass has grown to a height of 3 inches, prop up one end of both pans on a block or brick 1 to 2 inches high. (Both pans should be propped up on blocks of the same height.) Then place an empty pan in front of the lower end of each pan containing soil. Slowly pour one half-gallon of water into the higher end of each pan. Measure how much water and soil runs off into each of the empty pans. What is the variable in this experiment, and what could you learn by controlling it? ____

3. Place four identical leafy green houseplants in a sunny spot. Each plant should be in a 2-inch pot, be the same height (about 4 inches), and have about the same number and size of leaves. Label the pots *A*, *B*, *C*, and *D*. Water each pot with 8 ounces of water every day. Water Plant A with plain water. Add 1 teaspoon of distilled white vinegar to the water for Plant B every day. Add 1 tablespoon of distilled white vinegar to the water for Plant C every day. Add 3 tablespoons of distilled white vinegar to the water for Plant D every day. Observe the plants each day, making notes on their appearances. What is the variable in this experiment, and what could you learn by controlling it?

____

____

Use with page B97.

Name ______________________

Date ______________________

How Do People Change Ecosystems?

Lesson Concept

Human activity can change ecosystems. Some ecosystems can recover from the changes, while other ecosystems are altered forever.

Vocabulary

pollution (B99) **acid rain** (B99)

Complete the sentences below by writing the letter of a phrase from the chart.

A	paper products damage forest ecosystems and destroy habitats	**E**	corn, barley, wheat, or oats reduces the diversity of life
B	nitrogen oxides and sulfur dioxide that mix with water vapor and cause acid rain	**F**	strip mining, all the communities and many nonliving parts of an ecosystem are destroyed
C	roads, homes, schools, and office buildings, habitats for other organisms are destroyed	**G**	destroy habitats completely or change conditions so much that natural communities can't survive
D	kill unwanted plant and animal pests can damage natural ecosystems	**H**	birds, fish, and other water animals

1. Replacing the natural producers in a grassland ecosystem with ______.

2. Using pesticides and herbicides to ______.

3. As human communities grow and people build ______.

4. Cutting down trees to make wood and ______.

5. Energy stations and motor vehicles give off ______ .

6. Runoff from acid rain kills ______.

7. When topsoil and rock layers are removed in the process of ______.

8. Large-scale construction projects on fragile ecosystems may ______.

Use with page B101.

Name ______________________

Date ______________________

What Happens in a Landfill

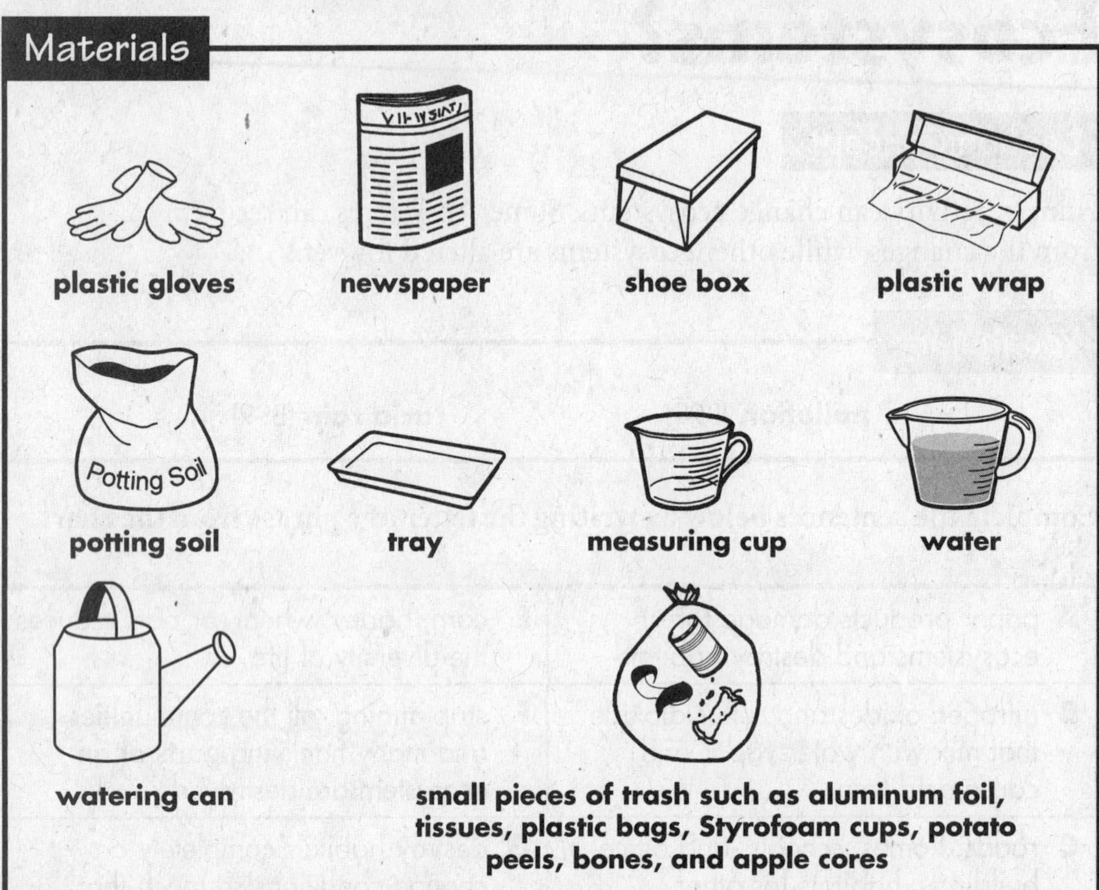

CAUTION

Activity Procedure

1. Make a chart listing ten different items of trash. Allow space in your chart to **record** observations you will make later.
2. **CAUTION** **Put on the plastic gloves.** Spread newspaper on your work surface. Choose the ten items of trash listed on your chart to put in the model landfill. Lay the trash on the newspaper.
3. Now prepare the model landfill. First, line the shoe box with plastic wrap. Then put a layer of potting soil on the bottom of the box.
4. Take the pieces of trash from the newspaper and place them on top of the soil. Then cover the trash completely with another layer of soil.
5. Set the model landfill on the tray. Use the watering can to sprinkle the surface of the soil each day with 50 mL of water.

Name ______________________

Investigate Log

6. After two weeks, put on plastic gloves and remove the top layer of soil. **Observe** the items of trash, and **record** your observations.

   My observations: ______________________

Draw Conclusions

1. Did you **observe** anything starting to decay? What items decayed the most? What items decayed the least? ______________________

2. Things that decay are said to be *biodegradable*. What items in your trash are biodegradable? ______________________

3. What do you **infer** might eventually happen to trash that is not biodegradable? ______________________

4. **Scientists at Work** Scientists often **draw conclusions** based on observations made while **using a model.** From your observations of a model landfill, what conclusions can you draw about using paper trash bags instead of plastic trash bags? ______________________

Investigate Further In many places, items that are not biodegradable are removed from trash before it is collected. **Predict** how quickly trash in landfills would decay if it were all biodegradable. **Make a model** to test your prediction.

My prediction: ______________________

My model: ______________________

My results: ______________________

Name ______________________

Date ______________________

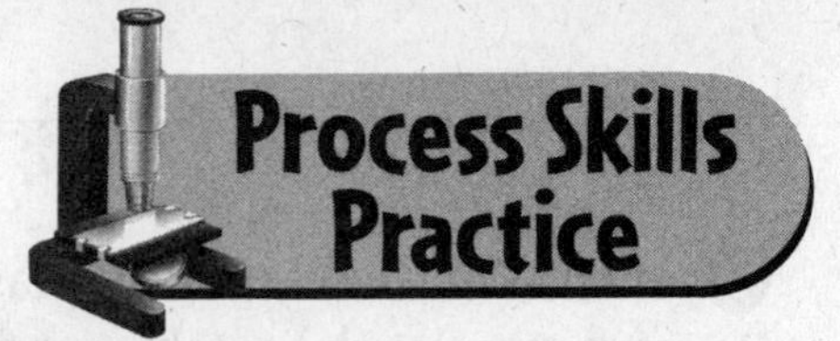

Using a Model to Draw Conclusions

Using a model involves making or using a representation of a process or structure to better understand how the process works. Examples of models include maps, diagrams, three-dimensional representations, and computer simulations.

Think About Using a Model to Draw Conclusions

The table below is a simple model showing how many plastic bags Mark would save in a year by using the same bag to carry things from the store instead of getting a new bag two times a week. Each cell lists a month and the number of bags Mark will save by the end of that month if he starts carrying a bag on January 1. Study the model, and answer the questions to draw a conclusion.

January:	8	April:	34	July:	60	October:	86
February:	16	May:	42	August:	68	November:	94
March:	24	June:	50	September:	76	December:	104

1. How many bags would Mark save in a year? ______________________

How did the model help you reach that conclusion? ______________________

____

2. Suppose three of Mark's friends think he has a good idea and decide to carry their own bags. These friends buy things about as often as Mark does. Use multiplication to figure out how many bags Mark and his three friends would save in a year. ______________________

3. Another friend decided to follow Mark's example, but half the time he forgot to take his bag to the store. About how many bags would this friend save?

____

4. From this mathematical model, draw a conclusion about reusing plastic bags. Use the information to argue for or against Mark's practice. ______________________

____

____

 Use with page B103.

Name ______________________

Date ______________________

How Can People Treat Ecosystems More Wisely?

Lesson Concept

People can treat ecosystems more wisely by reducing pollution, protecting ecosystems, and conserving resources.

Vocabulary

conserving (B104) **reduce** (B104) **reuse** (B105) **recycle** (B105)

Listed below are several things Carla does to treat ecosystems wisely. After each behavior, tell what resource she is reducing the use of, reusing, or recycling. Some behaviors may accomplish more than one of these goals.

1. Carla rides her bike to the library instead of riding in a car.

____

2. Instead of buying a new CD, Carla asks Bob if she can borrow his CD.

____

3. Carla's neighbor, Ms. Esposito, has a yard sale to sell used books, CDs, clothes, and other items. Carla buys a used chair to put in her living room.

____

____

4. Instead of turning the thermostat to a higher setting, Carla puts on a sweater and a pair of thick socks to keep warm in the winter. ______________________

____

5. Carla needs notebook filler paper for class. She buys paper made from postconsumer waste paper. ______________________

____

6. Carla buys organically grown oranges from the farmers' market to make marmalade. ______________________

____

Use with page B107.

Name ______________________

Date ______________________

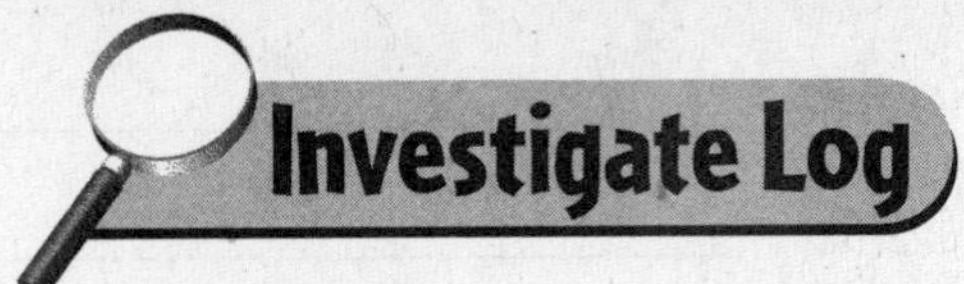

How Waste Water Can Be Cleaned

Materials

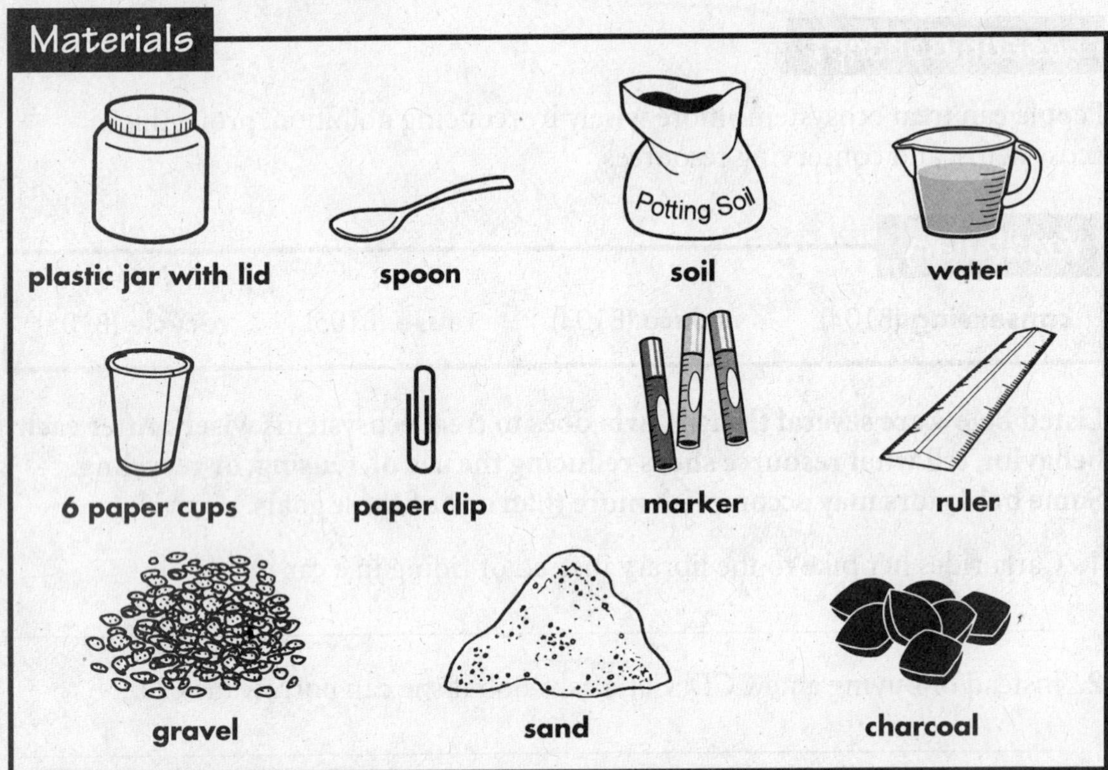

Activity Procedure

1. Put several spoonfuls of soil in the jar. Then fill the jar with water and put the lid on.
2. Shake the jar for 15 sec. Then put the jar aside for about 5 min. A process called *sedimentation* is taking place in the jar. It is the first step in waste-water treatment. **Observe** the water in the jar. **Record** your observations.

   My observations: ____

   ____

3. Unbend the paper clip. Use it to punch 10 small holes each in the bottoms of 3 paper cups. Using the marker, label the cups *A*, *B*, and *C*.
4. Using the spoon, put a 2.5-cm layer of gravel in Cup A. Put a 2.5-cm layer of sand and then a 2.5-cm layer of gravel in Cup B. Put a 2.5-cm layer of charcoal, and then a 2.5-cm layer of sand, and finally a 2.5-cm layer of gravel in Cup C.

Use with pages B108–B109.

Name ______________________

Investigate Log

5 Put each cup with holes inside a cup without holes. Label the outer cups *A*, *B*, and *C* to match the inner cups. Then carefully pour equal amounts of water from the jar into each set of cups. Try not to shake the jar as you pour. A process called *filtering* is taking place in the cups. It is the second step in waste-water treatment.

6 Separate each set of cups, allowing all the water to drain into the outer cups. **Observe** the water in the outer cups. **Record** your observations.

My observations: ______________________

____

Draw Conclusions

1. What did you **observe** happening during sedimentation?

____

2. What combination of materials did the best job of filtering the water?

____

3. What materials do you **infer** might not be filtered out of waste water?

____

____

4. **Scientists at Work** Scientists must **identify and control variables** when they **experiment.** In a real waste-water treatment plant, what variables might affect the filtering process?

____

____

Investigate Further **Plan and conduct a simple investigation**, using water that is "polluted" with food coloring. Decide what equipment you will need. Test several different kinds of filters.

My design: ______________________

____

My observations: ______________________

____

My results: ______________________

____

Name ______________________

Date ______________________

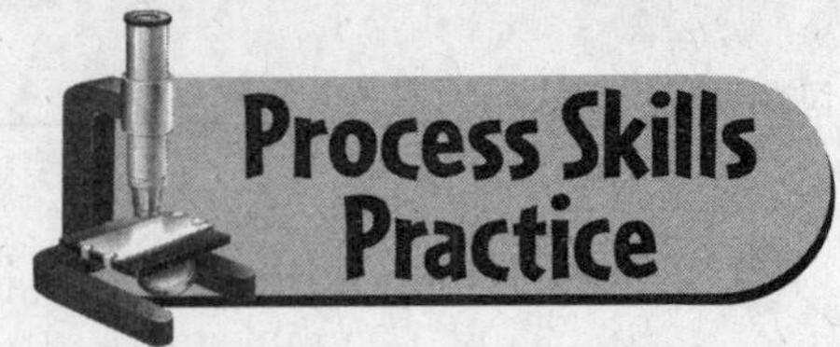

Experiment

When you experiment, you design procedures for gathering data. An experiment tests a hypothesis under conditions in which variables are controlled or manipulated.

Think About Experimenting

Experiments must be designed carefully so the people running the experiment will know the meaning of the experiment's outcome. Everything that happens in an experiment can affect the outcome. Something the experimenter doesn't notice—like a 2 degree difference in temperature—could have an impact on what happens. That's why experiments must be repeated over and over, with the same results, before experimenters have proved anything. The first step, however, is to design an experiment to test the thing about which the experimenter wants to learn.

Read the problem that follows, and then design an experiment that will help you find the solution to the problem.

Rachael plants native bushes and flowers in her yard to attract insects, birds, and other creatures native to her ecosystem. She doesn't use pesticides in her garden. One year, however, she notices small black bugs on a berry bush. She has read about people using soap or garlic on plants to get rid of pests, but she doesn't know how much to use or which would be more effective. She has five bushes of this type, in three different sunny locations in her yard. Design an experiment for Rachael that would let her test these remedies. ______________________

____

____

____

____

____

____

____

Use with page B109.

Name ____________________

Date ____________________

How Can People Help Restore Damaged Ecosystems?

Lesson Concept

People can help restore damaged ecosystems by rebuilding them.

Vocabulary

reclamation (B110) **wetlands** (B111)

Fill in the chart below to describe some of the typical problems found in damaged ecosystems and the solutions people have used.

Ecosystem	Problems	Solutions
River		
Wetlands		
Backyard		

Use with page B113.

Name ____________________

Date ____________________

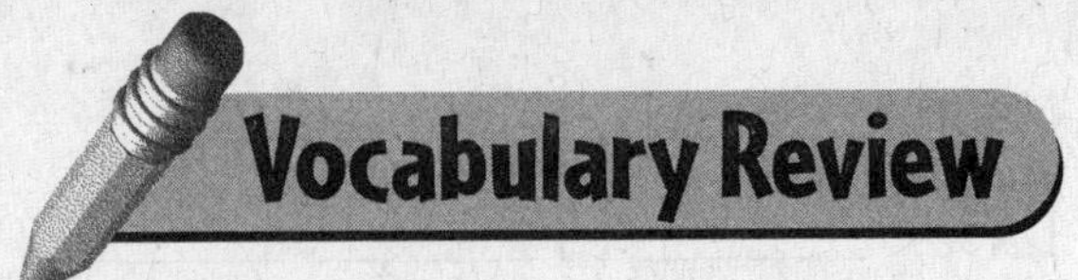

Recognize Vocabulary

succession	pioneer plants	climax community	pollution
acid rain	conserving	reduce	reuse
recycle	reclamation	wetlands	

Fill in the blanks below with the vocabulary terms above to complete the paragraphs about protecting ecosystems.

Even if most of the plants in an ecosystem are destroyed, hardy ____________________ will return and begin to grow, building up the soil and attracting animals. Over time, through natural ____________________, the area will change. The last stage of these slow changes occurs when a ____________________ is achieved. If no disasters occur, this ecosystem will remain unchanged for thousands of years. Unfortunately, ____________________ from human activities like manufacturing can kill organisms and break food chains. Activities like manufacturing, generating electricity, and operating motor vehicles produce gases that mix with water vapor in the atmosphere and fall back to Earth as ____________________.

We can all work to protect ecosystems by buying fewer things and using less energy. Instead of throwing things away, ____________________ them a second or third time. Do you really need a fresh plastic bag every time you buy something? If you don't need a bag when you buy something, don't get one. If everyone did this, we would ____________________ the number of plastic bags we throw away. A lot of towns and cities encourage people to ____________________ newspapers, glass, and plastics.

It's not hard to think of things that individuals and communities can do if they care about ____________________ resources. There are many inspiring stories about people who work together on ____________________ projects to restore damaged ecosystems. If everybody did just a little, it would help protect our ecosystems and preserve our resources.

Use with pages B90–B113.

Name ______________________ Date ______________

Chapter 1 • Graphic Organizer for Chapter Concepts

Changes to Earth's Surface		
LESSON 1 SURFACE PROCESSES THAT CHANGE LANDFORMS	LESSON 2 PROCESSES THAT BEGIN IN EARTH'S INTERIOR	LESSON 3 STAGES IN CONTINENTAL DRIFT
1. ______	1. ______	1. ______
2. ______	2. ______	2. ______
3. ______	3. ______	3. ______

Name ______________________

Date ______________________

How Water Changes Earth's Surface

Materials

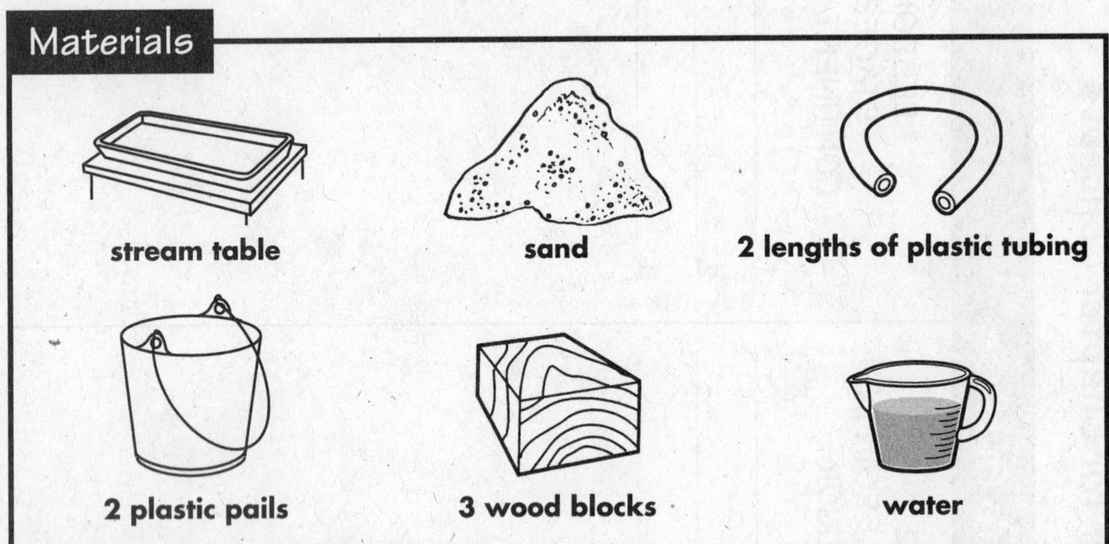

stream table
sand
2 lengths of plastic tubing
2 plastic pails
3 wood blocks
water

Activity Procedure

1. Place the stream table on a classroom table. Make sure the front end of the stream table is even with the edge of the table. Put the stream-table support under the back end of the stream table.
2. Fill the stream table with sand.
3. Using two fingers, make a path, or channel, down the middle of the sand.
4. Connect one end of one length of tubing to the front of the stream table. Let the other end of the tubing hang over the edge of the table. Place an empty pail on the floor under the hanging end of the tubing.
5. Place the other pail on two wood blocks near the raised end of the stream-table channel. Fill this pail $\frac{3}{4}$ full of water.
6. Put the second length of tubing into the pail, and fill it with water.
7. Start the water flowing through the tube from the pail to the stream table by lowering one end of the filled tube.
8. **Observe** any changes the water makes to the sand in the stream table. **Record** your observations.
9. Place the third wood block on top of the support under the stream table. Repeat Steps 7 and 8.

Name ___________________________

Draw Conclusions

1. In which setup was the speed of the water greater? ______________

____

2. In which setup did you **observe** greater movement of sand from the channel?

____

3. **Scientists at Work** Scientists learn by **observing.** What did you learn about the way water can change the land by observing the channel in the stream table?

____

____

Investigate Further Hypothesize what would happen if you replaced the sand with soil. **Experiment** to test your hypothesis.

____

____

____

Name ______________________

Date ______________________

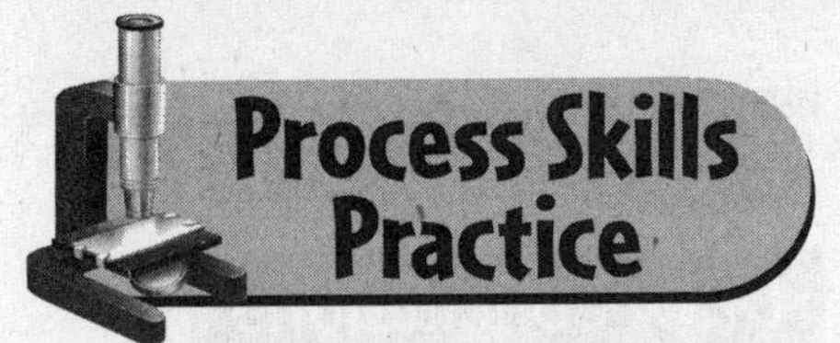

Observe

You observe by using your senses to see, hear, smell, and feel the world around you.

Think About Observing

Think about the things you see every day that may have been changed by moving water or ice. You may observe the dirt and gravel that pile up at the end of the street or the holes in the street that have to be repaired every year. What kinds of changes have you seen? Fill in the chart below with your observations and the possible causes for them. Two examples have been provided.

Observation	Possible Cause
1. Roots of plants growing on the side of a drainage ditch have been exposed.	1. Rushing water during heavy rain has washed soil away from the roots.
2. Bits of gravel have piled up under the downspout that comes from the roof.	2. Rainwater has washed bits of gravel off the roof shingles.
3.	3.
4.	4.
5.	5.
6.	6.

1. What do you think would happen if rain continued to wash away the soil in Observation 1 on the chart? ______________________

____

____

2. What do you think would happen to the roof in Observation 2?

____

3. How do you think the scenes you observed will change over the passing of many years? ______________________

____

____

Use with page C5.

Name ______________________

Date ______________________

What Processes Change Landforms?

Lesson Concept

The action of water, wind, ice, and gravity break down Earth's crust and change landforms.

Vocabulary

landforms (C6) **weathering** (C7) **erosion** (C7)
deposition (C7) **mass movement** (C9)

Answer each question with one or more complete sentences.

1. Most of the time, changes to landforms are slow. What are some examples of very fast changes? ______________________

2. What are two landforms that can be caused by glaciers? ______________________

3. Why has wind erosion shaped so many landforms in the American Southwest? ______________________

4. Name three kinds of mass movement. ______________________

5. How is a river delta formed? ______________________

Harcourt

Use with page C11.

Name ____________________

Date ____________________

Journey to the Center of Earth

Materials

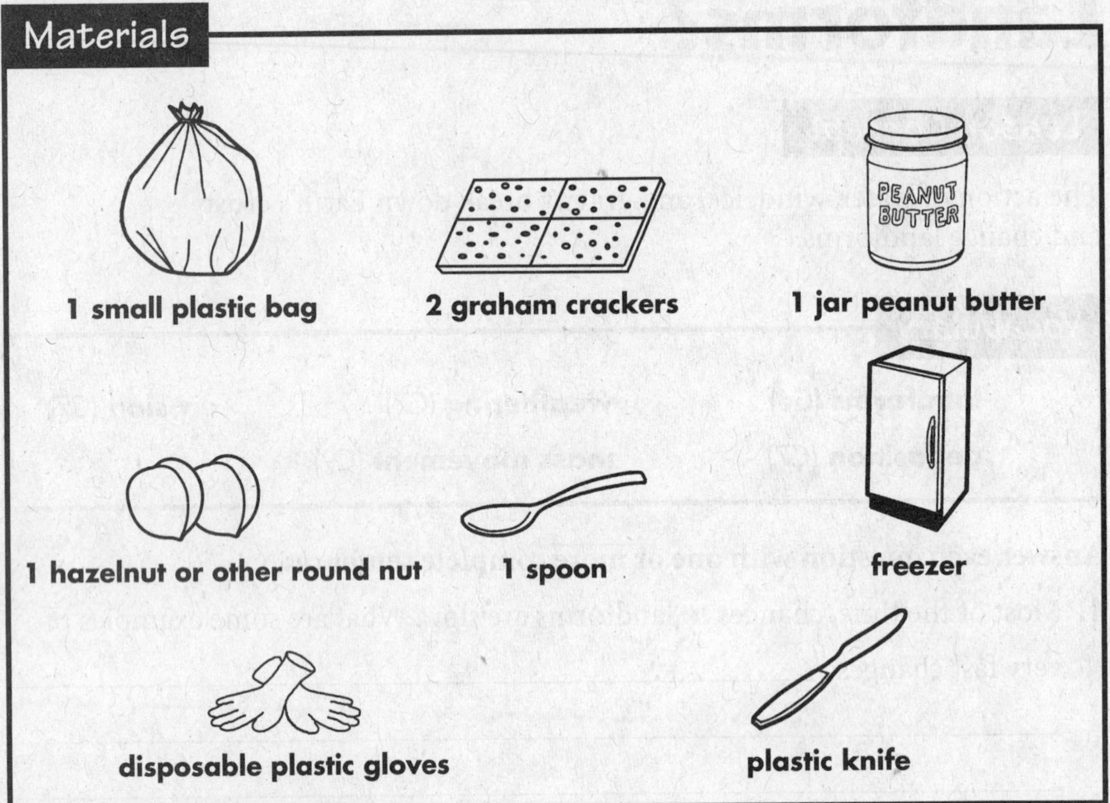

Activity Procedure

1. Put the graham crackers in the plastic bag. Close the bag and use your hands to crush the crackers into crumbs. Then set the bag aside.
2. Put on the plastic gloves. Use the spoon to scoop a glob of peanut butter from the jar and put it in your gloved hand. Place the nut in the center of the peanut butter. Cover the nut with more peanut butter until there is about 2.5 cm of peanut butter all around the nut. Using both hands, roll the glob of peanut butter with the nut at its center into a ball.
3. Open the bag of crushed graham crackers, and roll the peanut-butter ball in the graham cracker crumbs until the outside of the ball is completely coated.
4. Put the ball in the freezer for about 15 minutes. Remove the ball and cut into your model with the plastic knife. **Observe** the layers inside. You might want to take a photograph of your model for later review.

Name ______________________

Draw Conclusions

1. The peanut-butter ball is a model of Earth's layers. How many layers does Earth have in this model? ______________________

2. Which layer of Earth do the crushed graham crackers represent? Why do you think your model has a thick layer of peanut butter but a thin layer of graham cracker crumbs? ______________________

3. **Scientists at Work** Scientists can see and understand complex structures better by **making models** of them. What does the model show about Earth's layers? What doesn't the model show about Earth's layers? ______________________

Investigate Further Some geologists, scientists who study the Earth, say that Earth's center is divided into a soft outer part and a hard inner part. How could you **make a model** to show this? ______________________

Name ______________________

Date ______________________

Process Skills Practice

Make and Use Models

Sometimes making a model can give you a better understanding of a process. This is especially so when you are trying to understand an Earth process, which takes millions of years to occur.

Think About Making and Using Models

Suppose you are using biscuit dough to model the movement of Earth's surface. First you would roll the dough flat and cut two blocks out of it. Those blocks would model two opposing plates of Earth's crust. Suppose you put them together as shown and push them against one another. Then think of trying to slide them past one another.

1. What is the dough modeling when the two blocks are pushed together?

____

____

2. What do you think happens when you try to slide the blocks of dough past one another? What do you think this models? ______________________

____

____

____

3. You have seen how this model is similar to Earth's surface, or crust. How is this model different? ______________________________

____

 Use with page C13.

Name ______________________

Date ______________________

What Causes Mountains, Volcanoes, and Earthquakes?

Lesson Concept

Earth has three layers. The outer layer, or crust, is broken into tectonic plates. The movement of the plates results in mountains, volcanoes, and earthquakes.

Vocabulary

crust (C14)	**mantle** (C14)	**core** (C14)	**plate** (C15)
magma (C16)	**volcano** (C16)	**earthquake** (C18)	**fault** (C18)

Choose from the vocabulary list, and add the missing words to the paragraph below. Use each vocabulary term only once.

The ______________________ is Earth's center and its hottest layer. It is divided into two parts. The outer section is molten rock. Great pressure keeps the inner section solid. The middle layer of Earth is called the ______________________. It is made of hot, soft rock called ______________________. This hot, soft rock sometimes reaches Earth's upper layer through openings called ______________________. The hot, soft rock is called lava when it flows on Earth's surface. The outermost layer of Earth is called the ______________________. It is made of many ______________________ that float on the soft rock below them. When these pieces of Earth's surface crash together or scrape against one another, the release of energy causes an ______________________. The places where pieces of Earth's crust move can bend or break. These breaks can become ______________________.

Use with page C19.

Name ______________________

Date ______________________

Movement of the Continents

Materials

3 copies of a world map

scissors

globe or world map

glue

3 sheets of construction paper

Activity Procedure

1. Cut out the continents from one copy of the world map.
2. Arrange the continents into one large "supercontinent" on a sheet of construction paper. As you would with a jigsaw puzzle, arrange them so their edges fit together as closely as possible.
3. Label the pieces with the names of their present continents, and glue them onto the paper.
4. Use a globe or world map to locate the following mountains: Cascades, Andes, Atlas, Himalayas, Alps. Then draw these mountains on the supercontinent.
5. Use your textbook to locate volcanoes and places where earthquakes have occurred. Put a *V* in places where you know there are volcanoes, such as the Cascades. Put an *E* in places where you know that earthquakes have occurred, such as western North America.
6. Repeat Steps 1–5 with the second copy of the world map, but before gluing the continents to the construction paper, separate them by about 2.5 cm. That is, leave about 2.5 cm of space between North America and Eurasia, between South America and Africa, and so on.
7. Glue the third world map copy onto a sheet of construction paper. Then place the three versions of the world map in order from the oldest to the youngest.

Name ______________________________

Draw Conclusions

1. Where do the continents fit together the best? ______________________________

____

____

____

2. Where are most of the mountains, volcanoes, and earthquake sites in relation to the present continents? Why do you think they are there?

____

____

3. **Scientists at Work** Scientists use **models**, such as maps, to better understand complex structures and processes. How did your models of Earth's continents help you **draw conclusions** about Earth's past? ______________________________

____

What limitations did your models have? ______________________________

____

Investigate Further **Hypothesize** about the fact that the continents do not fit together exactly. Then **plan and conduct a simple investigation** to test your hypothesis. ______________________________

____

____

____

Name ______________________

Date ______________________

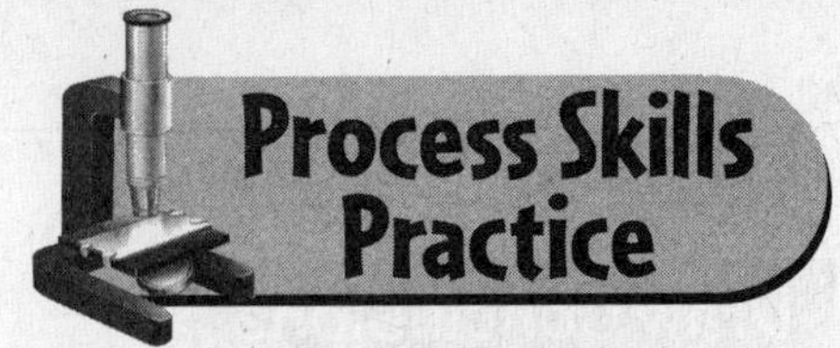

Make a Model

Making a model can help you understand an object or a process. You use models to find out about things all the time. When you use a map, you are using a model of a specific geographic area.

Think About Making a Model

In the space below, draw a map that someone could use to get from your house to your school. Show special landmarks, such as large buildings, trees, or other objects, that a person could use as help in following your map.

1. Write a paragraph telling someone how to get from your house to your school.

____

____

____

____

2. Do you think someone could use your map and get from your house to school without reading the paragraph you wrote? ______________________

____

____

3. Is your map a good model of the process of getting from your house to school? Why or why not? ______________________

____

4. What could you do to make your map more accurate? ______________________

____

____

Use with page C21.

Chapter 2 • Graphic Organizer for Chapter Concepts

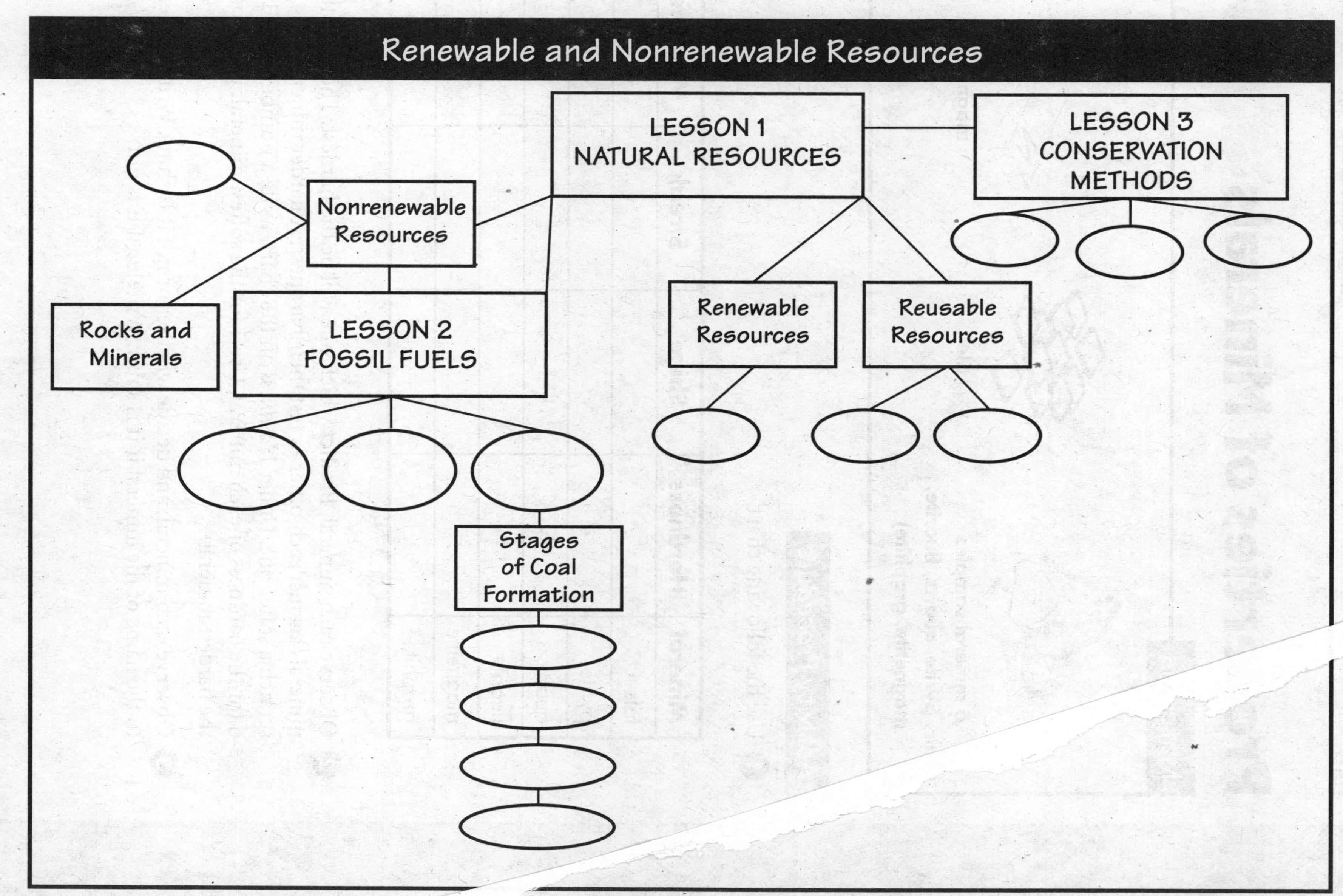

Name ______________________ Date ______________

Name ______________________

Date ______________________

Properties of Minerals

Materials

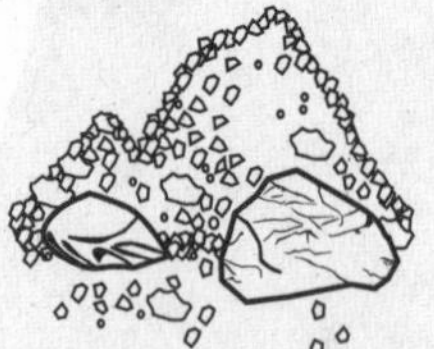

6 mineral samples (talc, pyrite, quartz, fluorite, magnetite, graphite)

tile

magnet

Activity Procedure

1. Use the following chart.

Mineral	Hardness	Shine	Streak	Magnetic
talc				
pyrite				
quartz				
fluorite				
magnetite				
graphite				

2. **Observe** each mineral. **Predict** which one will be the hardest. Then rub the minerals against each other to test their hardness. A harder mineral will scratch a softer one. Under *Hardness* on the chart, write a number from 1 to 6 for the hardness of each mineral. Use 1 for the softest mineral. Use 6 for the hardest mineral.

3. **Observe** each mineral, and decide whether or not it is shiny. Write *yes* next to the name of the mineral if it is shiny. Write *no* if it is not.

Name ______________________

4. Now **predict** the color of the streak each mineral will make. A streak is the colored line a mineral makes when it is rubbed on a tile. Then rub each mineral on the tile. If the mineral makes a streak, write the color of the streak next to the mineral's name. Write *none* if the mineral does not make a streak.

5. Finally, **predict** which minerals will be attracted to a magnet. Test each mineral with a magnet. Write *yes* next to the names of minerals that stick to the magnet. Write *no* next to the names of those that do not.

Draw Conclusions

1. Which mineral is the softest? **Compare** your test results with your predictions.

____

____

____

2. Which minerals make streaks? **Compare** your test results with your color predictions. ______________________

____

____

3. Which minerals are magnetic? **Compare** your test results with your predictions. ______________________

____

4. **Scientists at Work** Scientists often **predict** what might happen. How did careful observations of the mineral samples help you make better predictions about their properties? ______________________

____

____

Investigate Further Use the information you gathered on each mineral's properties to **infer** its uses. ______________________

____

____

____

Name ______________________

Date ______________________

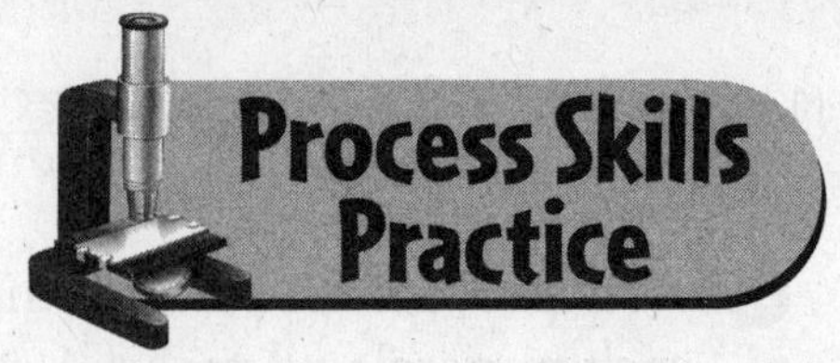

Predict

One way to check your understanding of something is to predict an outcome, and then see how closely your prediction matches the actual outcome. The first step is to interpret the data you have collected.

Think About Predicting

In 1955 each farm worker in the United States produced enough food to feed 20 people. By 1960 farming methods had improved, and one worker could supply 25 people. In 1965 that number became 40 people. In 1970 it was 45 people. In 1975 it increased to 60 people. In 1980 one farm worker could supply 75 people. Graph this data in the grid to the right to show how production increased with time. Then use the graph to help you predict.

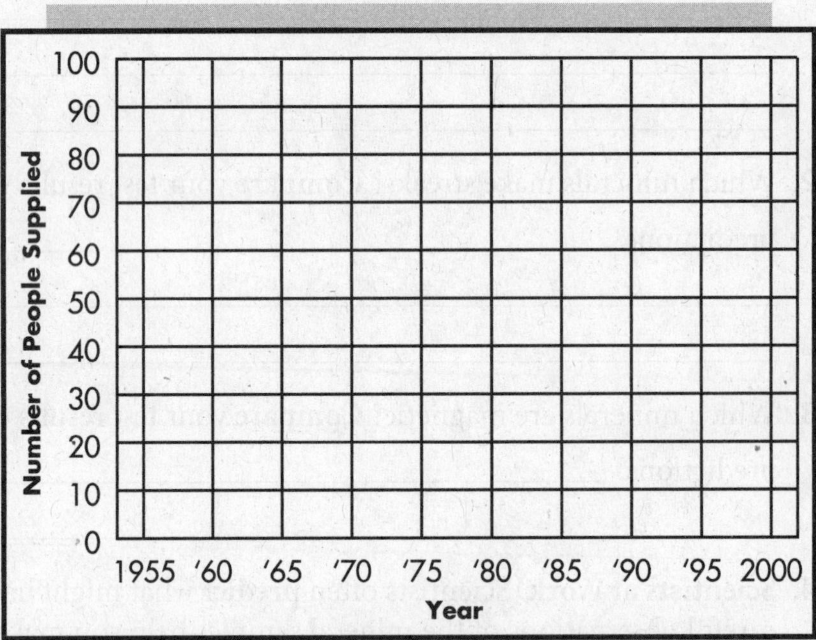

1. How many people do you think were supplied by one farm worker in 1990?

____

____

2. Will a graph like this help you predict far into the future? Why or why not?

____

____

____

Use with page C35.

Name ______________________

Date ______________________

What Are Natural Resources?

Lesson Concept

Natural resources are useful materials that people take from Earth. Some resources are renewable or reusable. Others are nonrenewable. Once nonrenewable resources are used, they cannot be replaced.

Vocabulary

natural resource (C36) **nonrenewable resource** (C36)
renewable resource (C38) **reusable resource** (C38)

Which kind of resources are these?

Next to each resource listed below, write whether the resource is renewable, reusable, or nonrenewable. Explain your answer.

Resource	Type and Explanation
1. water	______________________
2. oil	______________________
3. wood	______________________
4. soil	______________________
5. gasoline	______________________

Use with page C39.

Name ______________________

Date ______________________

What Kinds of Rocks Store Petroleum?

Materials

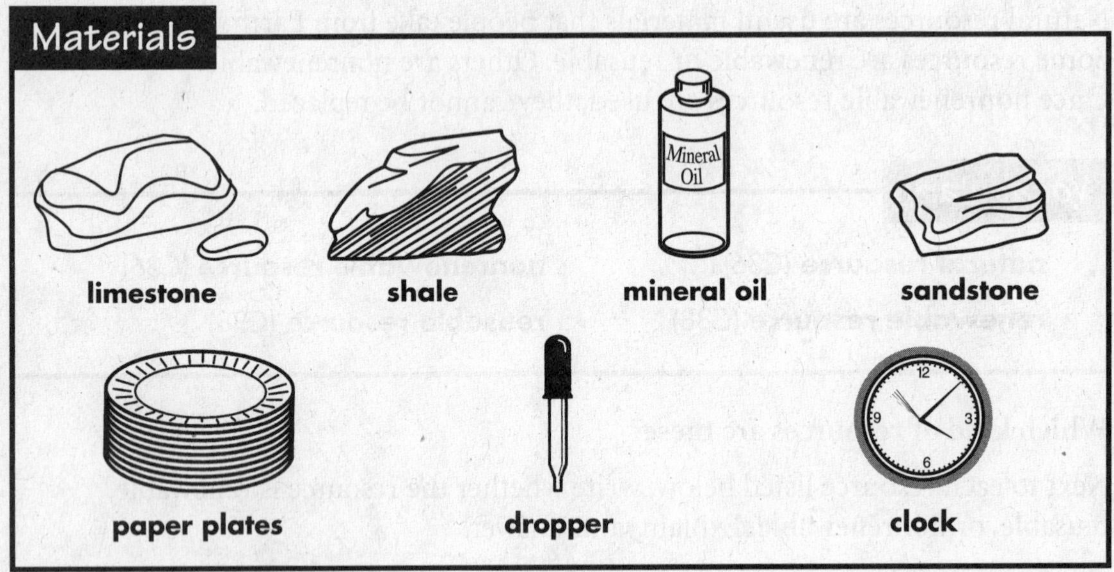

Activity Procedure

1. Place the rock samples on separate paper plates. **Observe** each rock. **Predict** which will be the best storage rock.
2. Fill the dropper with mineral oil. Put 5 drops of oil on the limestone sample.
3. **Observe** and **record** the time it takes for the 5 drops of oil to soak into the limestone.
4. Continue adding oil, counting the drops, until the limestone will hold no more oil. **Record** the number of drops it takes.
5. Repeat Steps 2–4 with the other rock samples.

Name ______________________

Draw Conclusions

1. Which rock soaked up the oil the fastest? What was the time?

____

____

2. Which rock soaked up the most oil? What was the number of drops?

____

____

3. Which rock is the best storage rock? Explain. ______________________

____

4. **Scientists at Work** Scientists often **use numbers** to **compare** things. How did you use numbers to compare the oil-storing ability of the rocks?

____

____

Investigate Further How could you determine which of the rocks is a source rock for petroleum? **Plan a simple investigation** to answer this question. Then decide what equipment you would need to carry out this investigation. ____________

____

____

____

Name ___________________________

Date ___________________________

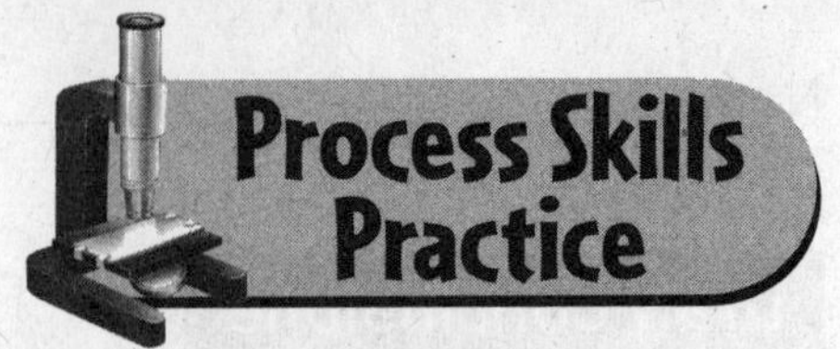

Use Numbers and Compare

Numbers give you a way to estimate things. They allow you to count, order, or compare information.

Think About Using Numbers and Comparing

The table below on the left shows how many quadrillion Btus (a way of measuring energy) were used in 1995 by the countries listed. Find the largest number in the "Btus" column. Put that number at the top of the Btus column in the table on the right. Next to that number, write the name of the country that used that amount of energy. Complete the table, ordering the numbers from largest to smallest.

Country	Btus
Germany	13.71
United Kingdom	9.85
China	35.67
Italy	7.42
Russia	26.75
Canada	11.72
United States	90.94
Japan	21.42
France	9.43
India	10.50

Btus	Country

1. What is the total energy used by the five European countries listed? What is the total energy used by the three Asian countries? How do these figures compare?

____

____

2. What did you learn from adding and comparing the numbers showing European and Asian energy use? ___________________________

____

____

Use with page C41.

Name ______________________

Date ______________________

How Do Fossil Fuels Form?

Lesson Concept

Fossil fuels form over millions of years from the decayed remains of organisms. Coal forms in four stages, first forming peat, then lignite, then bitumen, and finally anthracite.

Vocabulary

peat (C44)	**lignite** (C44)	**bitumen** (C45)
anthracite (C45)	**natural gas** (C46)	**fossil fuels** (C42)

Write the letter of the definition in Column B next to the word it defines in Column A.

Column A	Column B
_____ 70 percent	**A** coal, natural gas, and petroleum
_____ anthracite	**B** the most common fossil fuel
_____ the sun	**C** fossil fuel that formed when microorganisms died and fell to the bottoms of ancient seas
_____ sedimentary	**D** first stage of coal formation
_____ petroleum	**E** soft, brown rock that forms as layers of sand and mud cover peat
_____ bitumen	**F** mostly methane, usually found with petroleum
_____ swamps	**G** source of the energy in fossil fuels
_____ coal	**H** third stage of coal formation
_____ seams	**I** chemicals made from petroleum
_____ fossil fuels	**J** kind of rock in which fossil fuels are usually found
_____ natural gas	**K** layers of coal
_____ lignite	**L** fourth stage of coal formation
_____ peat	**M** places where peat can be found
_____ petrochemicals	**N** amount of carbon in lignite

Use with page C47.

Name ______________________

Date ______________________

How People Use Natural Resources

Materials

small bowl of paper clips

3 generation cards (parents, children, grandchildren)

Activity Procedure

1. Work in a group of three. Place your group's generation cards face down on a table. The bowl of paper clips stands for Earth's supply of a certain resource, such as iron.
2. Each person in the group now takes a generation card. Hold up your card so the other people in your group can see it. The card tells you your generation. It also tells you how many people are in your generation.
3. Each generation will now get paper clips from the bowl. The person from the parents' generation goes first. He or she takes five clips from the bowl for each person in his or her generation.
4. Next, the person from the children's generation takes five clips for each person in his or her generation.
5. Finally, the person from the grandchildren's generation takes five clips for each person in his or her generation.

Name ______________________

Draw Conclusions

1. Did everyone get the same number of clips? ______________________

2. Where did a problem occur? ______________________

____

3. What could be done to avoid the problem? ______________________

____

4. **Scientists at Work** Scientists **hypothesize** what the results of an investigation might be. Hypothesize what will happen if each person from a generation gets only three or four clips, instead of five. ______________________

____

____

____

Investigate Further With the members of your group, list the products people use that are made from a natural resource, such as a certain metal. Describe several things people could do to make sure that in the future there will be enough of this resource. Then **plan and conduct a simple investigation** using technology to simulate your plan. ______________________

____

____

____

Name ______________________

Date ______________________

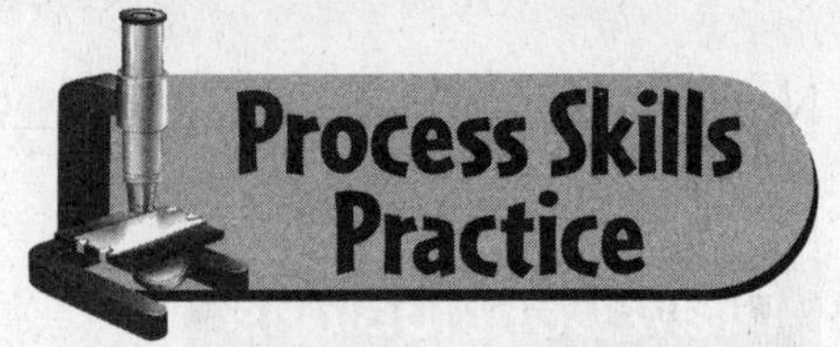

Hypothesize

A hypothesis is an educated "guess" about how one thing will be affected by another thing. A hypothesis is based on observation and prior knowledge. It can be tested in an experiment and changed depending on the result of the experiment.

Think About Hypothesizing

In some places trucks pick up newspapers, glass, cans, and plastics to be recycled. In other places people must take these items to a recycling center. In some states people get money back when they recycle certain types of glass or plastic bottles. Some towns put up billboards reminding people to recycle. What makes people more likely to recycle?

1. Think about the following hypothesis: If you pay people to recycle, then more people will recycle. How could you test this hypothesis?

2. What results would support the hypothesis?

3. Some people hypothesize that if you make recycling easier for people, then they will recycle. How can you test this hypothesis?

4. Some people hypothesize that if you educate people about the importance of recycling, then they will recycle. How can you test this hypothesis?

5. Hypothesize which of the three methods given above would be most effective in getting people to recycle. Support your hypothesis.

Use with page C49.

Name ______________________

Date ______________________

How Are Natural Resources Conserved?

Lesson Concept

Earth has a limited supply of natural resources that must be conserved so that they will last as long as possible.

Vocabulary

recycling (C52)

One way to conserve resources is to reduce the amounts that are used. Another way is to reuse things. Many things that can't be reused can be recycled. Think of things you could do to conserve resources by **reducing, reusing,** or **recycling.** Next to each resource below, describe what you could do to conserve that resource.

Reduce

1. Gasoline ____

____

____

2. Coal (Electricity) ____

____

____

____

Reuse

3. Plastics ____

____

____

____

Recycle

4. Trees (Paper) ____

____

Use with page C53.

Name ____________________

Date ____________________

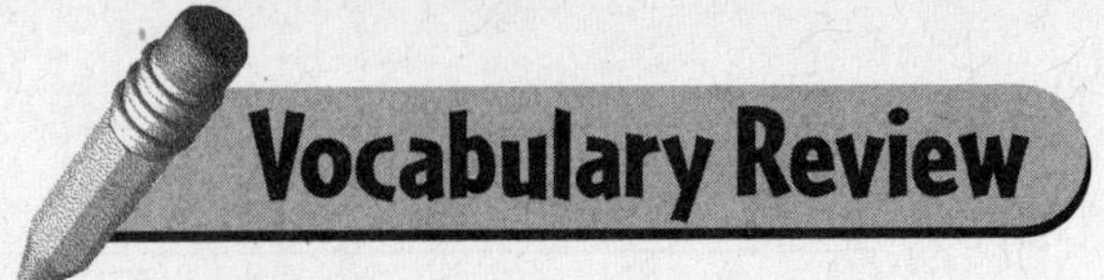

Recognize Vocabulary

Review the vocabulary terms for Chapter 2 by completing this word puzzle.

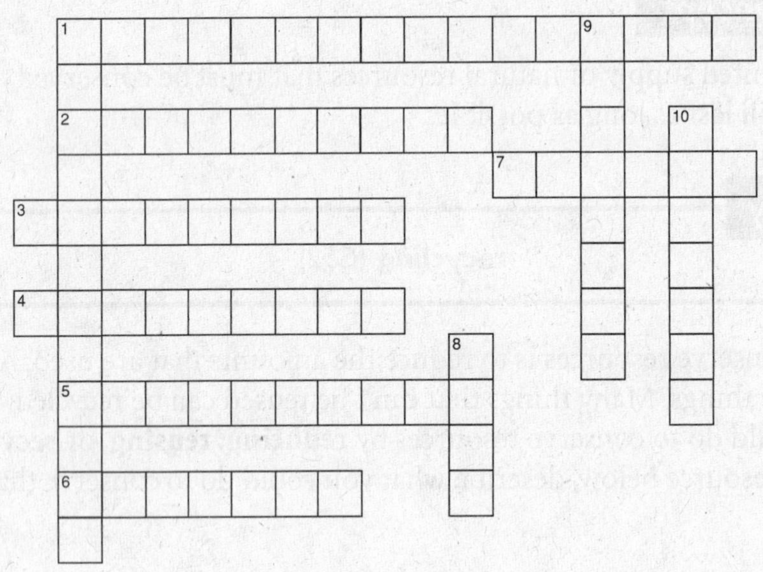

Across

1. Minerals and other useful materials that are taken from Earth (2 words)
2. A fossil fuel consisting mostly of methane (2 words)
3. A resource that's replaced as it is used is called a ____ resource.
4. The process of taking back the resource in a product
5. A very hard, black rock that is the most valuable form of coal
6. This is formed when pressure squeezes moisture out of peat
7. Burned to heat homes and produce electricity, ____ fuels are formed from decayed organisms in Earth.

Down

1. A resource that cannot be replaced is called a ____ resource.
8. A soft, brown material made up of partially decayed plants
9. A resource that can be used more than once is called a ____ resource.
10. The most common type of coal mined and used today

Use with pages C32–C59.

Name ______________________ Date ______________

Chapter 3 • Graphic Organizer for Chapter Concepts

Weather and Climate

LESSON 1 WEATHER FACTORS

Atmosphere

1. ______________________
2. ______________________

Air Pressure

1. ______________________
2. ______________________

Humidity

Precipitation

Water Cycle

evaporation → condensation →

Clouds

1. ______________________
2. ______________________
3. ______________________
4. ______________________

LESSON 2 WIND

Caused by Sun's Uneven Heating of Earth

1. ______________________
   ____
2. ______________________
   ____
3. ______________________

Types of Wind

1. ______________________
2. ______________________

LESSON 3 CLIMATE

Average of All Weather Over Time

Climate Zones

1. ______________________
2. ______________________
3. ______________________
4. ______________________
5. ______________________

Climate Changes

1. ______________________
2. ______________________
3. ______________________

Name ______________________

Date ______________________

Measuring Weather Conditions

Materials

weather station

Activity Procedure

1. Use the Weather Station Daily Record chart below to **record** the date, the time, the temperature, the amount of rain or snow, the wind direction and speed, and the cloud conditions each day for five days. Try to **record** the weather conditions at the same time each day.
2. Place the weather station in a shady spot, 1 m above the ground. **Record** the temperature.
3. Be sure the rain gauge will not collect runoff from any buildings or trees. **Record** the amount of rain or snow (if any).
4. Be sure the wind vane is located where wind from any direction will reach it. **Record** the wind direction and speed. Winds are labeled with the direction from which they blow.

Weather Station Daily Record					
Date					
Time					
Temperature					
Rainfall or snowfall					
Wind direction and speed					
Cloud condition					

Name ______________________

5 Describe and **record** the cloud conditions by noting how much of the sky is covered by clouds. Draw a circle and shade in the part of the circle that equals the amount of sky covered with clouds.

6 Use the temperature data to make a line graph showing how the temperature changes from day to day.

Draw Conclusions

1. Use your Weather Station Daily Record to **compare** the weather conditions on two different days. Which conditions were about the same? Which conditions changed the most? ______________________

____

____

____

2. From the **data** you **gathered** in this activity, how might scientists use weather data to **predict** the weather? ______________________

____

____

____

3. Scientists at Work Scientists learn about the weather by **measuring** weather conditions and **gathering data**. What did you learn by measuring the amount of rain your area received during the week of your observations?

____

____

____

Investigate Further Find a newspaper weather page, and note the temperatures in various cities throughout the United States. Why are there different temperatures in different cities? **Plan and conduct a simple investigation** using technology to find out. ______________________

____

____

Name ______________________

Date ______________________

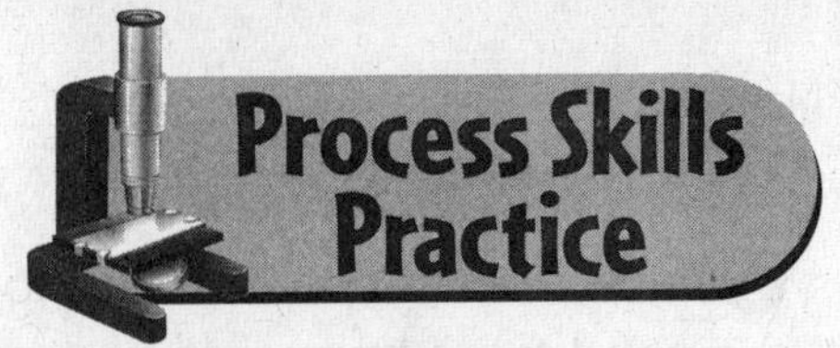

Measure and Collect Data

Measurements are a kind of observation. You measure when you use a tool, such as a thermometer, a clock, or a ruler.

Think About Measuring and Collecting Data

When you measure, you are actually comparing. For example, if you measure a rope and find that the rope is 1.5 m long, you are comparing the length of the rope to a standard length. The standard is, in this case, the meter. If you weigh the rope and find that it weighs 20 newtons, you are comparing the rope to a standard weight, the newton. Of course, it's important to use the right measuring unit, too. For example, you wouldn't measure a 5-m rope in kilometers. You would use meters. Think about setting a new standard for measuring lengths as shown below.

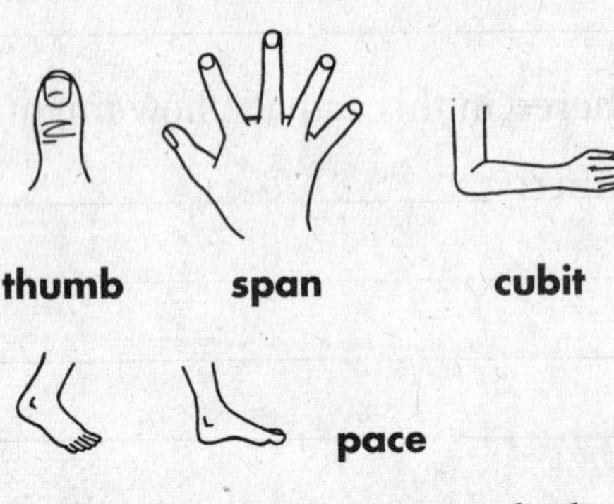

1. Which of these units would you use to measure the length of a swimming pool?

____

2. Which would you use to measure your height? ______________________

____

3. How many spans equal a cubit? ______________________

____

4. Why do you think no one uses a measuring system like this one?

____

____

____

5. How could you make this measuring system work as a standard?

____

____

Use with page C63.

Name ______________________

Date ______________________

How Can You Observe and Measure Weather Conditions?

Lesson Concept

Weather conditions such as temperature, air pressure, humidity, wind speed and direction, and precipitation can be observed and measured.

Vocabulary

atmosphere (C64)	**air pressure** (C65)	**humidity** (C65)
precipitation (C65)	**evaporation** (C67)	**condensation** (C67)

Answer each question with one or more complete sentences.

1. Where in the atmosphere does most weather occur? ______________________

2. Why does most weather occur only in one layer of the atmosphere? ______________________

3. What is the largest source of water for the water cycle? ______________________

4. Fog is actually a cloud that is low enough to touch the ground. What kind of cloud is fog? ______________________

5. What are you measuring when you measure air pressure? ______________________

6. Why do people measure atmospheric conditions? ______________________

7. If you see cumulus clouds in the sky, what type of weather are you likely to have? ______________________

Use with page C69.

Name ______________________

Date ______________________

The Sun's Energy Heats Unevenly

Materials

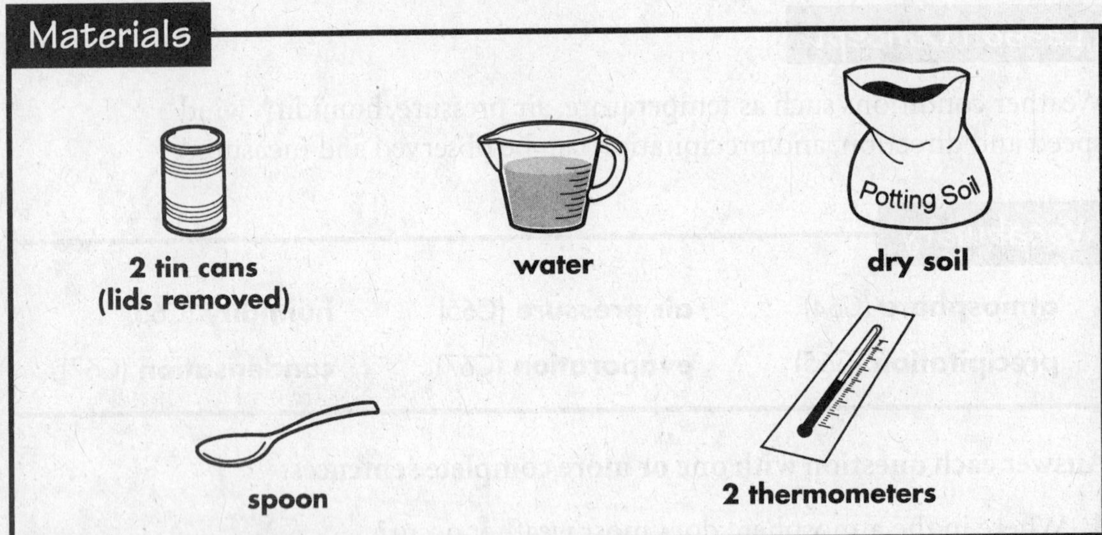

Activity Procedure

1. Fill one can about $\frac{3}{4}$ full of water and the other can about $\frac{3}{4}$ full of soil.
2. Place one thermometer in the can of water and the other in the can of soil. Put the cans in a shady place outside. Wait for 10 minutes, and then **record** the temperatures of the water and the soil.
3. Put both cans in sunlight. **Predict** which of the cans will show the faster rise in temperature. **Record** the temperature of each can every 10 minutes for 30 minutes. In which can does the temperature rise faster? Which material—soil or water—heats up faster?
4. Now put the cans back in the shade. **Predict** in which of the cans the temperature will drop faster. Again **record** the temperature of each can every 10 minutes for 30 minutes. In which can does the temperature drop faster? Which material—soil or water—cools off faster?
5. Make line graphs to show how the temperatures of both materials changed as they heated up and cooled off.

Name ______________________________

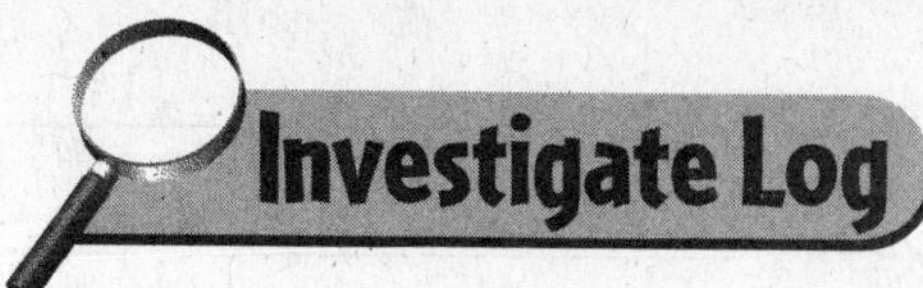

Draw Conclusions

1. How did your results match your predictions? Which material—water or soil—heated up faster? Which cooled off faster? ______________________________

2. From the results you **observed** in this investigation, which would you **predict** heats up faster—oceans or land? Which would you predict cools off faster? Explain. ______________________________

3. Scientists at Work Scientists learn by **predicting** and then testing their predictions. How did you test your predictions about water and soil?

____

Investigate Further Predict how fast other materials, such as moist soil, sand, and salt water, heat up and cool off. **Plan and conduct a simple** investigation to test your predictions. ______________________________

Name ______________________

Date ______________________

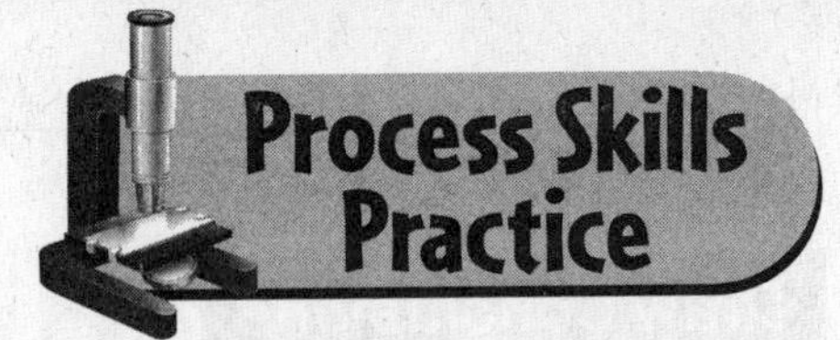

Predict

When you predict, you make a statement about what you think will happen. To make a prediction, you think about what you've observed before. You also think about how to interpret data you have.

Think About Predicting

Robert wanted to see if he could predict the weather if he knew which way the wind was blowing and whether the barometer was rising or falling. He decided to find out. All through the winter, he kept records of wind direction, air pressure, and the weather that followed his observations. Then he made this chart.

Wind Direction (From)	Barometer	Weather
varies	neither rising nor falling	pleasant weather, no changes in temperature
south, changing to southeast	falling	wind picks up, rain after a few hours
southeast, changing to northeast	falling	windy and colder
east, changing to northeast	falling slowly	rain the next day
east, changing to northeast	falling rapidly	wind increases, and it snows
south, changing to southwest	rising slowly	the skies clear, and the sun comes out
southwest, changing to west	rising rapidly	the skies clear, and it gets really cold

1. Using Robert's chart, what kind of weather would you predict if the wind is from the southwest and the barometer is neither rising nor falling?

____

2. Using Robert's chart, what kind of weather would you predict if the barometer is rising and the wind direction has changed from the south to the southwest?

____

3. The wind direction has changed from the east to the northeast, and the barometer is falling fast. Using Robert's chart, what kind of weather would you predict?

____

Use with page C71.

Name ______________________

Date ______________________

What Causes Wind?

Lesson Concept

Changes in air pressure, caused by uneven heating of Earth's surface and the air above it, cause the wind to blow. There are local winds and prevailing winds.

Vocabulary

local winds (C73)	**prevailing winds** (C73)

You know that weather conditions are caused by factors like temperature, humidity, and air pressure. The combinations of these factors form weather systems. A weather system can be a storm, very cold air, or pleasant, sunny weather. Weather systems are moved by prevailing winds from west to east across the United States.

1. Suppose weather conditions in your area are hot and dry. Do you think local winds are blowing toward the center of the hot area or away from it? Explain. ______________________

2. In which general direction is the hot and dry air mass in Question 1 most likely to move? Why? ______________________

3. Suppose it is raining today in Ohio and Michigan. What kind of weather would you expect to find in New York state tomorrow? ______________________

4. What causes prevailing winds? ______________________

Name ______________________

Date ______________________

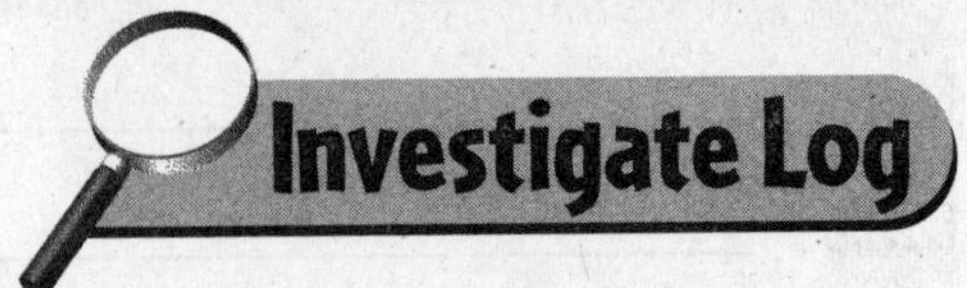

Local Weather Conditions

Materials

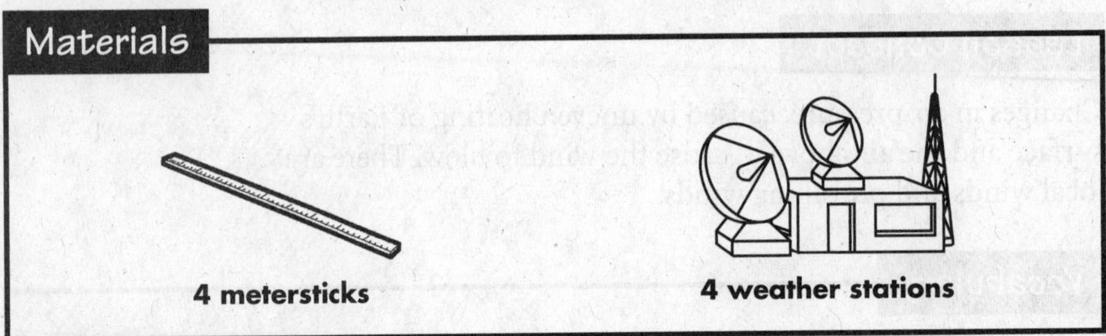

Activity Procedure

1. Use the table below.

Local Weather Conditions			
Location	**Temperature**	**Wind Direction**	**Wind Speed**
1			
2			
3			
4			

2. Choose four locations near your school to study. Select different kinds of locations, such as a shady parkway, a sunny playground, a parking lot on the south side of your school, and a ball field on the north side. For the same time on any given day, **predict** whether the temperature, wind direction, and wind speed will be the same or different at the different locations.

3. At the chosen time, four people should each take a meterstick and a weather station to a different one of the selected locations. Use the meterstick to locate a point 1 m above the ground. **Measure** and **record** the temperature at that point. Use the weather station to determine the wind direction and speed, too. Record the data in your table.

4. Make a double-bar graph to show the temperatures and wind speeds recorded at all the locations. Write the wind direction at each location on the appropriate wind-speed bar.

Name ______________________

Draw Conclusions

1. Use your table to **compare** the temperature, wind direction, and wind speed at the different locations. What differences, if any, did you find? What conditions were the same? ______________________

2. Local weather conditions affect the organisms that live in a location. Do you think wind speed or temperature is more likely to affect living organisms? Explain. ______________________

3. Based on your investigation, how would you define the phrase *local weather conditions*? ______________________

4. **Scientists at Work** Scientists learn about local weather conditions by **comparing** weather data from different locations. **Draw conclusions** about local weather conditions, based on the locations you studied.

Investigate Further What other factors, in addition to temperature, wind direction, and wind speed might affect local weather conditions? **Hypothesize** about a factor that might affect local weather conditions. Then **plan and conduct a simple investigation** to test your hypothesis. ______________________

Name ____________________

Date ____________________

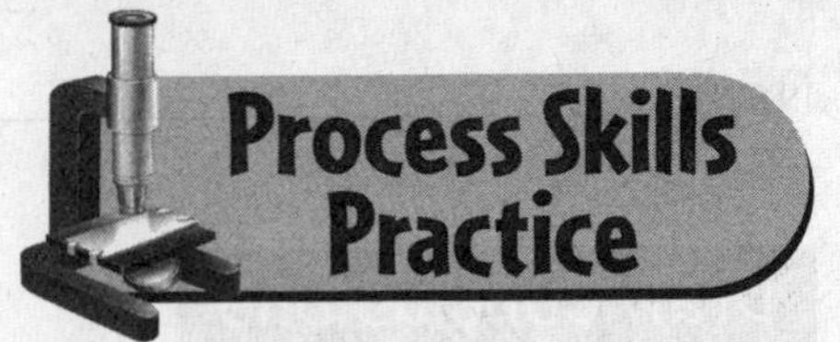

Compare and Draw Conclusions

When you compare objects or events, you look for what they have in common. You also look for differences between them.

Think About Comparing and Drawing Conclusions

Earth's climates can be grouped into five major climate zones. In this activity you can compare three of those climate zones. Use the map and the descriptions of three world climates to answer the questions below.

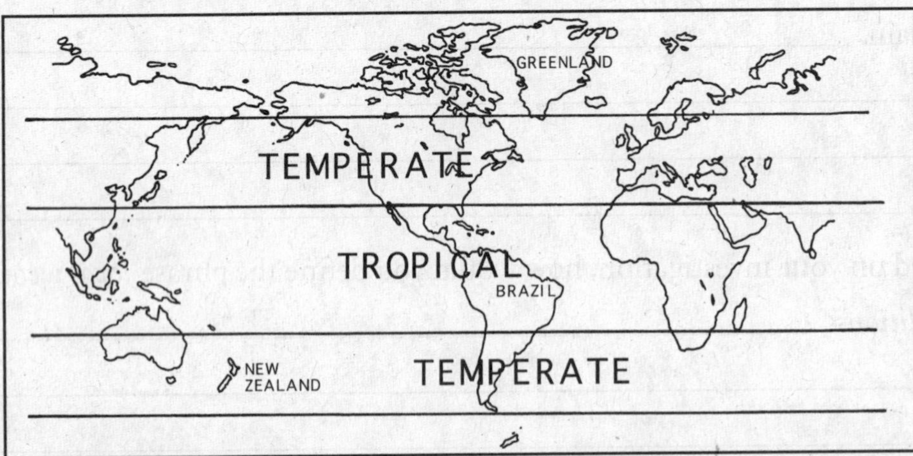

Polar climates are the world's coldest. Winter temperatures fall below −50°C.
Temperate climates have four seasons a year, with a warm or hot summer and a cool or dry winter. Average daily temperatures range between −3°C in the winter and 18°C in the summer. These areas have an average amount of precipitation.
Tropical climates are found in most of Earth's rain forests and savannas. These areas have an average daily temperature of 27°C and high rainfall.

1. Do you think the climate of Brazil is similar to or different from that of Greenland? Explain. ____________________

____

2. Do you think the climate in New Zealand would be very different from the climate in New Jersey? ____________________

____

____

Use with page C77.

Name ____________________

Date ____________________

What Is Climate and How Does It Change?

Lesson Concept

Climate is the average of all weather conditions through all seasons over a period of time. Earth's climate has changed over time as average temperatures have risen and fallen. Human activities can affect climate.

Vocabulary

climate (C78) **microclimate** (C78) **El Niño** (C81)

greenhouse effect (C82) **global warming** (C82)

Fill in the chart with information from your textbook and answer the questions.

Climate Zones	Summer Temp.	Winter Temp.	Precipitation	Where Found?
Polar	cool	cold	snow	near North and South Poles
Mountain				
Temperate				
Tropical				

1. Which climate zones are coldest? ____________________

2. Which climate zone is wettest? ____________________

3. Which climate zone shows the most variation over a year? ____________________

4. How did putting information in a chart help you compare the climate zones?

____

Use with page C83.

Name ______________________

Date ______________________

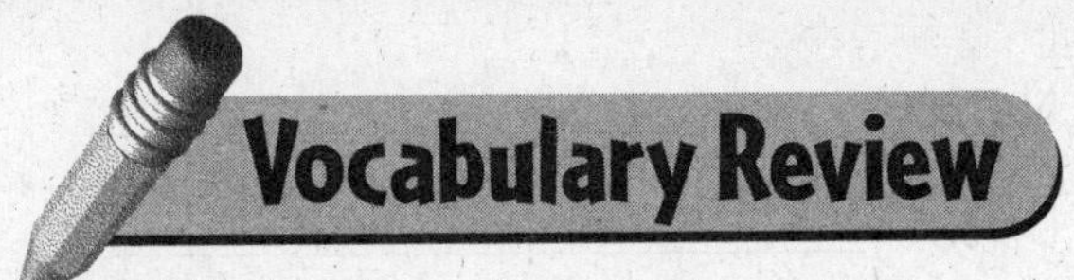

Recognize Vocabulary

Listed below are scrambled vocabulary terms. Use the clues to unscramble them. Write the unscrambled terms on the lines provided.

1. D S L O W N L C I A (2 words) ______________________ horizontal movement of air resulting from local changes in temperature

2. N N O L E I (2 words) ______________________ short-term change in climate occurring around the Pacific Ocean every two to ten years

3. S T R P O E M H A E ______________________ blanket of air surrounding Earth

4. O I R L C E I M M A T C ______________________ the climate of a very small area

5. A E M T C L I ______________________ the average of all weather conditions through all seasons over a period of time

6. P C E I I O N P T A T R I ______________________ rain or snow

7. I I P N S V A G L N W I R E D (2 words) ______________________ global winds that blow constantly from the same direction and cover a large part of Earth's surface

8. B G L W A L M O G I R N A (2 words) ______________________ an abnormally rapid rise in Earth's average temperature caused by excess carbon dioxide in the atmosphere

9. A S R R E R I S U P E (2 words) ______________________ the weight of air

10. Y H M I I U T D ______________________ water or moisture in the air

Use with pages C62–C83.

Chapter 4 • *Graphic Organizer for Chapter Concepts*

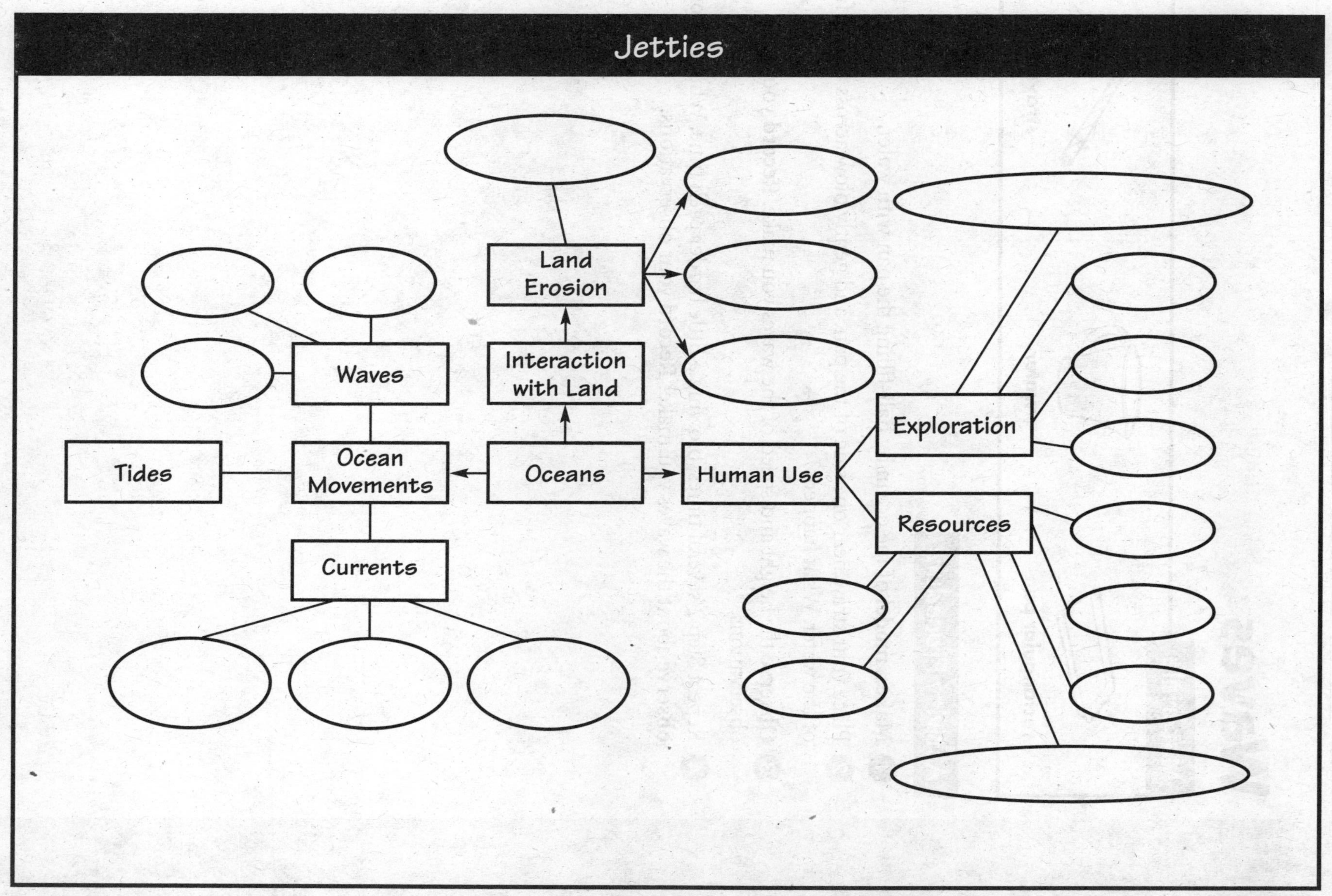

Name ______________________________ Date ____________________

Name ______________________

Date ______________________

Waves

Materials

Activity Procedure

1. **Make a model** of the ocean by half-filling the pan with water.
2. Place your straw near one side of the pan, and gently blow across the surface of the water. What happens?
3. **Observe** the height and speed of the waves you make. **Record** your observations.
4. Repeat Step 2 several times, blowing a little harder each time. What do you **observe** about the waves you make? **Record** your observations.

Name ____________________

Draw Conclusions

1. Use your observations to describe a relationship between how hard you blow and the height and speed of the waves. ____________________

2. From what you observed in this activity, what can you **infer** about the cause of waves on oceans and other bodies of water? ____________________

3. Scientists at Work Scientists often **use models** to learn about things they cannot **observe** directly. What did your model help you observe about waves?

Investigate Further Predict how high the waves on a pond, a lake, or the ocean will be on a calm day and on a stormy day. Then test your predictions by **using a model.** ____________________

Name ______________________

Date ______________________

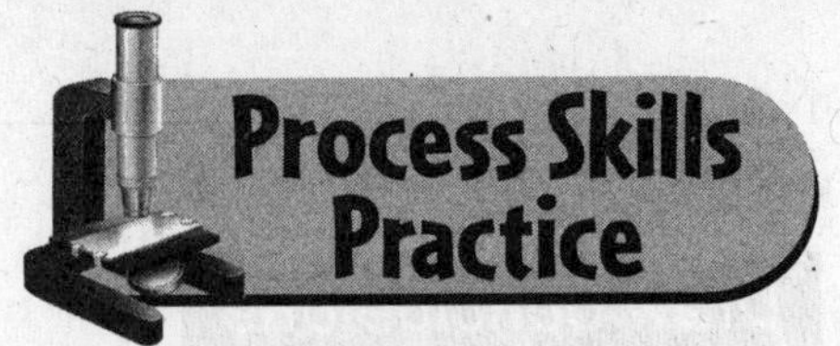

Observe

You observe when you use your senses to note the properties of an object or event. You can observe directly, or you can use instruments such as microscopes or hand lenses.

Think About Observing

When you observe something, you often ask questions about what you are observing. Observing then leads to other process skills, such as measuring, comparing, recording data, inferring, or drawing conclusions. Beneath the drawing below, you will see that some conclusions have been drawn. What can you observe in the drawing that would help you reach those conclusions?

Conclusion	Observation
1. It is either morning or evening.	
2. It is dark under the water.	
3. The diver does not have to come to the surface to breathe and can probably stay underwater for a long while.	

Use with page C93.

Name ____________________

Date ____________________

How Do Ocean Waters Move?

Lesson Concept

Ocean waters move as waves, currents, and tides. Most waves are caused by wind. Currents are caused by prevailing winds and differences in water temperature. Tides are caused by the gravitational pull of the sun and the moon.

Vocabulary

wave (C94)	**current** (C96)	**tide** (C98)

Choose the short answer that best completes each sentence below.

1. Most of the movement of water on the ocean's surface is caused by ______.

A waves **B** currents **C** tides

2. Earthquakes and volcanoes cause ______.

A some of the biggest waves **B** some of the strongest currents **C** tropical storms

3. A stream of water that flows through the ocean like a river is called a ______.

A rogue wave **B** tsunami **C** current

4. The Gulf Stream is a surface current that ______.

A strikes the shore at an angle **B** carries warm water to cold regions **C** is a cold, deep-ocean current

5. Surface currents are caused by ______.

A differences in water temperature **B** long ridges of sand that form near the shoreline **C** prevailing winds

6. Deep-ocean currents are caused by ______.

A differences in water temperature **B** long ridges of sand that form near the shoreline **C** prevailing winds

7. Tides are caused by ______.

A powerful deep-ocean currents **B** the pull of gravity from the sun and the moon **C** prevailing winds

Use with page C99.

Name ______________________

Date ______________________

The Effect of Waves on a Beach

Materials

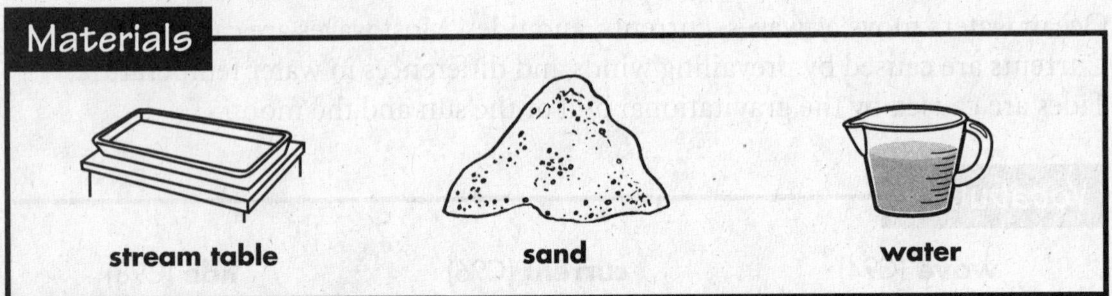

Activity Procedure

1. Use sand to **make a model** of a beach at one end of the stream table. The beach should have a gentle slope.
2. Slowly add water to the stream table until it is about half full. Try not to disturb the beach.
3. Make a wave by lifting the sand end of the stream table about 2 cm above the tabletop and then dropping it. What do you **observe** about the beach and the water? Repeat this several times. **Record** your observations.
4. Repeat Steps 1–3, but this time build a beach that is much steeper than the first one. **Record** your observations.

Name ______________________

Draw Conclusions

1. Use your observations to explain how waves affect a beach. ______________________

2. Does the slope of the beach matter? Explain. ______________________

3. Scientists at Work Scientists often **make a model** to study how natural processes work. How did your model help you **observe** how waves affect a beach? ______________________

What couldn't you observe about wave action with your model?

Investigate Further If possible, study the shore of a pond, a lake, or an ocean in your area. What do you **observe** about the shore? What questions do you have about how waves affect the shore? **Plan and conduct a simple investigation** to help you answer your questions. Decide what equipment you will need to use in your investigation. ______________________

Name ______________________

Date ______________________

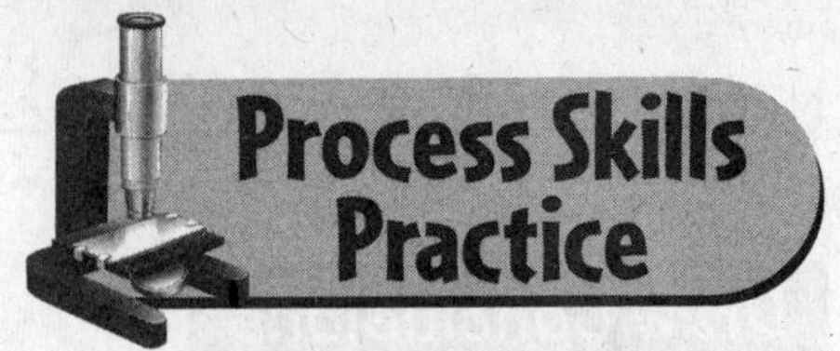

Use a Model

Sometimes the best way to investigate a process is to make and use a model. This is especially true when you want to take a closer look at large-scale Earth processes such as ocean currents.

Think About Using a Model

You have already learned that Earth's rotation causes ocean currents to bend to the right in the Northern Hemisphere and to the left in the Southern Hemisphere. You can model this effect with a very simple experiment. Suppose you are riding on a carousel and you have a tennis ball in your hand. You toss the ball to a friend who is standing in the grass beside the carousel.

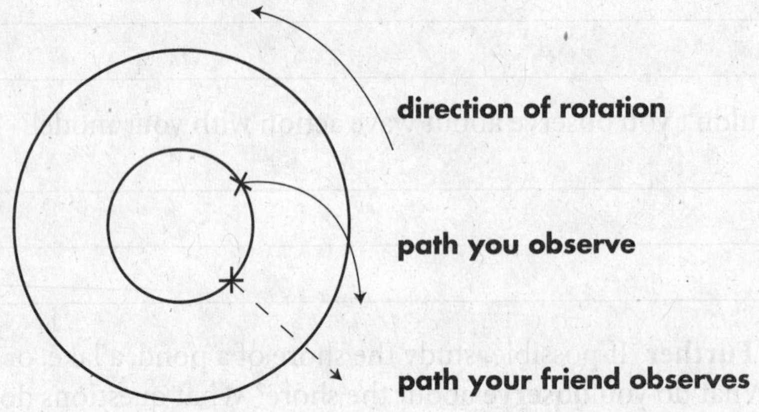

1. Does the path of the ball seem curved to your friend? ______________

2. Why does the path seem curved to you? ______________

____

____

3. Has some force acted on the ball to make its path curve? Explain.

____

____

4. How is this model like Earth and the ocean currents? How is it different?

____

____

____

Use with page C101.

Name ____________________

Date ____________________

How Do Oceans Interact with the Land?

Lesson Concept

The shore is changed by waves, currents, and human activities. Waves erode beaches and cliffs, longshore currents deposit material along the shore, and human-made structures affect the natural process of shore change.

Vocabulary

shore (C102) **estuary** (C102) **headland** (C103)

tide pool (C103) **jetty** (C104)

Ocean waves, ocean currents, and human activity all have an effect on the shore. Read this list of things that can be done to the shore. Decide whether each one is the result of waves, currents, or human activity. Mark the effects of waves with a *W*. Mark the effects of currents with a *C*. Mark the effects of human activity with an *H*.

__________ **1.** beach material being pushed along the shore

__________ **2.** structures built to block longshore currents

__________ **3.** rock along the shore slowly dissolved by a weak acid

__________ **4.** the formation of sand spits by beach material that has been pulled sideways

__________ **5.** jetties building up the beach by catching sand

__________ **6.** the bottom of a cliff eroding, causing the cliff to break apart and fall into the ocean

__________ **7.** structures built to protect beaches from erosion

__________ **8.** pebbles and small rocks loosened through water pressure and carried out to the ocean

__________ **9.** the formation of a new beach or the addition of material to an existing beach

Use with page C105.

Name ______________________

Date ______________________

How Scientists Measure Ocean Depths

Materials

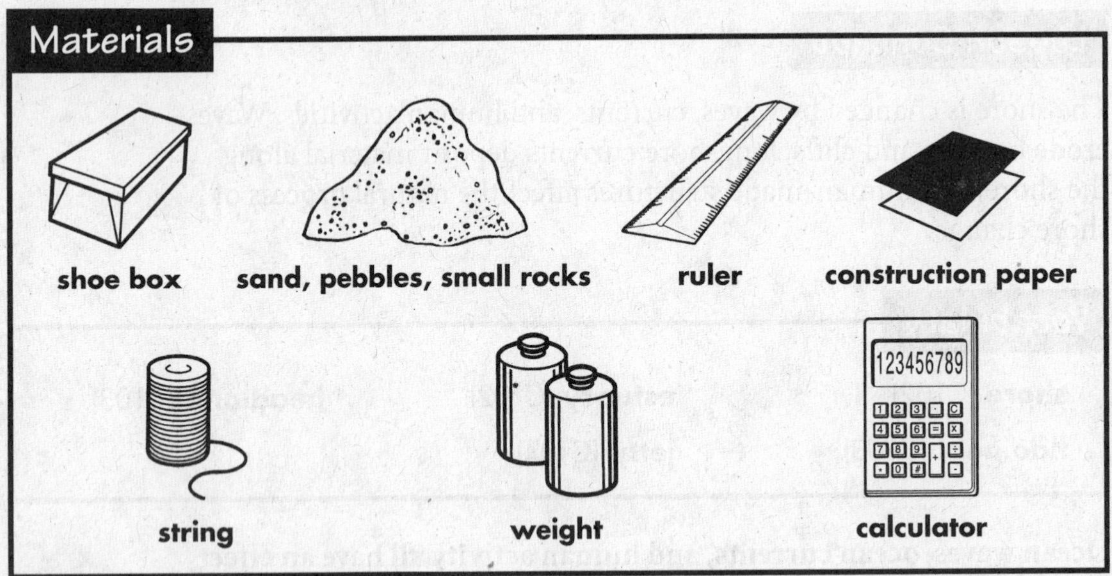

Activity Procedure

1. **Make a model** of the ocean floor by pouring sand and pebbles into the shoe box. Then scatter a few small rocks on top of the sand.
2. Cut a piece of construction paper large enough to cover the top of the box. This will stand for the sea surface.
3. With a pencil and ruler, draw a grid on the paper 4 squares wide by 8 squares long. Number the squares 1 through 32, and tape the lid onto the box. Tie the weight to a piece of string about twice as long as the box is deep.
4. Make a hole in the first square in any row and lower the weighted end of the string until the weight just touches the ocean floor.
5. Hold the string at sea level. **Measure** the length of string you pinched off to find the depth of the ocean. **Record** your measurement. Repeat Steps 4 and 5 for the remaining squares in that row.
6. Use the Sonar Data table on page WB169. The "Time" is the number of seconds it takes for a sound to travel from a boat to the bottom of the ocean and back to the boat.

Name ___________________________

7 Use a calculator to multiply the Location 1 time by 1500 m/s (the speed of sound in water). Then divide the product by 2. This number is the depth of the water in meters at Location 1. This one has been done for you.

8 Repeat Step 7 for each location in the table. Then make a line graph of the depths. The graph will be a profile of the ocean floor.

Sonar Data

Location	Time (s)	Depth (m)
1	1.8	1350
2	2.0	
3	3.6	
4	4.5	
5	5.3	
6	2.3	
7	3.1	
8	4.6	
9	5.0	
10	5.2	

Draw Conclusions

1. Why do you think scientists today use sonar rather than weighted ropes to **measure** the depth of the ocean? ___________________________

____

____

2. When using sonar, why must you divide each product by 2 to calculate the depth of the water? ___________________________

____

____

3. Scientists at Work How could a scientist use sonar to **measure** the size of large objects on the ocean floor? ___________________________

____

Investigate Further How could you find the depth of a pond, lake, or river? **Plan and conduct a simple investigation** to find out. Select the equipment you would need to use. ___________________________

____

____

Name ______________________

Date ______________________

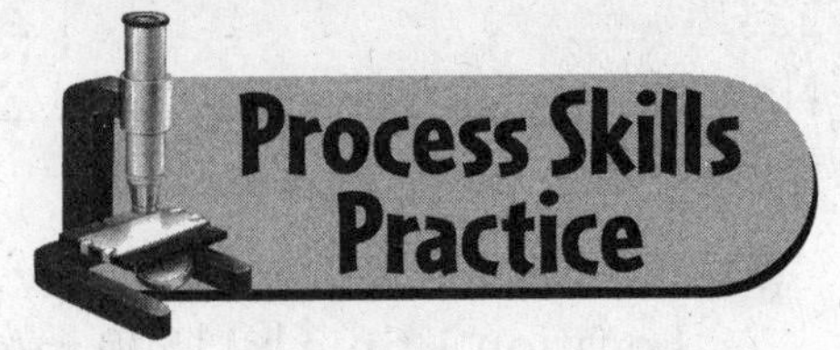

Measure

When you measure something, you are determining what its length, weight, volume, or some other quality is. You do this by using measuring standards, such as meters, inches, grams, or pounds.

Think About Measuring

Olden is a world where there are no roads, cars, airplanes, or any type of modern transportation. The only way to get from one place to another on Olden is by walking. The people who live there have no idea how big their world is. They have no idea what a mile or a kilometer is. They measure distance by the amount of time it takes to walk from one place to another.

1. Assuming that it takes you about one hour to walk two miles, how would you tell someone living on Olden that you live one mile away from school?

____

2. How would you describe the distance between New York and Chicago, which is about 800 miles? ______________________

____

3. Finish the table by filling in the Olden units of distance (that is, time) between New York and the cities listed in the left column.

	Miles	Olden Units
Cincinnati to New York	600	
Indianapolis to New York	700	
Little Rock to New York	1300	
Las Vegas to New York	2500	

4. Scientists on Earth use a unit called a light-year to measure the distances between the stars. Light travels about 186,000 miles in one second. What do you think a light-year is? ______________________

____

____

Use with page C107.

Name ______________________

Date ______________________

How Do People Explore the Oceans and Use Ocean Resources?

Lesson Concept

A wide range of technology is used to explore the ocean, including scuba equipment, submersibles, satellites, and sonar. The oceans contain valuable natural resources, such as fish, petroleum, minerals, and sea water.

Vocabulary

scuba (C109) **sonar** (C109) **submersible** (C109) **desalination** (C112)

Match the dates in the left column with the events in the right column. Write the letter of the event that matches each date in the space next to the date.

_____ 1690

_____ 1872

_____ 1912

_____ 1942

_____ 1956

_____ 1960

_____ 1977

_____ 1986

_____ 1987

A Jacques Piccard and Donald Walsh go down to the deepest place in the Pacific Ocean (10, 920 m) in the *Trieste II.*

B The RMS *Titanic* strikes an iceberg in the North Atlantic and sinks to the bottom of the ocean.

C Scientists in *Alvin* discover hot springs deep under the ocean. The springs come from vents in the ocean floor over volcanically active areas.

D Sir Edmund Halley, an English astronomer, builds a diving bell that traps air for divers to use.

E *Nautile* brings up some objects from the *Titanic* wreck.

F Six scientists spend more than three years at sea on the voyage of the HMS *Challenger.*

G Allyn Vine convinces the United States government that scientists need deep-diving vessels that can hold small crews.

H *Alvin* is used to explore the wreckage of the sunken RMS *Titanic.*

I French explorer Jacques Cousteau invents an aqua-lung that allows a diver to move about freely under water to a depth of about 100 m.

Use with page C113.

Name ____________________

Date ____________________

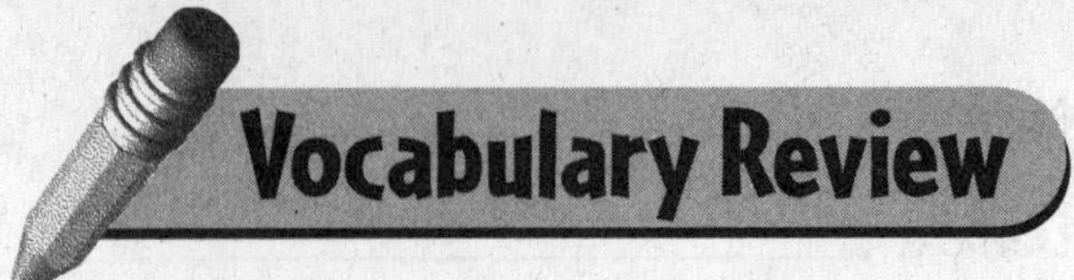

Recognize Vocabulary

Look at the vocabulary terms in the box. Choose the term that best completes each sentence. Write your answers on the lines. Use each term only once.

wave	**scuba**	**headland**	**jetty**
desalination	**shore**	**tide pool**	**sonar**
current	**tide**	**submersible**	

I love to go to the beach. It's fun to splash in a (up-and-down movement of surface water) ________________, but there's a lot more to do at the (area where the ocean and land meet and interact) ________________.

I look for stuff washed up from distant lands by a (stream of water that flows through the ocean) ________________. Once I found a can with writing I couldn't read! The (rise and fall in ocean level) ________________ makes the beach look different at different times of day. I study the variety of plants and animals in a (pool of sea water found along a rocky shoreline) ________________. Some days we climb the (process of hard rock left behind after softer rock has eroded) ________________, exploring caves and other formations, and we walk out along the (wall of rocks that sticks out into the ocean) ________________ to enjoy the crash of the sea and wind.

The ocean is an important resource. In some places people use (process of removing salt from sea water) ________________ to provide water for drinking.

Next year, I'm going to take lessons on how to dive using (self-contained underwater breathing apparatus) ________________ gear. When I get older, I want to be an oceanographer. I hope some day I'll be able to use (reflected sound waves) ________________ to learn more about the ocean depths. Maybe I'll get to travel in a (small underwater vehicle) ________________ to learn more about the mysteries of the deep!

Use with pages C92–C113.

Name ______________________ Date ______________

Chapter 1 • Graphic Organizer for Chapter Concepts

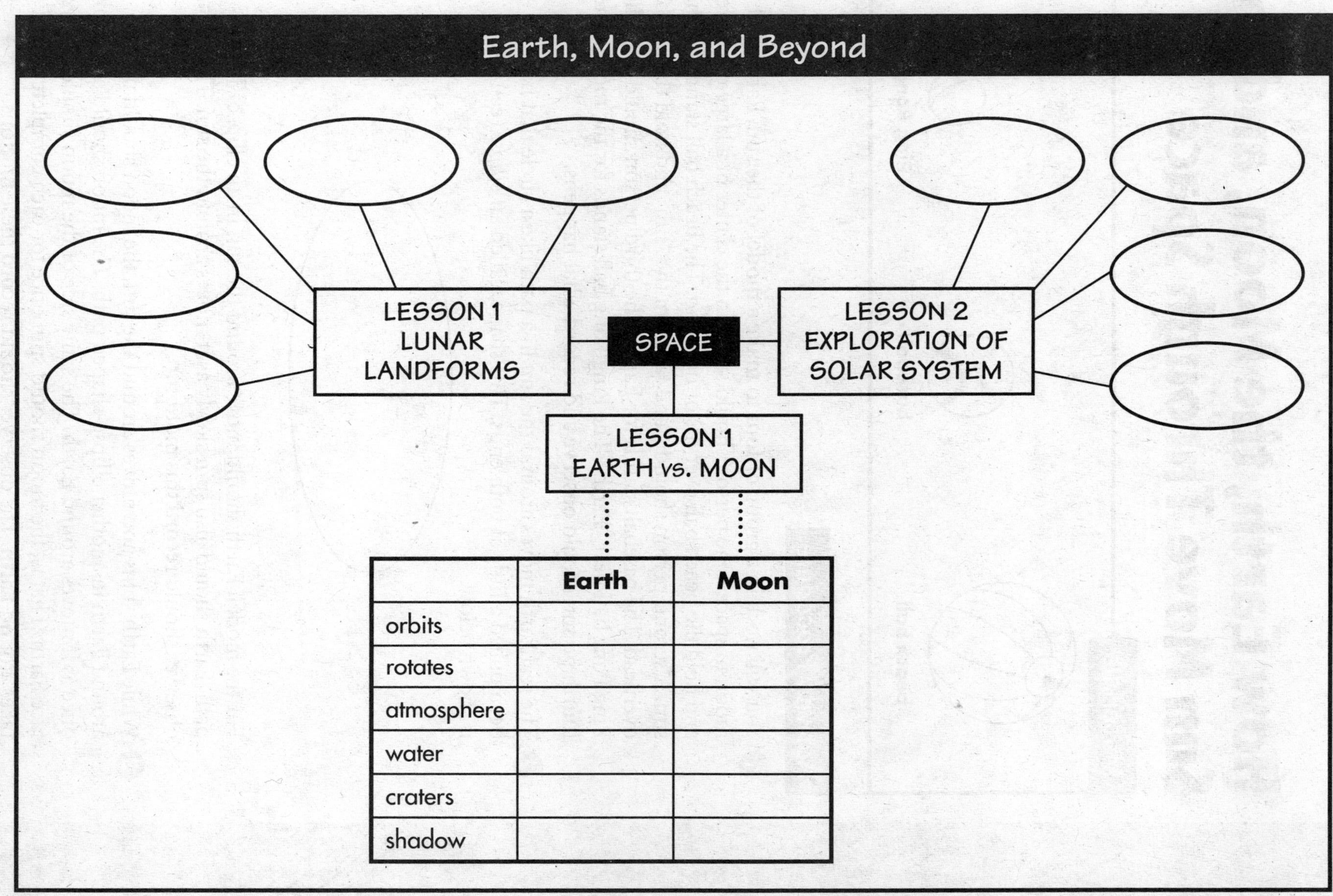

	Earth	Moon
orbits		
rotates		
atmosphere		
water		
craters		
shadow		

Name ______________________

Date ______________________

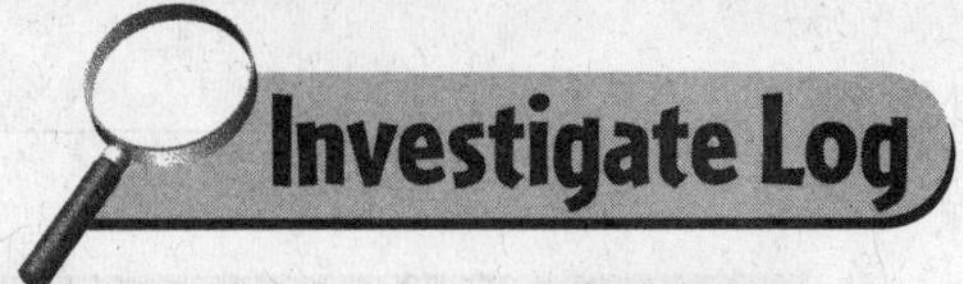

How Earth, the Moon, and the Sun Move Through Space

Materials

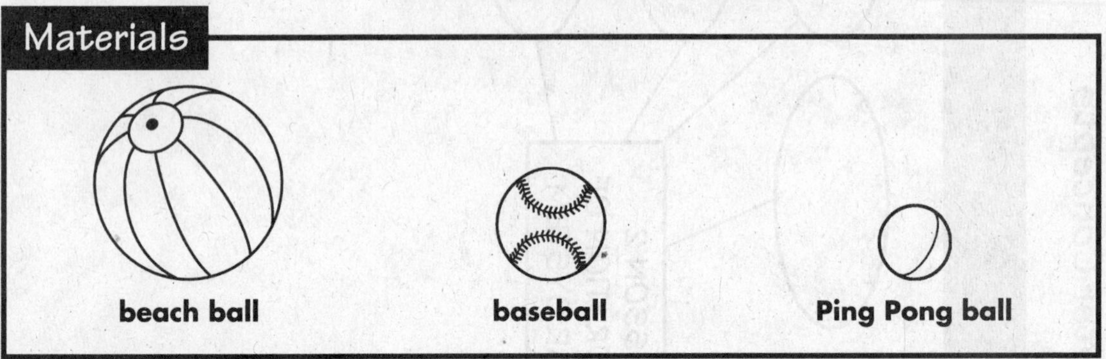

Activity Procedure

1. You will work in a group of four to **make a model** of the sun, Earth, and the moon in space. One person should stand in the center of a large open area and hold the beach ball over his or her head. The beach ball stands for the sun. A second person should stand far from the "sun" and hold the baseball overhead. The baseball stands for Earth. The third person should hold the Ping Pong ball near "Earth." The Ping Pong ball stands for the moon. The fourth person should **observe** and **record** what happens.

2. The real Earth moves around the sun in a path like a circle that has been pulled a little at both ends. This shape, called an *ellipse* (ee•LIPS), is shown below.

For the model, Earth should move around the sun in an ellipse-shaped path. Earth should also spin slowly as it moves around the sun. The observer should **record** this motion.

3. While Earth spins and moves around the sun, the moon should move around Earth in another ellipse-shaped path. The moon should also spin once as it moves around Earth. The same side of the moon should always face Earth. That is, the moon should spin once for each complete path it takes around Earth. The observer should **record** these motions.

Name ______________________

Draw Conclusions

1. Your model shows three periods of time—a year, a month, and a day. Think about the time it takes Earth to spin once, the moon to move around Earth once, and Earth to move around the sun once. Which period of time does each movement stand for? ______________________

2. **Compare** the movements of the moon to the movements of Earth.

3. **Scientists at Work** Scientists often **make models** to show **time and space relationships** in the natural world. However, models can't always show these relationships exactly. How was your model of Earth, the moon, and the sun limited in what it showed? ______________________

Investigate Further You could **make a model** to show how the sun shines on Earth. **Plan and conduct a simple investigation** to show how the amount of sunlight reaching Earth changes as Earth moves around the sun.

Name ______________________

Date ______________________

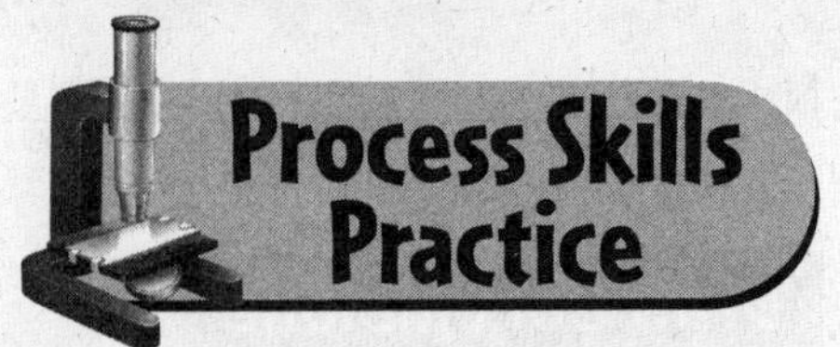

Use Time and Space Relationships

Time relationships tell you the order of events. Space relationships tell you about locations of objects. Understanding these relationships can help you make accurate models.

Think About Using Time and Space Relationships

Suppose you are a space traveler from Earth and you have just discovered a new solar system. You want to make an accurate map for those who will follow you. Answer these questions to plan your map. Use a separate sheet of paper if you need more space.

1. Think about mapping a new solar system. What space relationships will you show? ______________________

____

____

2. Seven large objects orbit a single star. Three of them have smaller objects orbiting them. What do the locations of the orbits tell you about the objects?

____

____

3. One of the seven larger orbiting objects is very close to the star. Three are a little farther away. Three are very far away. In which group are you most likely to find a planet to colonize? Explain. ______________________

____

4. Why is it important to show the locations of the planets accurately?

____

____

____

5. What would happen if you made a mistake in showing the locations of some of the planets or moons? ______________________

____

____

Use with page D5.

Name ______________________

Date ______________________

How Do Earth and the Moon Compare?

Lesson Concept

The moon revolves around Earth. The Earth-moon system revolves around the sun. Both Earth and the moon rotate on axes and have day-night cycles. Many features on Earth and the moon are different, but some landforms occur on both.

Vocabulary

revolve (D6)	**orbit** (D7)	**rotate** (D7)
axis (D7)	**eclipse** (D8)	

Select words from the box below to label the diagram. Watch out! Not every word in the box can be used to label the diagram, so you'll have to pick and choose.

lunar mare	**gibbous**	**orbit**	**moon**	**full moon**
day-night cycle	**sun**	**Earth**	**eclipse**	**crater**
quarter moon	**half moon**	**axes**	**revolve**	**rotation**

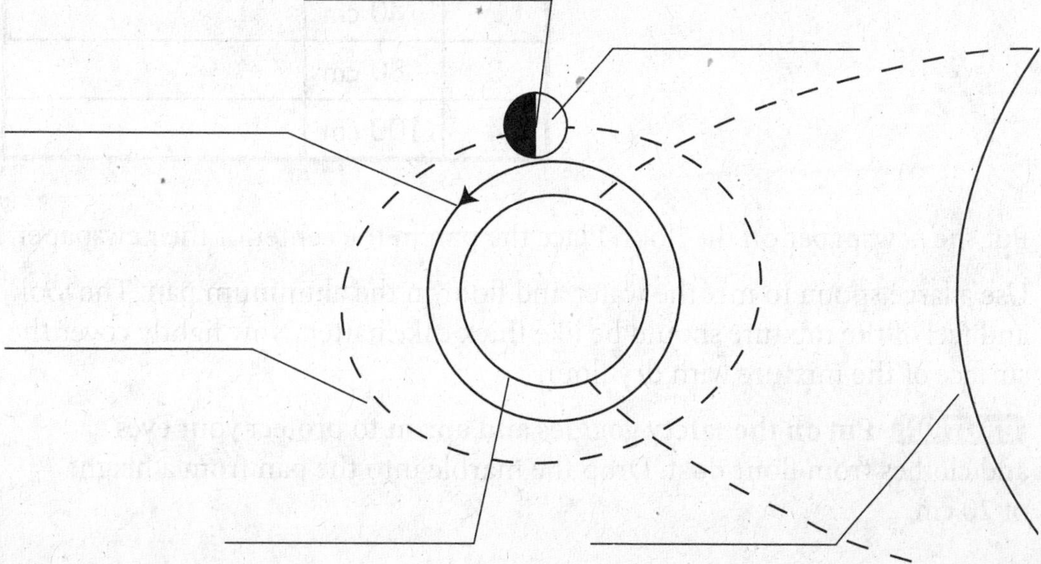

Harcourt

Use with page D11.

Name ______________________

Date ______________________

The Moon's Craters

Materials

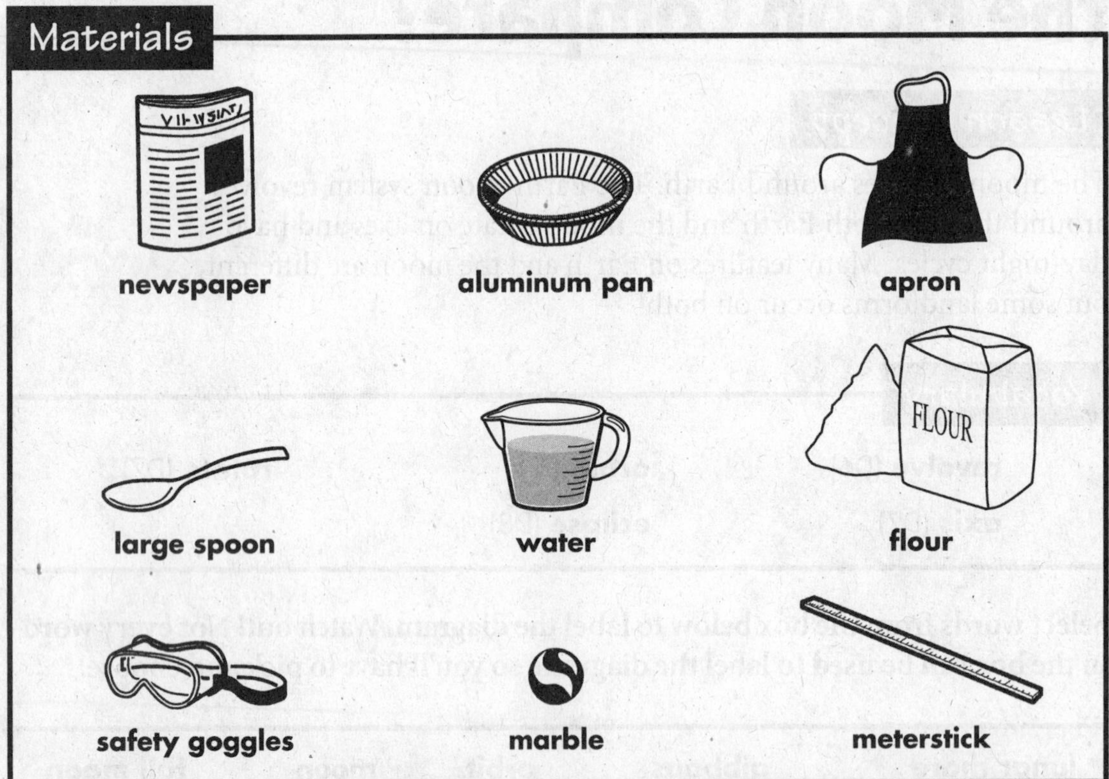

Activity Procedure

1. Use the following table.

Trial	Height	Width of Craters
1	20 cm	
2	40 cm	
3	80 cm	
4	100 cm	

2. Put the newspaper on the floor. Place the pan in the center of the newspaper.
3. Use a large spoon to mix the water and flour in the aluminum pan. The look and feel of the mixture should be like thick cake batter. Now lightly cover the surface of the mixture with dry flour.
4. **CAUTION** **Put on the safety goggles and apron** to protect your eyes and clothes from flour dust. Drop the marble into the pan from a height of 20 cm.

Name ______________________

5. Carefully remove the marble and **measure** the width of the crater. **Record** the measurement in the table. Repeat Steps 4 and 5 two more times.

6. Now drop the marble three times each from heights of 40 cm, 80 cm, and 100 cm. Measure the craters and record the measurements after each drop.

Draw Conclusions

1. **Compare** the height from which each marble was dropped to the size of the crater it made. How does height affect crater size? ______________________

____

____

2. The Copernicus (koh•PER•nih•kuhs) crater on the moon is 91 km across. Based on your model, what can you **infer** about the object that formed this crater?

____

____

____

3. **Scientists at Work** Most of the moon's craters were formed millions of years ago. Scientists **use models** to **infer** events that occurred too long ago to **observe** directly. What did you infer from the model about how the moon's craters formed? ______________________

____

____

Investigate Further **Hypothesize** how using larger or smaller marbles would affect the size and shape of the craters. **Plan and conduct a simple investigation** to test your hypothesis. ______________________

____

____

____

____

____

Name ______________________

Date ______________________

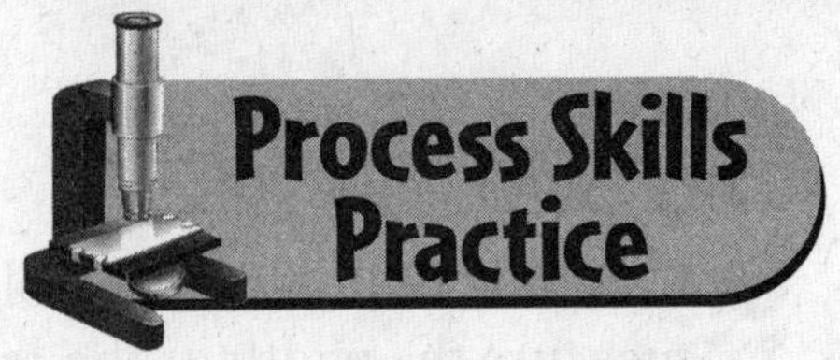

Infer

You infer when you use logical reasoning to draw conclusions based on observations. An inference based on logical reasoning and observation is always valid, even though it may not be correct.

Think About Inferring

Imagine you are in a spacecraft flying over the surface of an unexplored planet that is about the same size as Earth. Crewless probes have reported that the planet is composed of material that is common to both the moon and Earth. You are the first human to see this planet. Looking down through thin, moving clouds, you notice that there are craters and a lot of areas that look like the maria of the moon. Most of the craters look worn and old, but a few have high, sharp sides and look new. Some of the craters have steam rising from them and are surrounded by a plain made of fresh material. Others are in rougher areas and are surrounded by material that has been thrown out over the ground. You also notice very large fields of what look like sand dunes.

1. From your observations of the new planet, what can you infer about how the craters were formed? Explain. ______________________

____

____

____

____

2. What can you infer about life on this planet? ______________________

____

____

____

____

3. What can you infer about weather on this planet? ______________________

____

____

____

____

Use with page D13.

Name ______________________

Date ______________________

How Have People Explored the Solar System?

Lesson Concept

People have studied objects in space since ancient times. They began by using their unaided eye and then the telescope. Today they also use satellites and space probes. In the future, people may live and work on space stations and moon bases.

Vocabulary

telescope (D15) **satellite** (D15) **space probe** (D16)

Write the letter of an event next to the year it occurred.

_____ 900

_____ 1609

_____ 1668

_____ 1936

_____ 1957

_____ 1961

_____ 1969

_____ 1977

_____ 1981

A The Soviet Union launches *Sputnik 1*, the first artificial satellite.

B *Voyager I* and *Voyager II* space probes are launched. They have sent back pictures of Jupiter, Saturn, Uranus, and Neptune and are traveling beyond the solar system.

C The Mercury program sends the first Americans into space.

D Mayan people build an observatory for viewing the stars and planets at Chichén Itzá, in Mexico, around this date.

E Beginning of the use of space shuttles to lift heavy cargoes into orbit; to provide labs for scientific research in space; and to launch, bring back, and repair satellites

F Galileo uses a telescope to observe four moons orbiting Jupiter.

G American astronaut Neil Armstrong is the first person to walk on the moon.

H Sir Isaac Newton designs a telescope that uses a mirror as well as lenses to produce sharper images than those produced by Galileo's telescope.

I The first radio telescope is built and detects radio waves coming from objects in space.

Use with page D19.

Name ____________________

Date ____________________

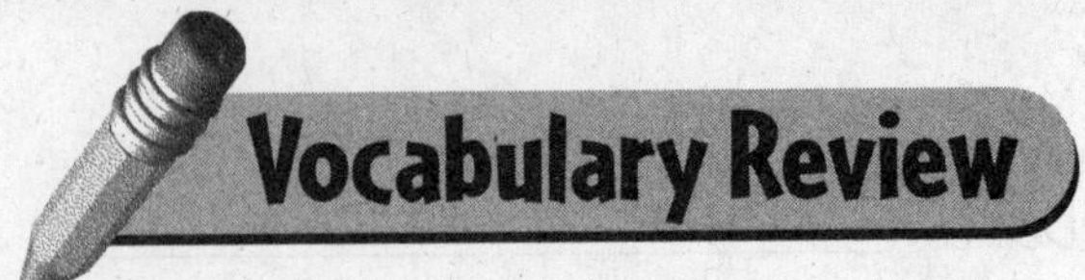

Recognize Vocabulary

Read the following sentences. On each line, write the letter for the word or phrase that could be substituted for the vocabulary term in italics.

_____ **1.** In 1609 Galileo used a *telescope* to observe craters on the moon.

A artificial satellite
B robot vehicle used to explore space
C instrument that makes distant objects appear nearer

_____ **2.** As it travels around the sun, Earth *rotates.*

A spins on its axis
B travels in a closed path
C moves in an ellipse

_____ **3.** The *Voyager space probes* have sent pictures of distant planets back to Earth.

A artificial satellites
B robot vehicles used to explore space
C instruments that make distant objects appear nearer

_____ **4.** Earth's *axis* travels through its North Pole and South Pole.

A imaginary line that passes through Earth's center
B elliptical path that Earth travels around the sun
C shadow that Earth casts over the moon at some points in its orbit

_____ **5.** Gravity makes the Earth-moon system *revolve* around the sun.

A spin on its axis
B travel in a closed path
C face the sun as it moves

_____ **6.** A total lunar *eclipse* lasts more than two hours and can be seen from any place on Earth that is facing the moon.

A passage through Earth's shadow
B trip around Earth in an elliptical path
C volcanic eruption that leaves pools of dark lava on the moon

_____ **7.** Earth's *orbit* around the sun is an ellipse, a shape that is nearly but not quite circular.

A path as it revolves
B imaginary line that passes through the center and the poles
C shadow cast that causes an eclipse

Use with pages D4–D19.

Chapter 2 • *Graphic Organizer for Chapter Concepts*

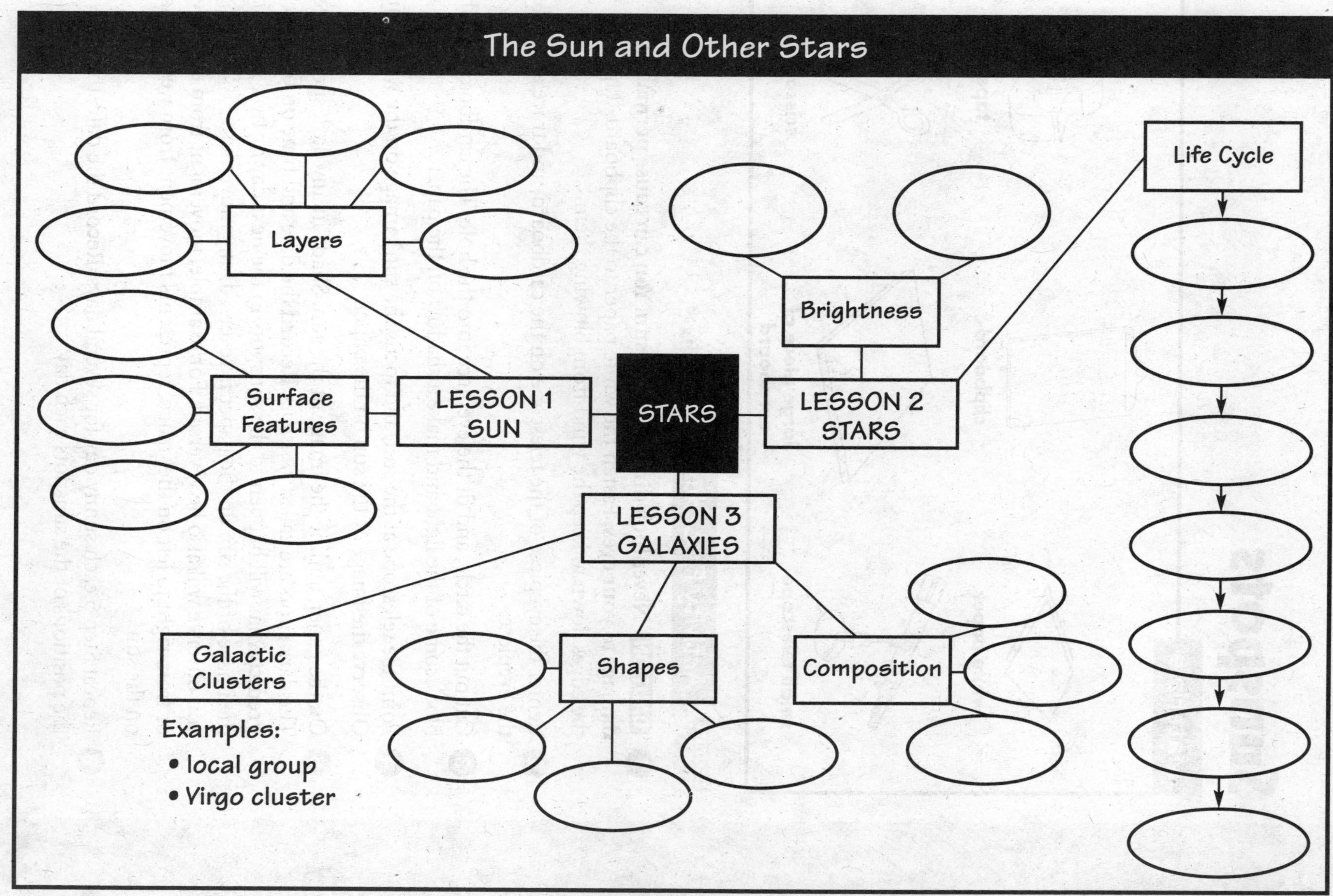

Name ______________________ Date ______________

Name ______________________

Date ______________________

Sunspots

Materials

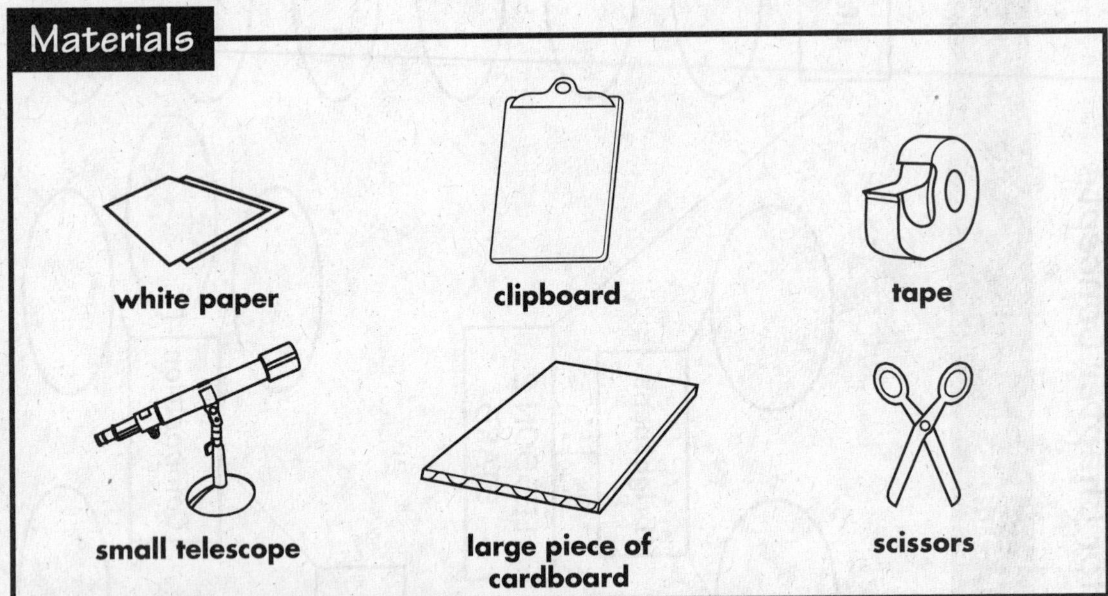

Activity Procedure

1. **CAUTION** **Never look directly at the sun. You can cause permanent damage to your eyes.** Fasten the white paper to the clipboard. Tape the edges down to keep the wind from blowing them.
2. Center the eyepiece of the telescope on the cardboard, and trace around the eyepiece.
3. Cut out the circle, and fit the eyepiece into the hole. The cardboard will help block some of the light and make a shadow on the paper.
4. Point the telescope at the sun, and focus the sun's image on the white paper. **Observe** the image of the sun on the paper.
5. On the paper, outline the image of the sun. Shade in any dark spots you see. The dark spots are called *sunspots.* **Record** the date and time on the paper. **Predict** what will happen to the sunspots in the next day or two. *Note:* Since the image of the sun on the paper is reversed, any movement you **observe** will also be reversed. For example, movement from east to west, or from right to left on the image, represents movement from west to east on the sun.
6. Repeat Step 5 each sunny day for several days. **Record** the date, the time, and the positions of the sunspots each day.

 Use with pages D28–D29.

Name ______________________

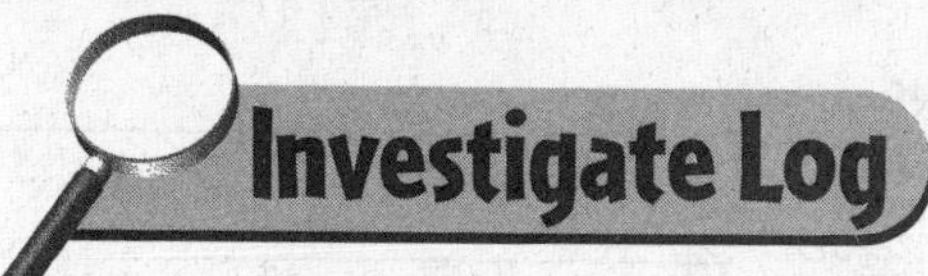

Draw Conclusions

1. How did the positions of the sunspots change over several days?

____

2. What can you **infer** from the movement of sunspots? ______________________

____

3. Scientists at Work Scientists **draw conclusions** from what they **observe.** Galileo was the first scientist to observe that it takes a sunspot about two weeks to cross from the left side of the sun's surface to the right side. Two weeks later, the sunspot appears on the left side of the sun's surface again. From this information, what conclusions can you draw about the time it takes the sun to make one complete rotation? ______________________

____

Investigate Further Does the sun always have the same number of spots? Do sunspots change in size? **Plan and conduct a simple investigation** to find answers to these and any other questions you might have about sunspots.

____

Name ________________________

Date ________________________

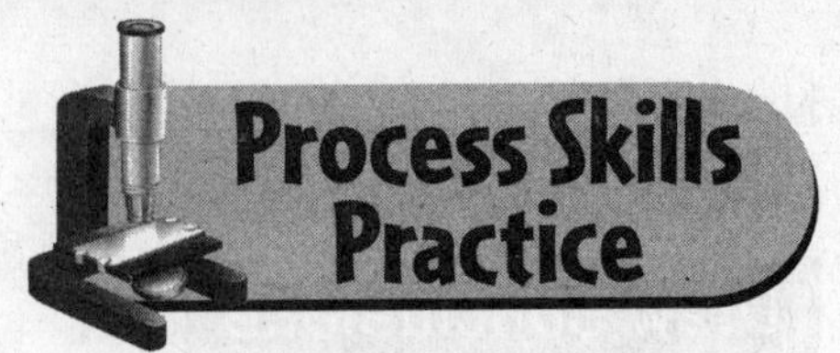

Draw Conclusions

Drawing conclusions involves the use of other process skills, such as observing. Unlike inferences, conclusions are usually based on much more data and should be tested repeatedly.

Think About Drawing Conclusions

In ancient times two astronomers were watching sunspots. The first astronomer concluded the spots were planets orbiting the sun. The second astronomer watched the sunspots more closely than the first. He noticed the spots changed shape as they approached the edge of the sun's image. They became compressed and then seemed to disappear. The second astronomer concluded the spots were part of the sun's surface.

1. Why do you think the two astronomers came to such different conclusions?

____

____

2. What other data could the astronomers have gathered to support their conclusions? ________________________

____

____

3. Astronomers over the ages have kept records of sunspots. The following is a graph showing the appearance of sunspots from 1900 to 2000. What conclusions can you draw from the graph? ________________________

____

____

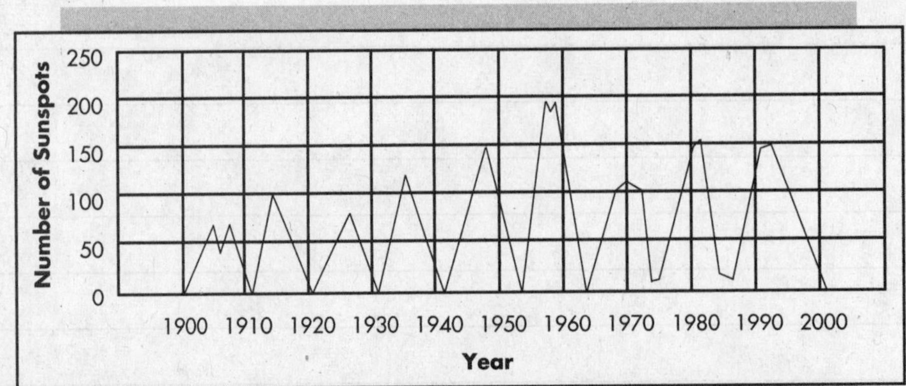

Use with page D29.

Name ______________________

Date ______________________

What Are the Features of the Sun?

Lesson Concept

The sun is the source of almost all the energy on Earth. The sun has layers and visible surface features.

Vocabulary

photosphere (D33)	**corona** (D33)	**sunspot** (D34)
solar flare (D34)	**solar wind** (D34)	

Vocabulary terms and other words from this lesson are listed in the chart below. Choose the correct term for each blank attached to a part of this diagram of the sun.

corona	**core**	**solar flare**	**convection zone**
solar wind	**photosphere**	**sunspot**	**radiation zone**

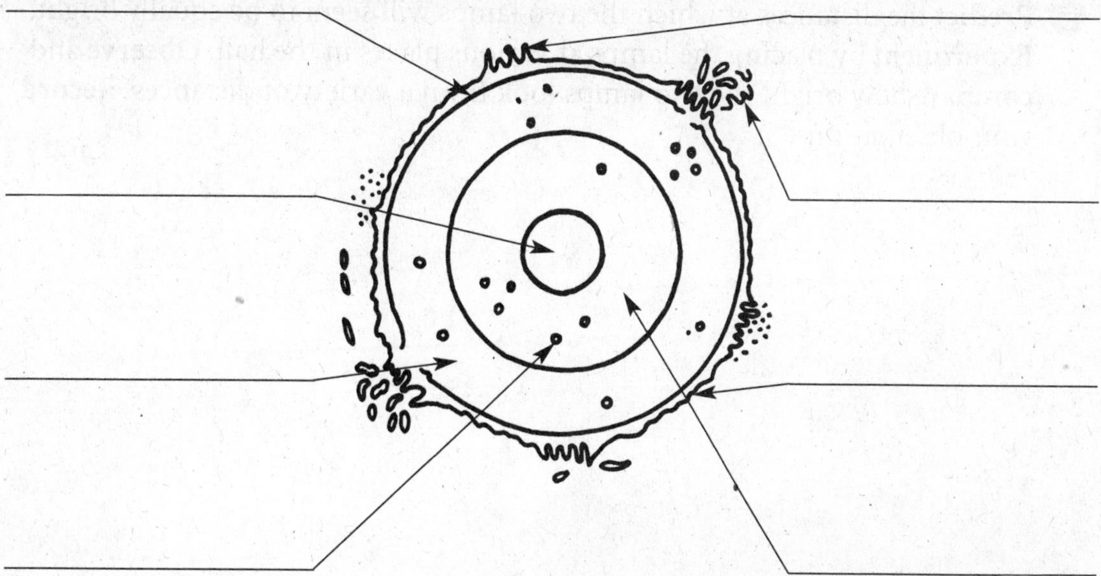

Harcourt

Name ______________________

Date ______________________

The Brightness of Stars

Materials

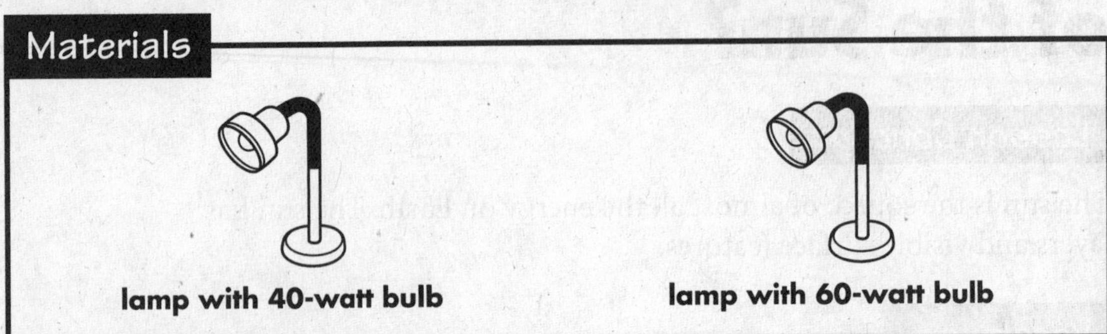

Activity Procedure

1. Place the two lamps near the middle of a darkened hall. Turn the lamps on.
2. **Observe** the lamps from one end of the hall. **Compare** how bright they look. **Record** your observations.
3. Move the lamp with the 60-watt bulb to one end of the hall. **Observe** and **compare** how bright the two lamps look from the other end of the hall. **Record** your observations.
4. Now place the lamps side by side at one end of the hall. Again **observe** and **compare** how bright the two lamps look from the other end of the hall. **Record** your observations.
5. **Predict** the distances at which the two lamps will seem to be equally bright. **Experiment** by placing the lamps at various places in the hall. **Observe** and **compare** how bright the two lamps look from a variety of distances. **Record** your observations.

Name ______________________

Draw Conclusions

1. What two variables did you test in this experiment? ______________________

____

____

____

2. From what you **observed**, what two factors affect how bright a light appears to an observer? ______________________

____

____

3. Scientists at Work Scientists often **draw conclusions** when **experimenting**. Use the results of your experiment to draw conclusions about how distance and actual brightness affect how bright stars appear to observers on Earth.

____

____

____

____

____

____

Investigate Further Why can't you see stars during the day? Use the lamps and a brightly lighted room. **Plan and conduct a simple investigation** to show how the sun can make it seem that stars don't shine during the day. ______________________

____

____

____

____

Name ___________________________

Date ___________________________

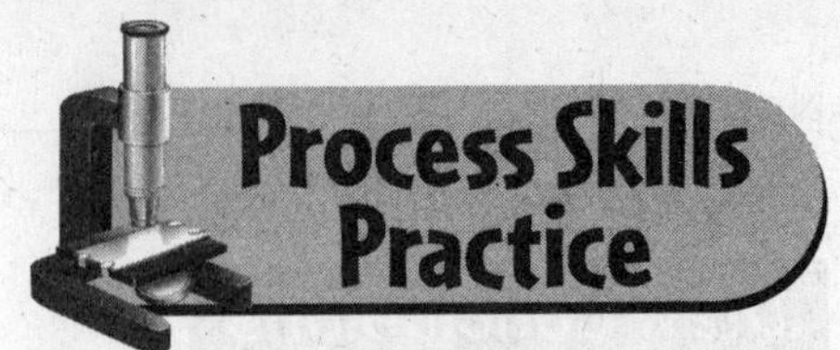

Experiment and Draw Conclusions

You draw conclusions after you have experimented and collected data. Drawing conclusions is usually the last step in an investigative process. When you draw a conclusion, you pull together what you have learned from observation or experimentation.

Think About Experimenting and Drawing Conclusions

You are involved in a search for extraterrestrial intelligence. You build a gigantic radio antenna on top of the highest building near your home. You let it scan the sky, hoping someone on another planet is sending signals to Earth. After you experiment with your antenna, you begin gathering data and drawing conclusions.

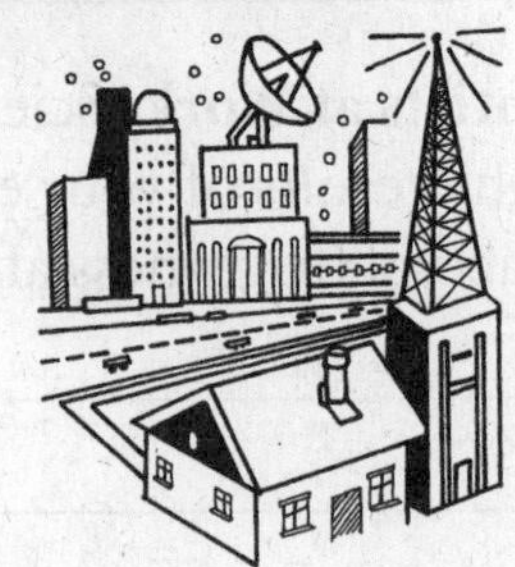

1. You receive a burst of radio noise, called static, at the same time every day. You suspect it's coming from a local radio station. Can you draw any conclusions?

   Explain. ___________________________

   ____

2. You notice the radio noise is coming from a fixed point in the sky and is actually a series of pulses. If you keep your antenna aimed at that spot, the pulses continue without stopping. Can you draw any conclusions? Explain.

   ____

   ____

3. You aim a telescope at the source of the pulses and see a small white star. Can you draw any conclusions? Explain. ___________________________

   ____

   ____

4. You check a star map. The star you have been observing is a pulsar, which is a star that spins very, very fast and sends out a radio signal as it spins. Can you draw any conclusions? Explain. ___________________________

   ____

Use with page D37.

Name ______________________

Date ______________________

How Are Stars Classified?

Lesson Concept

Stars are classified by absolute magnitude, surface temperature, size, and color. Stars change from nebula to protostar to main-sequence star to expanding star to red giant to planetary nebula and white dwarf. Most stars are main-sequence stars.

Vocabulary

magnitude (D38) **main sequence** (D39)

Match the star type in Column A with its description in Column B by writing the letter of the correct description next to the star type.

Column A

_____ main-sequence star

_____ nebula

_____ red giant

_____ expanding star

_____ planetary nebula

_____ protostar

_____ white dwarf

Column B

A An object with the mass of the sun shines for billions of years. Then, as its hydrogen runs low, it starts to get bigger.

B The star's atmosphere expands a million times.

C After several million years, the temperature at the center of the object gets hot enough to release various kinds of energy.

D The object continues to shine dimly for billions of years as it slowly cools.

E Attracted to each other by gravity, the particles squeeze together. The object grows, gets hotter, and starts to glow.

F A star begins within a huge cloud of hydrogen, helium, and tiny particles of dust.

G The star may expand to 100 times its former size.

Name ___________________________

Date ___________________________

The Sun's Location in the Milky Way Galaxy

Materials

scrap paper

Activity Procedure

1. Make about 70 small balls from scrap paper. These will be your "stars."
2. On a table, **make a model** of the Milky Way Galaxy. Arrange the paper stars in a spiral with six arms. Pile extra stars in the center of the spiral. Use fewer stars along the arms.
3. Look down at the model. Draw what you **observe**.
4. Position your eyes at table level. Look across the surface of the table at the model. Again, draw what you **observe**.
5. Look at the photographs at the bottom of page D47. One is of a spiral galaxy viewed from the edge. The other shows the galaxy viewed from the "top." **Compare** the pictures you drew in Steps 3 and 4 with the photographs of a spiral galaxy. Then look at page D46. **Observe** the photograph of a ribbon of stars. This is our view of the Milky Way Galaxy from Earth. Using your drawings and the photographs, **infer** where in the Milky Way Galaxy the sun is.

Name ____________________

Draw Conclusions

1. Suppose the sun were located "above" the Milky Way Galaxy. What view of the galaxy might we see from Earth? ____________________

2. If the sun is in one of the arms, what view might we see of the galaxy then?

3. From your drawings and the photographs of a spiral galaxy, where in the Milky Way Galaxy do you **infer** the sun is? ____________________

4. **Scientists at Work** Scientists often **infer** when **using models** like the one you made. How did your model of the Milky Way Galaxy help you infer the sun's location in the galaxy? ____________________

Investigate Further Observe the Milky Way Galaxy in the night sky. You will need a clear, dark night, far away from city lights. Binoculars or a telescope will help you see some of the fainter stars. ____________________

Name ______________________________

Date ______________________________

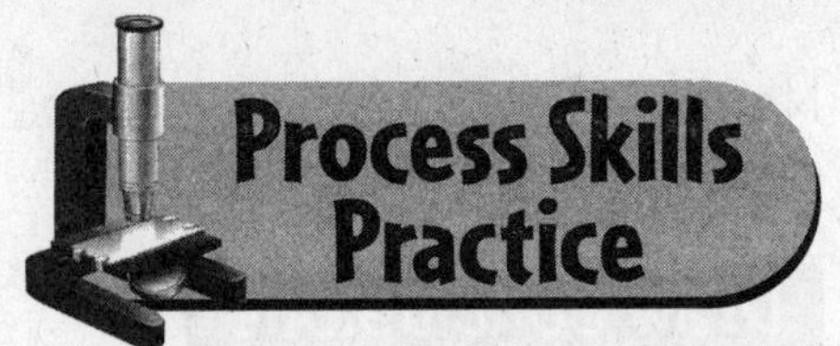

Use Models

You can use a model to study something that is too big to study in your classroom. For example, you may use a wall chart to study the solar system, or projections of stars on the ceiling to study the night sky.

Think About Using Models

When you want to see where you live in relation to the rest of the city, you can look at a map. A map is a model of your city. You can find the street you live on and, if the map is detailed enough, you can even figure out where your house is on the street. Astronomers have carefully measured the light from stars in our galaxy and have figured out how far away they are from the sun. They have used this information to draw maps of the galaxy as it would look from the side and from above.

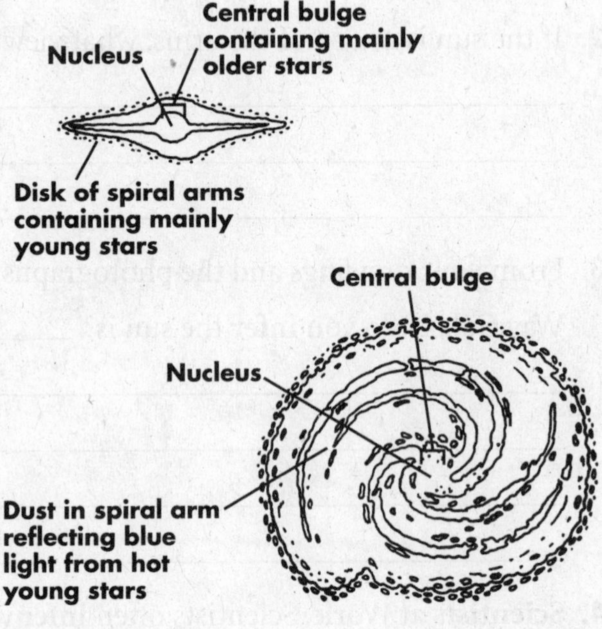

1. Looking at the map, where in our galaxy do you think you would find most of the matter (that is, stars, gas, and dust)? ______________________________

____

2. Which of the two views shown do you think most resembles the Milky Way Galaxy as seen from Earth? Explain. ______________________________

____

____

3. The entire galaxy is rotating. The inner stars are moving faster than the outer stars. How fast is the sun moving when compared to the rest of the galaxy?

____

____

____

Use with page D45.

Name ____________________

Date ____________________

What Are Galaxies?

Lesson Concept

A galaxy is a group of stars, gas, and dust. The sun is in the Milky Way Galaxy, which is part of a galactic cluster called the Local Group.

Vocabulary

universe (D46) **galaxy** (D46) **light-year** (D47)

Answer each question with one or more complete sentences.

1. How are galaxies classified? ____________________
2. You are looking through your telescope at the night sky, and you see a pinwheel-shaped object. What do you think it is? ____________________
3. What shape do irregular galaxies have? ____________________

____

Mark the following statements with *True* or *False.* If the statement is false, write a correction next to it.

_____ 4. Many galaxies rotate around a core. ____________________

____

_____ 5. A nebula has no light of its own. ____________________

____

_____ 6. A light-year is a unit of time. ____________________

____

_____ 7. Most galaxies are elliptical. ____________________

____

_____ 8. The Milky Way is an irregular galaxy. ____________________

____

_____ 9. Elliptical galaxies probably don't rotate. ____________________

____

Name ____________________

Date ____________________

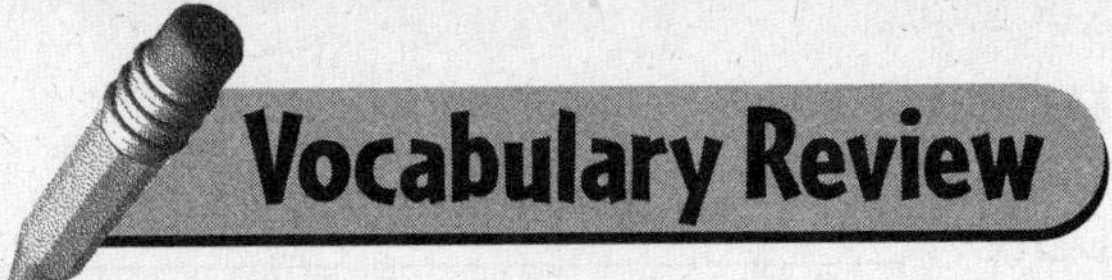

Recognize Vocabulary

Listed below are the vocabulary terms from this chapter. Match the terms in Column A with the definitions in Column B by writing in the space next to the term the letter of the correct definition.

Column A

_____ **1.** photosphere

_____ **2.** corona

_____ **3.** sunspot

_____ **4.** solar flare

_____ **5.** solar wind

_____ **6.** magnitude

_____ **7.** main sequence

_____ **8.** universe

_____ **9.** galaxy

_____ **10.** light-year

Column B

A a fast-moving stream of particles released into space from the surface of the sun

B dark places on the surface of the sun that are cooler than the areas surrounding them

C the brightness of a star

D the part of the sun that we see

E everything that exists: planets, stars, dust, gases, and energy

F a group of stars, gas, and dust

G the sun's atmosphere

H the distance light travels in one Earth year, about 9.5 trillion kilometers

I the most common combinations of color, size, magnitude, and temperature of stars; plotted on a special diagram, they appear in a band stretching from the upper left of the diagram to the lower right

J brief burst of energy from the sun's atmosphere

Use with pages D28–D49.

Name ______________________ Date ______________

Chapter 1 • *Graphic Organizer for Chapter Concepts*

Matter and Its Properties

LESSON 1 PHYSICAL PROPERTIES	LESSON 2 CHANGES OF STATE	LESSON 3 CHEMICAL PROPERTIES
1. ____________	1. ____________	1. ____________
2. ____________	2. ____________	2. ____________
3. ____________	3. ____________	
4. ____________	4. ____________	
5. ____________	5. ____________	
	6. ____________	

Name ____________________

Date ____________________

Using Physical Properties to Identify Objects

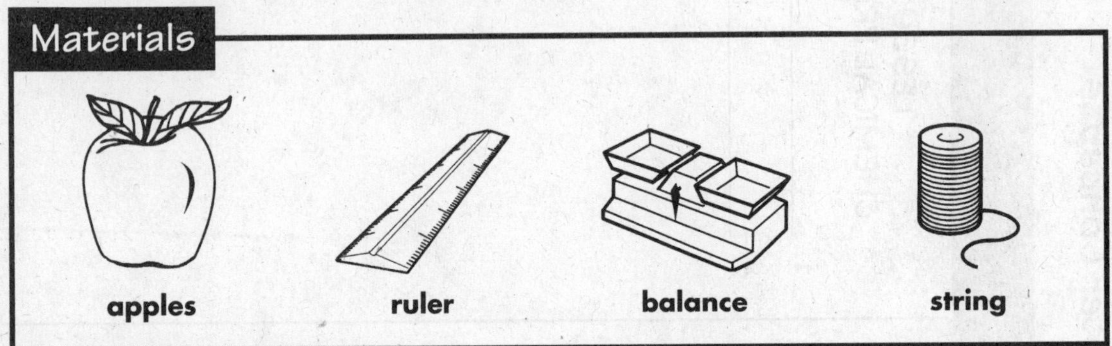

Activity Procedure

1. Carefully **observe** the apple your teacher gave you. What properties of your apple can you discover just by observing it? **Record** all the properties you observe.
2. Use the balance, ruler, and string to **measure** some characteristics of your apple. **Record** the properties you measure.
3. Put your apple in the pile of apples on your teacher's desk. Don't watch while your teacher mixes up the apples.
4. Using the properties that you recorded, try to identify your apple in the pile.
5. Using the balance, ruler, and string, **measure** this apple. **Compare** the measurements to those you recorded earlier. Then decide whether the apple you chose from the pile is yours. If someone else chose the same apple, comparing measurements should help you decide whose apple it really is.

Name ______________________

Draw Conclusions

1. **Compare** your apple with a classmate's apple. How are the two apples alike? How are they different? ______________________

2. Why was it helpful to **measure** some characteristics of your apple in addition to **observing** it? ______________________

3. How did you use the string to **measure** the apple? ______________________

4. **Scientists at Work** Scientists use both observations and measurements to identify substances. Which is faster, **observing** or **measuring**? Which provides more exact information? ______________________

Investigate Further **Compare** the list of your apple's properties with a classmate's list. Then, using your classmate's list, try to find his or her apple. Talk with your classmate about how he or she made the list. Did you and your classmate do things the same way? ______________________

Name ______________________

Date ______________________

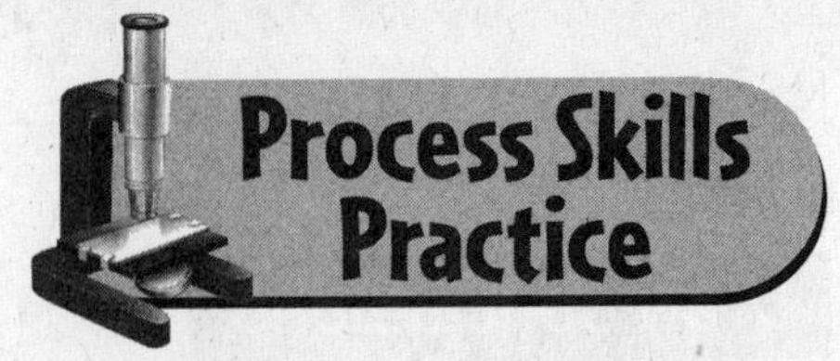

Observe and Measure

Observing is learning facts about something by using your senses. Measuring, a form of observation, is learning facts by using instruments that can be used to extend your senses.

Think About Observing and Measuring

Tanya's science teacher told the class that chemical elements do not break down during normal laboratory reactions. Then she said that the iron in fortified cereal is not an iron compound, but pure iron! To demonstrate, she poured the contents of a box of iron-fortified cereal into a large bowl and crushed the cereal into a powder. She mixed water into the powder until it was very thin and watery. Then she took a small bar magnet taped to a glass rod and stirred the cereal and water mixture for several minutes. When she pulled the bar magnet out, tiny bits of iron were clinging to it.

1. Tanya observed the iron clinging to the magnet. How could her class measure the amount of iron in the box of cereal? ______________________

____

____

2. Tanya and her classmates read on the side panel of the cereal box that one serving of the cereal met the recommended daily allowance for iron and that one cup of cereal was one serving. What observation and measurement could they do to see if the cereal really provided the recommended daily allowance for iron? ______________________

____

____

____

____

3. How did the iron become separated from the cereal? Did the chemical elements of the cereal break down when Tanya's teacher mixed it with water? Explain.

____

____

____

Use with page E5.

Name ______________________

Date ______________________

How Can Physical Properties Be Used to Identify Matter?

Lesson Concept

Matter has mass and takes up space. Physical properties can be used to identify different types of substances. Some physical properties, such as mass, volume, and density, can be measured.

Vocabulary

matter (E6) **physical properties** (E6) **mass** (E7) **weight** (E7)
volume (E8) **density** (E9) **solubility** (E10)

Choose the answer that best completes the statement.

1. The effect of gravity on matter is the measure of ______.
   A mass **B** weight **C** density
2. An object has a mass of 120 g on Earth. On the moon it would have a mass of ______.
   A 20 g **B** 60 g **C** 120 g
3. The density of a steel hammer is 7.9 g/cm³ on Earth. On a spaceship it would have a density of ______.
   A 0 g/cm³ **B** 3.9 g/cm³ **C** 7.9 g/cm³.
4. Matter is anything that has mass and ______.
   A occupies space **B** properties **C** size

Decide whether the underlined term makes each statement true or false. If the statement is true, write the word *true* on the line. If the statement is false, write a word or phrase that makes the statement true.

false__________ **5.** Materials <u>are</u> changed when physical properties are measured.

True__________ **6.** A milliliter is a unit of <u>volume</u>.

false__________ **7.** In a <u>mixture</u>, the particles are evenly mixed.

Name ______________________

Date ______________________

Changing States of Matter

Materials

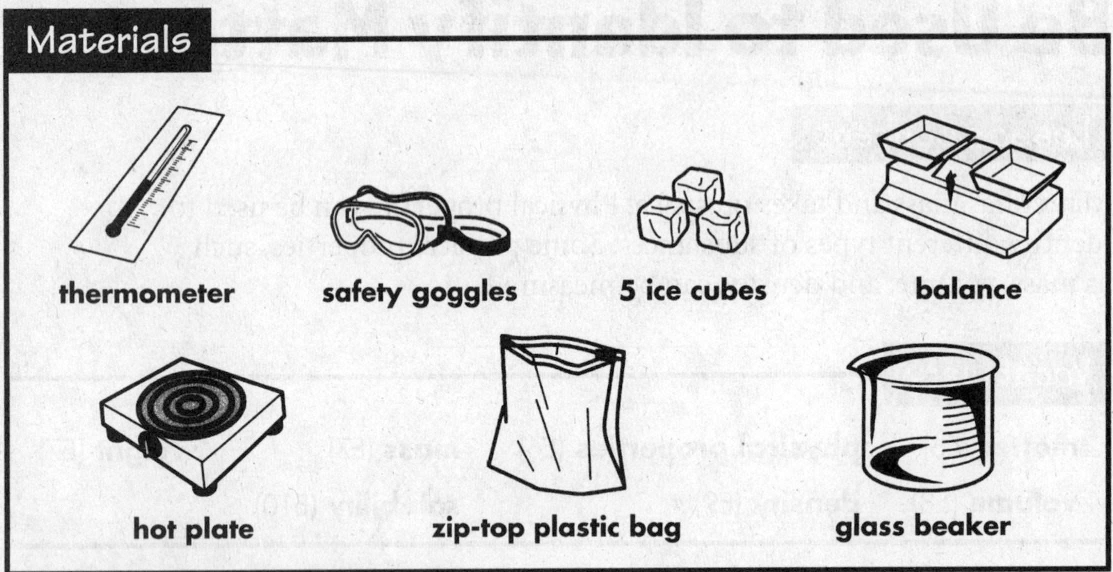

Activity Procedure

1. Place five ice cubes in a zip-top plastic bag. Be sure to seal the bag. Use the balance to **measure** the mass of the ice cubes and the bag. **Observe** the shape of the ice cubes. **Record** your observations and measurements.
2. Set the bag of ice cubes in a warm place. **Observe** what happens to the shape of the ice cubes. Use the balance to **measure** the mass of the melted ice cubes and the bag. Unzip the bag slightly and insert the thermometer. Measure the temperature of the water. **Record** your observations and measurements. Use your observations to **infer** that a change of state is occurring.
3. After the ice has completely melted, pour the water into a glass beaker. Put the thermometer in the beaker. **Observe** what happens to the water's shape, and **record** the water's temperature.
4. **CAUTION** **Put on the safety goggles.** Your teacher will use a hot plate to heat the water in the beaker until it boils. **Observe** what happens to the water when it boils. **Record** the temperature of the boiling water. Use your observations to **infer** that another change of state has occurred.

Name ______________________

Draw Conclusions

1. Identify the different states of water at different points in this investigation.

____

____

____

____

2. Compare the mass of the ice to the mass of water after it melted. What does this show about changes in state? ______________________

____

____

3. What temperatures did you **record** as the water changed states?

____

____

4. Scientists at Work After scientists use their senses to **observe** the properties of substances, they can **infer** whether a change in state has taken place. What did you observe in this investigation? What did you infer about a change of state from each observation? ______________________

____

____

Investigate Further The physical change that happens to water when it is boiled produces water vapor—an invisible gas. **Plan and conduct a simple investigation** to test the hypothesis that the mass of the water vapor is the same as the mass of the liquid water. ______________________

____

____

____

____

Name ______________________

Date ______________________

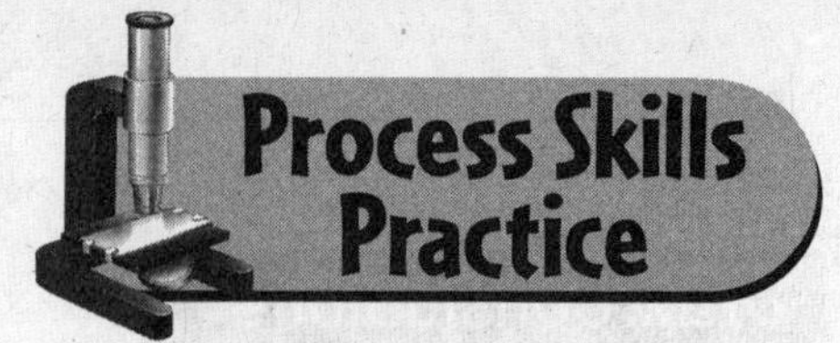

Observe and Infer

Observation is collecting information about something by using your senses. Inferences are assumptions you make after considering your observations. Observations are facts, but inferences are guesses and may not always be correct.

Think About Observing and Inferring

Every night Dan could hear strange creaking noises in his bedroom and from the hallway outside his door. He finally asked his father about the noises and if the house was haunted. "That's just the house," explained his father. When Dan seemed doubtful, his father reached into the recycle bin and found a long-necked bottle. "After the sun goes down," he explained to Dan, "the house cools and contracts, that is, it actually gets smaller." To demonstrate, he partially inflated a balloon and put it over the bottle's neck as shown in the drawing. When he put the bottle into a bowl of ice water, the balloon shrank and fell over. When he put the bottle outside in the sun, the balloon slowly became inflated again.

1. What was Dan's first inference when he observed the noises in his house? Was his observation a fact? Was his inference correct? ______________________

____

2. What did he observe about the balloon and the bottle? ______________________

____

____

3. Why would Dan's house make noise expanding and contracting although the balloon did not? ______________________

____

____

Use with page E13.

Name ____________________

Date ____________________

How Does Matter Change from One State to Another?

Lesson Concept

Three states of matter are solid, liquid, and gas. Changes in state are physical changes. Particles of matter move faster as heat is added and slow down as heat is removed. Every substance has a melting point, the temperature at which it changes from a solid to a liquid. It also has a boiling point, the temperature at which it changes from a liquid to a gas.

Vocabulary

solid (E14) **liquid** (E14) **gas** (E14)
evaporation (E16) **condensation** (E17)

Identify the following characteristics as belonging to solids (S), liquids (L), or gases (G). Some characteristics belong to more than one state of matter.

S 1. particles are held rigidly in place

L 2. takes the shape of the container

S 3. has a definite shape

S 4. particles are touching

L 5. particles slide over one another

G 6. particles are far apart

Choose the answer that best completes the statement.

7. The freezing point of a substance is the same as its _____ point.
   A melting **B** boiling **C** condensation

8. Evaporation changes a _____.
   A gas to a liquid **B** liquid to a solid **C** liquid to a gas

9. When a substance freezes, it _____.
   A gains energy **B** loses energy **C** stays the same

10. Boiling involves the same change of state as _____.
    A freezing **B** condensation **C** evaporation

Name ______________________

Date ______________________

Chemical Properties

Materials

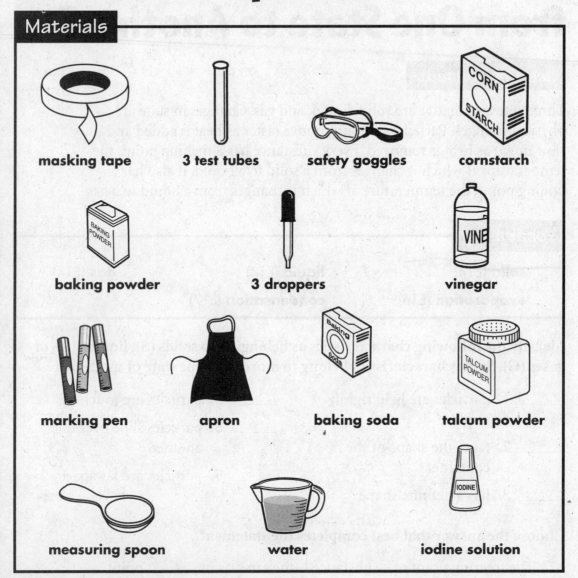

masking tape | 3 test tubes | safety goggles | cornstarch

baking powder | 3 droppers | vinegar

marking pen | apron | baking soda | talcum powder

measuring spoon | water | iodine solution

Activity Procedure

1. Use the masking tape and marking pen to label your test tubes *water*, *vinegar*, and *iodine*.
2. **CAUTION Put on the apron and safety goggles. Leave them on for the entire activity.**
3. Put about $\frac{1}{3}$ spoonful of baking soda in each test tube. Add a dropper of water to the test tube labeled *water*. **Observe** and **record** what happens.

Name ______________________

4. Add a dropper of vinegar to the test tube labeled *vinegar*. **Observe** and **record** what happens this time.

5. Add a dropper of iodine solution to the test tube labeled *iodine*. **CAUTION** **Iodine is poisonous if swallowed and can cause stains. Be careful not to spill or touch the iodine solution. Wash your hands if you get iodine on them. Observe** and **record** what happens.

6. Wash the test tubes with soap and water. Repeat Steps 3–5 three more times using cornstarch, talcum powder, and baking powder in the test tubes instead of baking soda. Be sure to wash the test tubes between tests. **Observe** and **record** what happens each time.

7. Get an "unknown" sample from your teacher. It will be one of the substances you have already tested. Test it with water, vinegar, and iodine solution, just as you did before. **Observe** and **record** what happens when you add each of the liquids. What is your unknown substance?

Draw Conclusions

1. How did you find out what your unknown sample was? ______________________

____

2. Vinegar is one of a group of substances called *acids*. Acids react with substances called *bases*. Of the substances you tested, which are bases? How can you tell?

____

3. Baking powder is not a pure substance. It is a mixture of two of the other substances you tested. Based on your results, what do you **infer** are the two substances in baking powder? ______________________

4. **Scientists at Work** Scientists **experiment** to find out if two substances react. What signs of reactions did your experiments produce? What **variables** did you **control**? ______________________

____

Investigate Further Suppose you wanted to discover some of the chemical properties of chalk. **Predict** whether chalk is an acid or a base. Then **experiment** to test your prediction. ______________________

____

____

____

____

Name ______________________

Date ______________________

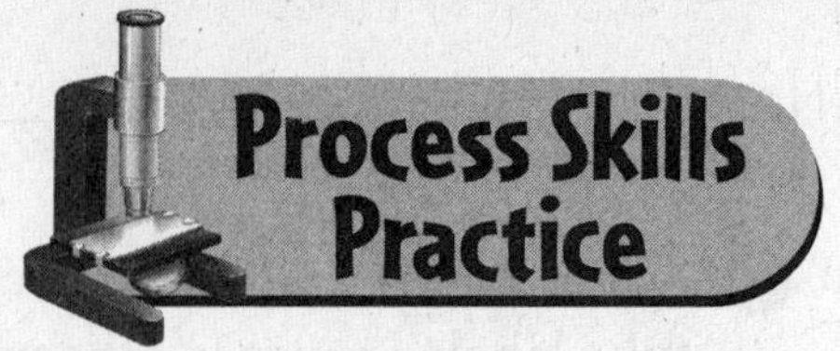

Experiment

One of the most basic of all activities in science is experimenting. Scientists state hypotheses and then design experiments to test them. Scientists change certain conditions in experiments and observe what happens. From these observations, they can see whether their hypotheses were correct.

Think About Experimenting

Sandra learned in science class that each substance has its own characteristic properties. One of those properties is density. Her teacher also said that the properties of a substance do not change even if the sample size changes. Sandra found that hard to believe. Sandra knew she could measure the density of a substance by putting it in water. If something floats, it is less dense than water. If it sinks, it is more dense than water. Sandra put some water in a clear jar and dropped in a piece of potato. The potato floated. Sandra hypothesized that a large enough piece of potato would sink. She put a large potato in the water and it also floated.

1. What was Sandra's hypothesis? ______________________

2. What did Sandra observe? Was her hypothesis supported by her experiment? Why or why not? ______________________

3. If the potato floats, then it is less dense than the water. Hypothesize what would happen if you could somehow make the potato more dense.

4. Design an experiment that would test your hypothesis. ______________________

Use with page E21.

Name ______________________________ Date ____________________

Chapter 2 • Graphic Organizer for Chapter Concepts

Atoms and Elements

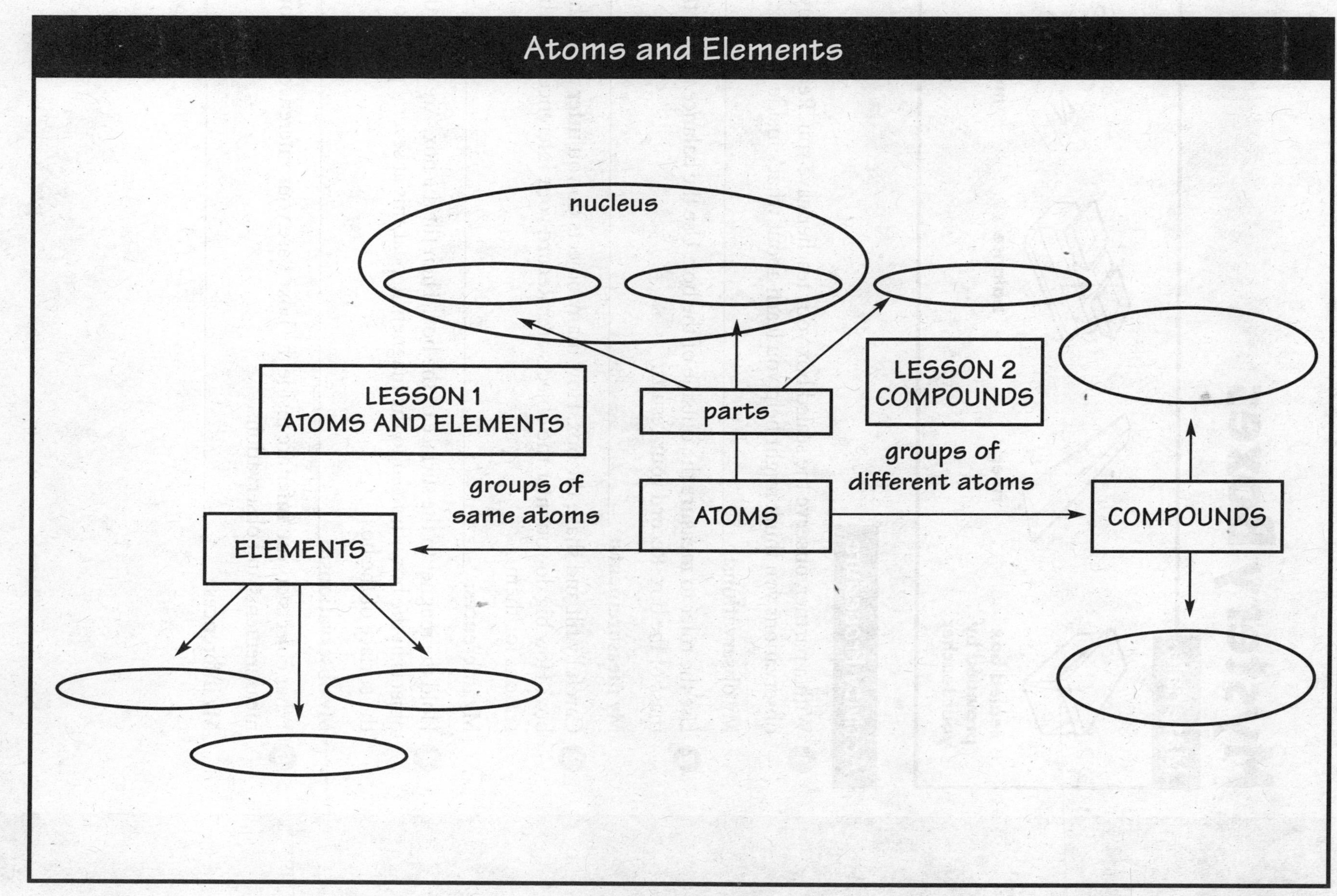

Name ______________________

Date ______________________

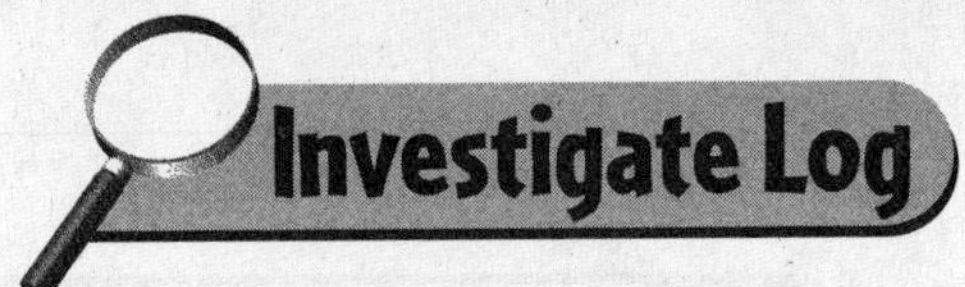

Mystery Boxes

Materials

sealed box provided by your teacher

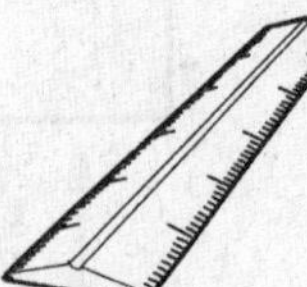

ruler

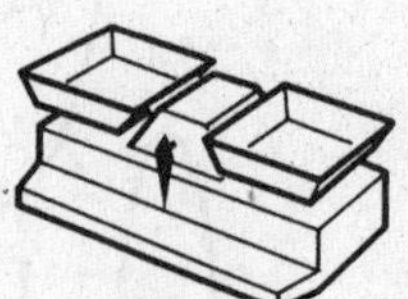

balance

magnet

Activity Procedure

1. With a partner, **observe** the sealed box your teacher gave you. **Record** any observations you think might help you learn about what's inside the box.

   My observations: ______________________

2. Use the ruler to **measure** the outside of the box. Use the balance to find the mass of the box. **Record** your results.

   My measurements: ______________________

3. Carefully tilt and shake the box. How many objects do you **infer** are in the box? How big do you infer the objects are? **Record** your inferences and the reasons for them.

   My inferences: ______________________

4. Hold the magnet to the surface of the box. Then tilt the box. Are any of the objects in the box attracted to the magnet? Repeat this at several places on the surface of the box.

   My observations: ______________________

5. What objects do you **infer** are inside the box? Base your inferences on your measurements and observations.

   My inferences: ______________________

Name ______________________

Investigate Log

6. What do you **infer** about the ide of the box? Draw a picture of wh you think the inside of the box looks like.

7. Now open the box. **Compare** your infer es about the objects in the box with the objects the box really contains. A compare your inferences about what the box looks like inside with what i ally looks like.

My comparisons: ______________________

Draw Conclusions

1. How did what you **inferred** about the objects inside box **compare** with what was really inside? ______________________

2. How did what you **inferred** about the inside of the box **co are** with the way it really looked inside? ______________________

3. **Scientists at Work** Different scientists may **infer** different thing out objects they can't **observe** directly. Compare your inferences about the co ents and the inside of the box with the inferences of other pairs. How were r inferences similar? How were they different? ______________________

Investigate Further Construct your own mystery box, and place various o cts inside it. Give your box to a classmate. Your classmate will **observe** the box a **infer** things about its contents and how it looks inside.

Name ______________________

Date ______________________

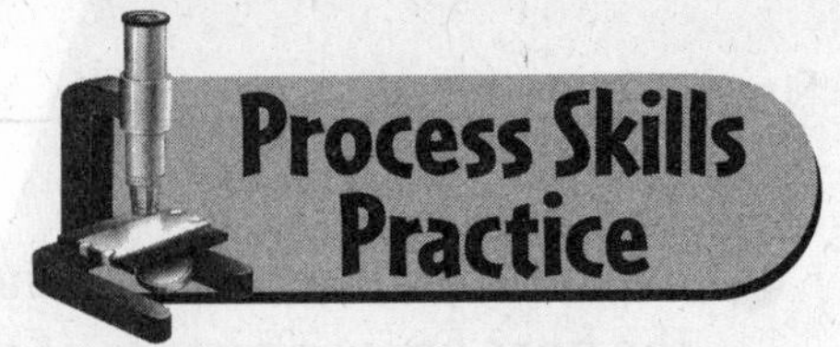

Observe and Infer

When you observe, you use one or more of your senses to perceive properties of objects and events. Observations can be made directly with the senses or indirectly through the use of instruments. When you infer, you use logical reasoning to draw conclusions based on observations. Inferences are explanations based on judgments and are not always correct.

Think About Observing and Inferring

During the investigation activity, you observed and inferred the characteristics of a mystery box. Below are some of the things you did during the investigation. After each action, write an *O* if you were observing or an *I* if you were inferring when you performed that step.

1. recorded things you noticed about the box	
2. used a ruler to measure the outside of the box	
3. listened to the sounds made and noticed the shifts in weight within the box when you tilted it and shook it	
4. drew a picture of what you thought the inside of the box looked like before you opened the box	

5. How did observing help you make an inference about the box?

____

____

____

6. Suppose you receive a large envelope in the mail. Before opening it, you observe it and infer what is in it. What might you observe about the envelope?

____

____

____

7. What are some things you could infer about an unopened letter?

____

____

Use with page E37.

Name ______________________

Date ______________________

What Are Atoms and Elements?

Lesson Concept

Atoms are tiny particles of matter. Elements are substances made up of only one kind of atom.

Vocabulary

nucleus (E39) **proton** (E39) **neutron** (E39) **electron** (E39)

element (E40) **atom** (E40) **molecule** (E40)

Below is a list of terms and names from this lesson. Put each term or name into the correct category by writing it under one of the headings below.

heat conductor **ductile** **sodium** **electron**

iron **oxygen** **Dalton** **neutron**

silicon **proton** **malleable** **Bohr**

electrical conductor

Subatomic Particles	Common Elements	Properties of Metals	Scientists Who Studied Atoms

Draw a picture of Bohr's model of an atom, and label each part.

Name ___________________________

Date ___________________________

Grouping Elements

Materials

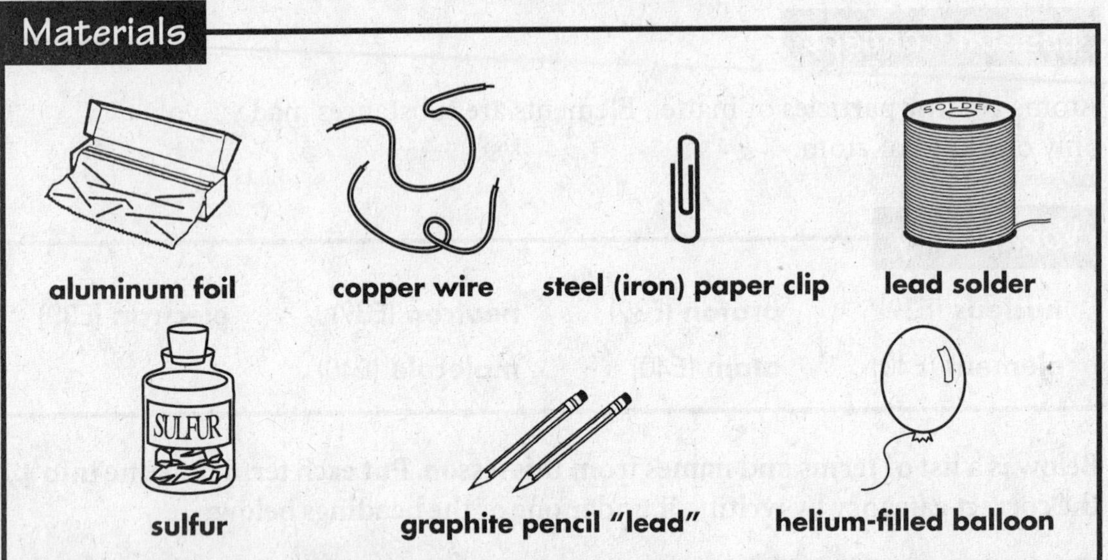

CAUTION

Activity Procedure

1. Use the chart below to **record** the properties of the elements you **observe**.

Object	Element	Phase	Color	Luster	Malleability
foil					
wire					
paper clip					
sulfur					
graphite					
solder					
balloon					

2. What elements do the objects represent? **Record** your answers in the second column of the chart.

3. **Observe** each element. Is it a solid, a liquid, or a gas at room temperature? **Record** your observations in the column labeled "Phase" of the chart.

Name ______________________

Investigate Log

4. What is the color of each element? (Carefully release some of the helium from the balloon.) **Record** what you **observe** in the chart.

5. Which elements have luster? (Which are shiny?) **Record** what you **observe** in the fifth column of the chart.

6. Which elements bend easily? **Record** what you **observe** in the column labeled "Malleability." **CAUTION** **Wash your hands after handling the objects in this investigation.**

Draw Conclusions

1. What similar properties did you **observe** in different elements?

____
____
____

2. Consider the properties you **observed** to form groups. Which elements could you group together? Explain. ______________________

____

3. **Scientists at Work** Scientists have made a periodic table, in which elements are grouped by their properties. Using your observations, **predict** which elements from the activity are near each other in the periodic table. ______________________

____
____

Investigate Further Think of other properties that could be used to group elements. Are there any you could test? **Plan and conduct a simple investigation** of one group of elements from this activity using these new tests.

____
____
____

Name ______________________

Date ______________________

Process Skills Practice

Observe and Predict

You can use observations to predict the outcomes of future events. Before making scientific predictions, you should think about previous observations you made of related events.

Think About Observing and Predicting

Observe the table below. Each element in the table is shown with its atomic number and atomic mass. The atomic mass is the mass of one mole (6.02×10^{23} atoms) of an element.

Element	Atomic Number	Atomic Mass in Grams
Helium	2	4
Carbon	6	12
Nitrogen	7	14
Oxygen	8	16
Sodium	11	
Iron		56

1. How many electrons circle around the nucleus of each atom of oxygen? ______
2. Describe the relationship between atomic number and atomic mass in the table. ______
3. The atomic mass of sodium is missing. What would you predict the atomic mass to be? ______
4. The atomic number of iron is missing. What would you predict the atomic number to be? ______
5. The atomic mass of sodium is actually 23 g. The atomic number of iron is actually 26. Compare these values to your predictions in Questions 3 and 4. What does this tell you about the relationship you saw between atomic number and atomic mass? ______

Use with page E45.

Name ____________________

Date ____________________

What Are Compounds?

Lesson Concept

Compounds are molecules made of two or more elements.

Vocabulary

periodic table (E47) **compound** (E48)

Chemists use shorthand to describe compounds. Use the table below to match each chemical symbol with the element it stands for.

C = carbon	Ca = calcium	Cl = chlorine	H = hydrogen
He = helium	O = oxygen	N = nitrogen	Na = sodium
Fe = iron			

1. One molecule of table salt (NaCl) has _____ atom(s) of ________________ and _____ atom(s) of ________________.

2. One molecule of water (H_2O) has _____ atom(s) of ________________ and _____ atom(s) of ________________.

3. One molecule of methane (CH_4) has _____ atom(s) of ________________ and _____ atom(s) of ________________.

4. One molecule of ammonia (NH_3) has _____ atom(s) of ________________ and _____ atom(s) of ________________.

Circle the choice that best completes each sentence below.

5. The order of elements in the periodic table is based on the *number of protons in one atom* / *atomic mass.*

6. Elements with properties of metals and nonmetals are called *metalloids* / *semi-metals.*

7. A Russian chemist named Dmitri Mendeleev organized elements by *atomic number* / *atomic mass.*

Use with page E49.

Name ______________________

Date ______________________

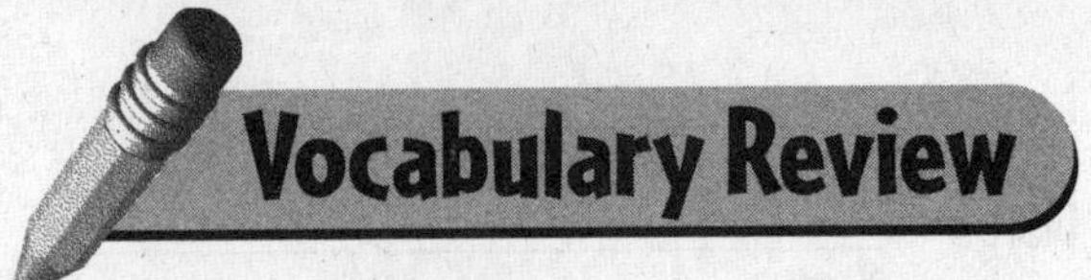

Recognize Vocabulary

On the line, write the letter of the answer that best completes each sentence.

1. The ______ is the center of an atom.

A nucleus **B** proton **C** compound **D** molecule

2. A(n) ______ is made up of only one kind of atom.

A compound **B** element **C** molecule **D** atomic number

3. A(n) ______ is a subatomic particle with a negative charge.

A electron **B** nucleus **C** neutron **D** proton

4. The smallest unit of an element that has all the properties of that element is a(n) ______.

A substance **B** compound **C** atom **D** molecule

5. The elements are arranged in order of atomic number in the ______ table.

A atomic **B** Mendeleev **C** periodic **D** atomic mass

6. A(n) ______ is made of atoms of two or more elements.

A neutron **B** compound **C** element **D** molecule

7. A(n) ______ is a subatomic particle with a positive charge.

A electron **B** nucleus **C** neutron **D** proton

8. When two or more atoms are linked together, they form a(n) ______.

A substance **B** compound **C** atom **D** molecule

9. A(n) ______ is a subatomic particle with no charge.

A electron **B** nucleus **C** neutron **D** proton

Use with pages E36–E49.

Name ____________________ Date ____________

Chapter 1 • *Graphic Organizer for Chapter Concepts*

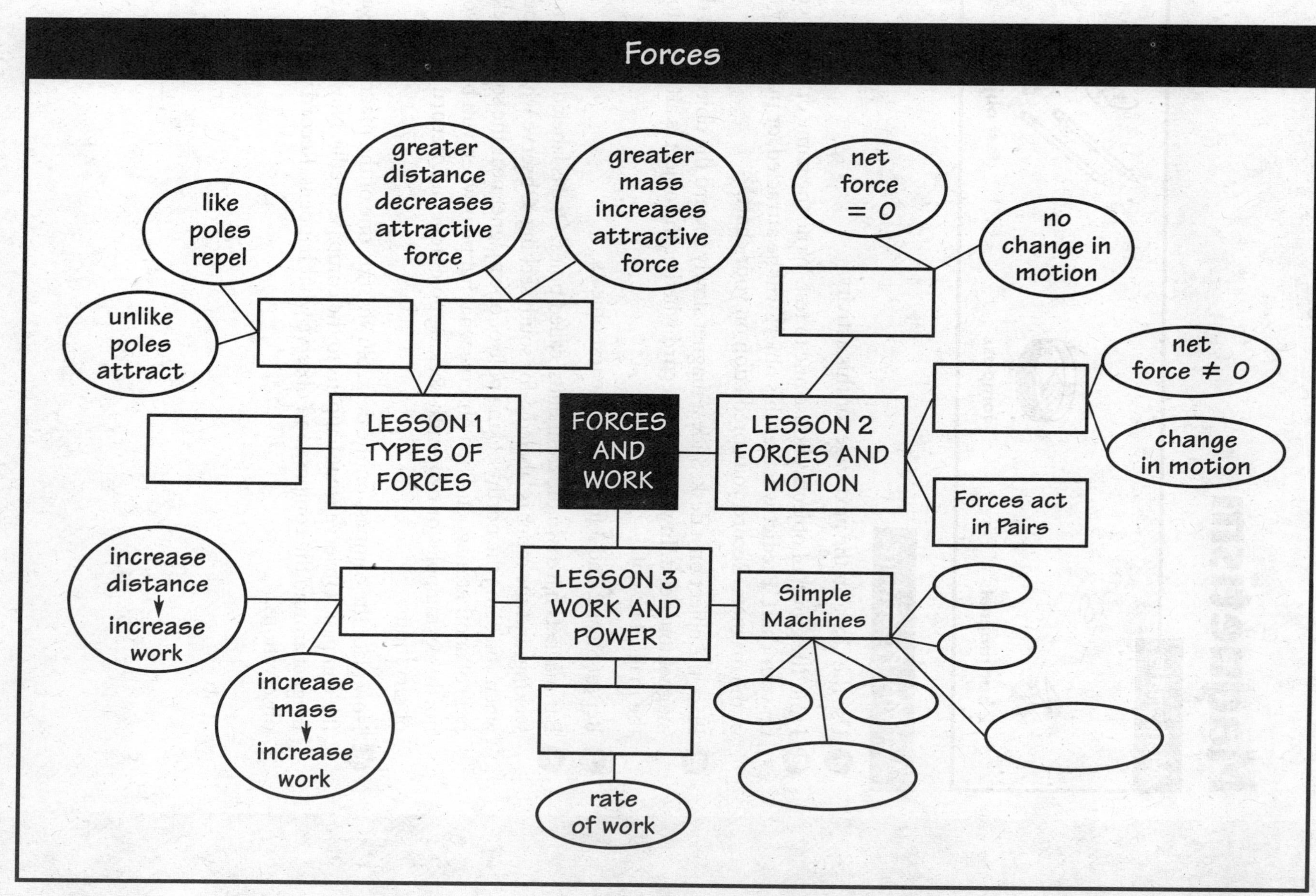

Harcourt

Name ______________________

Date ______________________

Magnetism

Materials

Activity Procedure

1. Use the chart on the next page for this activity.
2. From the group of objects, choose one to test. Write the name of the object on your chart. **Predict** whether this object will be attracted, or pulled, by one of the magnets. **Record** your prediction on your chart.
3. Place the object on a desk. Slide a magnet slowly toward the object until the magnet touches it. In your chart, **record** whether the object is attracted to the magnet or not.
4. Repeat Steps 2 and 3 for each of the test objects.
5. Bar magnets have two different ends, called poles. One is labeled *N* for north seeking, and the other is labeled *S* for south seeking. **Observe** what happens when you bring the north-seeking pole of one magnet near the south-seeking pole of another magnet. Then observe what happens when you bring two north-seeking poles or two south-seeking poles together. **Record** your observations.
6. Now place the compass on the desk. Slowly slide one of the magnets toward the compass. **Observe** what happens to the compass needle. Now move the magnet around the compass and observe what happens. **Record** your observations.

 Use with pages F4–F5.

Name ______________________

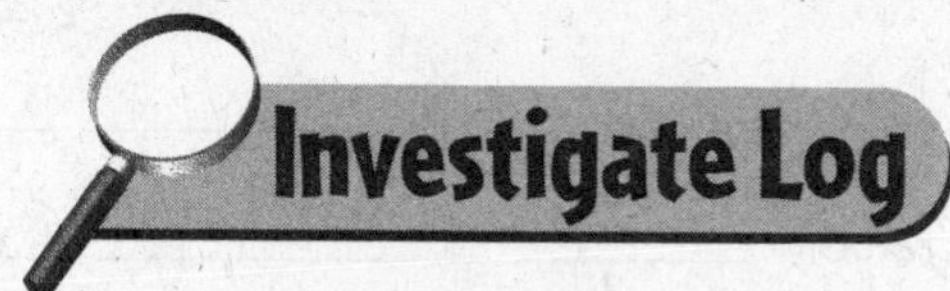

Object	Prediction	Test Result

Draw Conclusions

1. What characteristic of an object determines whether or not it is attracted by a magnet? ______________________

2. **Infer** what characteristic of a compass needle accounts for your observations of the compass and the magnet. ______________________

3. **Scientists at Work** Scientists often **hypothesize** about why things happen. Then they **plan and conduct investigations** to test their hypotheses. Form a hypothesis about why unlike magnetic poles attract each other while like magnetic poles repel, or push away, each other. Then plan and conduct an investigation to test your hypothesis. ______________________

Investigate Further Research to find out why a compass needle always points to the north. ______________________

Name

Date

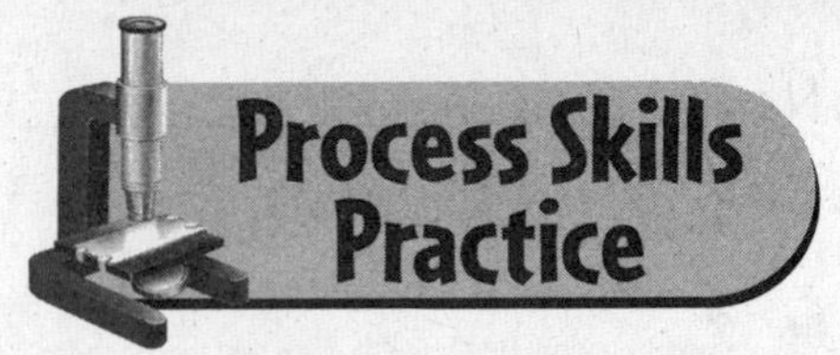

Hypothesize

When you hypothesize, you make an educated guess about the relationship between variables. A hypothesis must be something that can be tested. A hypothesis is often changed because of the outcome of experiments that test it.

Think About Hypothesizing

Leona's mother bought a small car because lightweight cars can go farther than heavy cars on the same amount of gasoline. Because weight is important to fuel efficiency, Leona wondered how the weight of the gasoline itself affects gas mileage. She hypothesized that a car probably gets better gas mileage when it has less gas in it. Therefore, to save both gas and money, it is better to fill the gas tank half-full than to fill it full. Her mother suggested they experiment to test the hypothesis.

1. How could Leona test her hypothesis?

2. What are some variables in this experiment?

3. Which of the variables should be held constant in this experiment?

4 What results would support Leona's hypothesis?

5. Suppose Leona and her mother discovered that their gas mileage increased by 0.5 mile per gallon of gas by driving with the tank half-full. How much more often would they have to stop at the gas station to get this extra mileage? Do you think it would be worth the extra stops at the gas station?

Use with page F5.

Name ______________________

Date ______________________

What Forces Affect Objects on Earth Every Day?

Lesson Concept

A force is a push or a pull that can move an object, stop it, or change its direction. Some forces are direct; others work at a distance. Where two surfaces rub against each other, the force of friction opposes motion. Magnetism pulls the poles of magnets together or pushes them apart. Gravity, which pulls objects toward each other, depends on the masses of the objects and how far apart they are.

Vocabulary

force (F6) **friction** (F6) **magnetism** (F7) **gravitation** (F8)

Complete each sentence below by writing the word *friction, magnetism,* or *gravitation* in the blank.

1. The moving parts of an automobile engine are coated in oil or grease to reduce the ______________________ between the metal parts.
2. Some toys let you draw hair, eyebrows, and other features with a special wand that moves iron filings around by ______________________.
3. A balance scale works by using ______________________ to compare the weights of two objects.
4. A parachute uses the force of air pushing up on a large area of silk to resist the force of ______________________.
5. When you apply the brakes on your bike, you are clamping down on the bike's wheel to increase the force of ______________________.
6. Hikers can use a compass to guide them along a trail because the compass needle is pulled to the north by ______________________.
7. You can tape lightweight objects to a wall, but if you try to tape something heavy to a wall and it falls off, you'll know the tape isn't strong enough to overcome the force of ______________________.

Name ____________________

Date ____________________

Forces That Interact

Materials

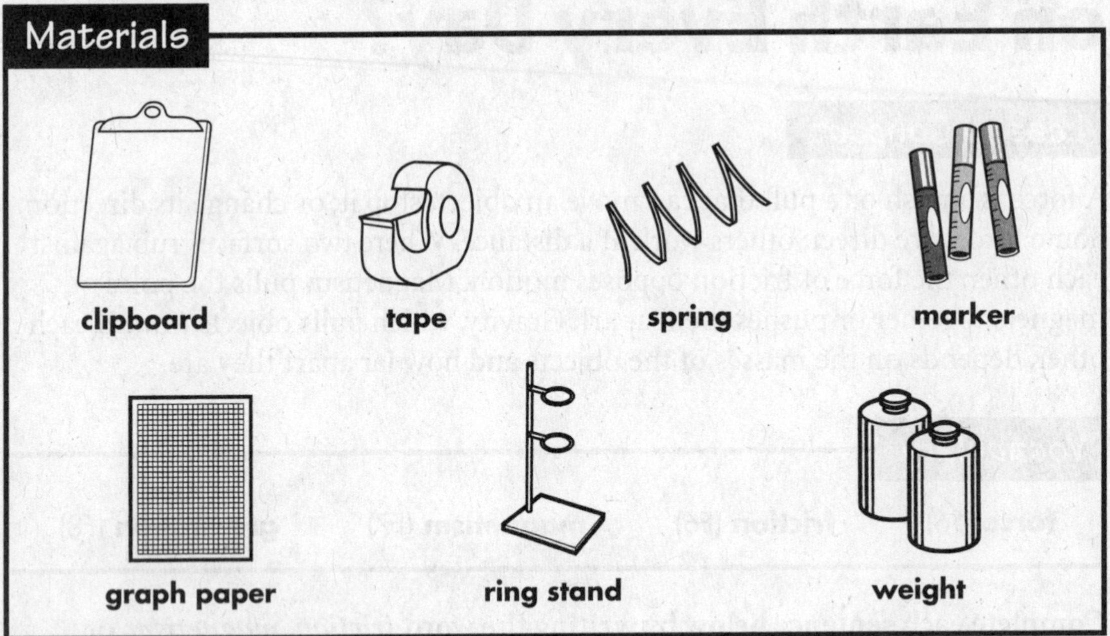

Activity Procedure

1. Tape the graph paper to the clipboard. Across the bottom of the graph paper, draw a line and label it *Seconds.* Starting at one end of the line, make a mark every 2.5 cm.
2. Attach the spring to the ring stand. Then attach the weight to the free end of the spring. Tape the marker to the bottom of the weight so that its tip points toward the back of the setup.
3. Have a partner hold the clipboard with the graph paper taped to it behind the weight. The marker point should just touch the graph paper. Pull the weight until the spring is fully stretched.
4. Have your partner slide the clipboard across a table at a steady rate of about 2.5 cm per second. As soon as the clipboard starts to move, drop the weight. As it bounces, it traces its movements on the graph paper.
5. **Interpret the data** on your graph. Identify and mark the points where the weight was not moving up or down for an instant. Identify and mark the direction (up or down) the weight was moving along each sloping line. Identify and mark the places where the weight was moving most rapidly.

Name ______________________

Draw Conclusions

1. At what points was the weight not moving? ______________________

2. At what point was the weight moving most rapidly? ______________________

3. From your graph, **infer** the point at which the force of the spring was the greatest. ______________________

4. Scientists at Work Scientists often **draw conclusions** after they **interpret data** they have collected. After studying your graph, draw conclusions to answer the following questions:

During which part of each cycle was the force of gravity greater than the force of the spring? ______________________

During which part of each cycle was the force of the spring greater than the force of gravity? ______________________

Investigate Further Hypothesize how your graph would look if you repeated the activity with a heavier weight. **Plan and conduct a simple investigation** to test your hypothesis. ______________________

Name ______________________

Date ______________________

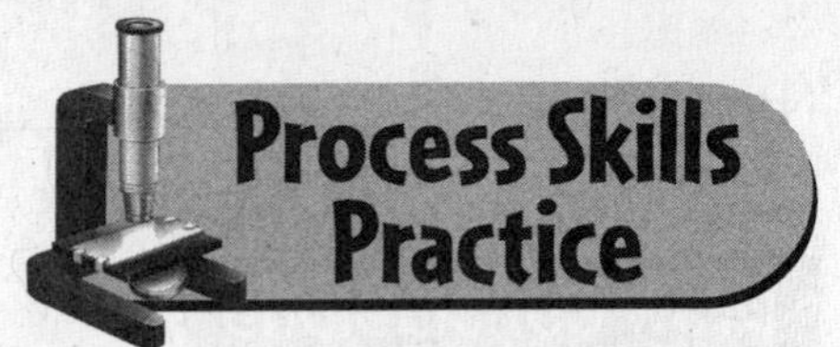

Interpret Data and Draw Conclusions

When you interpret data, you look for patterns or meaning in information that is given to you or information you have gathered from your own observations.

Think About Interpreting Data and Drawing Conclusions

The table below shows the force required to lift various objects on Earth as well as on two other planets, Planet X and Planet Y. The force is expressed in newtons (N). Study the data table, and then answer the questions that follow.

Force Needed to Lift Objects

Object	On Earth (N)	On Planet X (N)	On Planet Y (N)	Mass (g)
1	20.0	8	4	2040.8
2	7.5	3	1.5	765.3
3	12.5	5	2.5	1275.5
4	5.0	2	1	510.2
5	25.0	10	5	2551.0

1. Which of the three planets has the strongest gravitational pull? Explain.

____

2. Which of the three planets has the weakest gravitational pull? Explain.

____

3. List the objects in order, starting with the one having the greatest mass and ending with the one having the least mass. ______________________

4. How did you use your knowledge of interpreting data to help you decide what the information in the data table means? ______________________

____

____

____

 Use with page F11.

Name ______________________

Date ______________________

What Are Balanced and Unbalanced Forces?

Lesson Concept

Balanced forces occur when two forces acting on an object are equal in size and opposite in direction. Unbalanced forces occur when forces acting on the same object are not opposite and equal. When forces are unbalanced, a net force occurs, causing acceleration. When you calculate the net force on an object, you must account for both the size and the direction of the forces.

Vocabulary

balanced forces (F12) **unbalanced forces** (F13)

acceleration (F13) **net force** (F14)

Decide whether the underlined term or phrase makes each statement true or false. If the statement is true, write the word *true* on the line. If the statement is false, write a word or phrase that makes the statement true.

______________ **1.** Balanced forces are equal in size and opposite in direction and therefore cancel each other out.

______________ **2.** The change in motion of an object is always caused by a force or forces.

______________ **3.** If balanced forces are acting on an object, it will seem as if a net force is acting on the object.

______________ **4.** Forces always act alone.

______________ **5.** Balancing the forces acting on an object gives you the net force.

______________ **6.** When balanced forces act on an object, the object speeds up, starts to move, slows down, stops, or changes direction.

______________ **7.** If two equal forces act on an object in opposite directions, the net force will be balanced.

______________ **8.** Unbalanced forces can stop a moving object.

Name ___________________________

Date ___________________________

Measuring Work

Materials

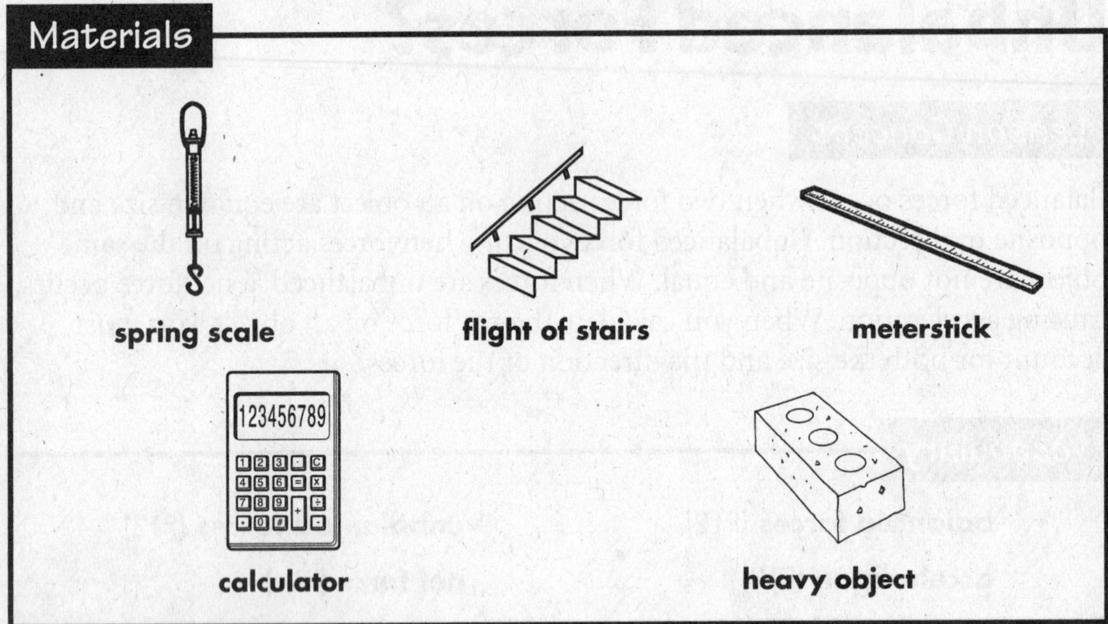

Activity Procedure

1. Use the table below for this activity.
2. Weigh the object using the spring scale and **record** its weight in the table, next to *Trial 1*.
3. **Measure** the total height of the flight of stairs in meters. **Record** the measurement in your table, also next to *Trial 1*.
4. Work can be **measured** as the product of force (in newtons) and distance (in meters). **Calculate** to find the number of newton-meters, or *joules*, of work you would do if you carried the object up the flight of stairs. **Record** the product in the table.
5. Suppose you carried the object up two flights of stairs. Beside *Trial 2* on the table, **record** the new height and **calculate** the work done.

Work

Trial	Weight (newtons)	Height (meters)	Work (joules)
1			
2			
3			
4			

Name ______________________

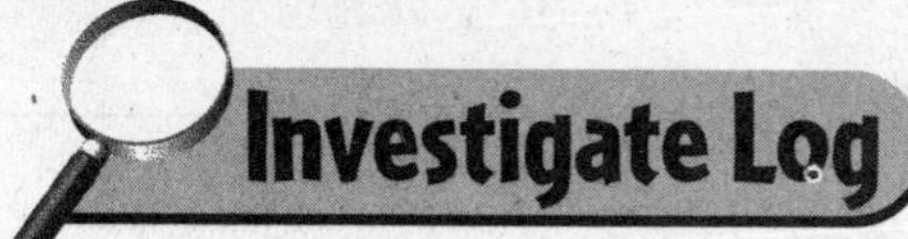

6 For *Trial 3*, **calculate** how much work you would do if you carried the object up three flights every day for a week.

7 For *Trial 4*, suppose your weight is 300 newtons. **Record** this new data and **calculate** the work you do climbing the stairs without carrying the object.

Draw Conclusions

1. **Compare** the amount of work a person weighing 300 newtons does climbing one flight of stairs to the total amount of work the same person does climbing three flights of stairs every day for a week. ______________________

2. **Interpret** your **data** and **draw conclusions** about how work is related to force and distance. ______________________

3. **Scientists at Work** When scientists **interpret data**, they often **draw conclusions** based on the data they collected. What can you conclude about the amount of work done by people who weigh more than 300 newtons?

____

Investigate Further *Power* is the measure of how quickly work is done. You can measure power in *joules per second.* **Plan and conduct a simple investigation** to calculate how much power you use walking up a flight of stairs compared to running up a flight of stairs. ______________________

Name ______________________

Date ______________________

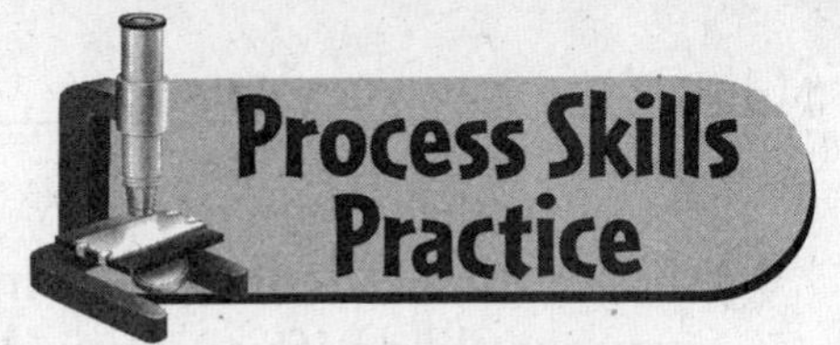

Interpret Data

When you interpret data, you look for patterns or meaning in information that has been given to you or information that you have gathered.

Think About Interpreting Data

The table below provides data about five students who participated in a fitness test. Look at the data, and then answer the questions that follow.

Name	Student Weight	Distance Run	Time
Darcy	369 N	500 m	120 seconds
Carla	392 N	500 m	116 seconds
Tyler	400 N	500 m	122 seconds
Tasha	382 N	500 m	126 seconds
Daniel	419 N	500 m	130 seconds

1. Which of the five students requires the most force to move his or her body? Explain. ______________________

____

2. Which of the five students did the most work? Explain. ______________________

____

____

3. Write a mathematical sentence that describes the amount of work done by Daniel. ______________________

4. Which student is the most powerful? Explain. ______________________

____

____

5. How did having the data in a table help you interpret it to answer the questions?

____

____

Use with page F17.

Name ______________________

Date ______________________

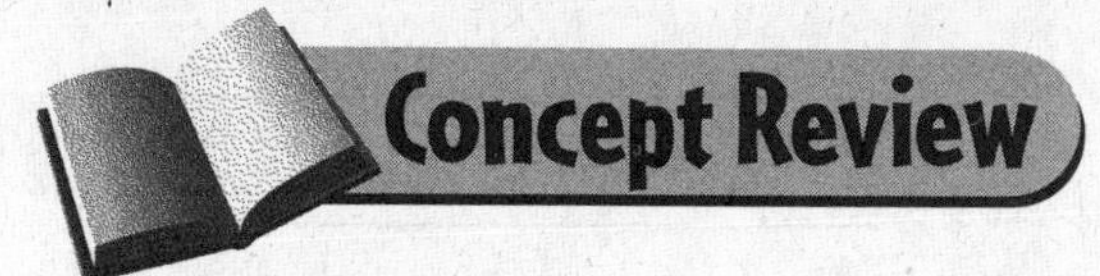

What Is Work and How Is It Measured?

Lesson Concept

Work is the force applied to an object times the distance the object is moved. Work is measured in joules. Power is a measure of the speed at which work is done. Power is measured in watts. Machines are devices that make work seem easier by changing the size or direction of a force. Pulleys, levers, wheels and axles, inclined planes, wedges, and screws are simple machines.

Vocabulary

work (F18) **power** (F19) **machine** (F20)

Rewrite the descriptions in Questions 1–4 as mathematical sentences. Express values in newtons (N), meters (m), joules (J), and watts (W). Do any calculations necessary to find these values.

1. Vanessa and her father have built a sandbox for a neighborhood playground. They need to fill the sandbox with 20 bags of sand. Each bag weighs 50 pounds.

   How many newtons of force will be needed to lift the sand? ______________

   ____

2. The closest Vanessa and her father can get the back of their truck to the sandbox is 5 meters. How much work will Vanessa and her father have to do to move all the sand to the sandbox? ______________________

3. Figure out how much work Vanessa's father must do to move one bag of sand.

   ____

   ____

4. It takes Vanessa's father three minutes to lift one bag of sand from the truck and carry it to the sandbox. How much power does Vanessa's father use to move one bag of sand?

   ____

   ____

Name ____________________

Date ____________________

Recognize Vocabulary

Choose from the following terms to solve each riddle. Use each term only once.

balanced forces	**work**	**power**	**forces**
net force	**magnetism**	**acceleration**	**gravitation**
friction	**machines**	**unbalanced forces**	

________________ **1.** I am a repulsing force, and my partner is an attracting force. Together we are forces between the poles of a magnet. What are we?

________________ **2.** I am a force pushing on an object, and you are a force pushing back on the object, but neither of us is moving the object. What are we?

________________ **3.** When you catch a football and run with it, I am what you are doing when you move the ball and yourself over the distance you run. What am I?

________________ **4.** We can change force into distance and distance into force. What are we?

________________ **5.** We are pushes or pulls. What are we?

________________ **6.** The faster you work, the more you have of me. What am I?

________________ **7.** I am a force, I oppose motion, and you find me where the surfaces of two objects meet. What am I?

________________ **8.** We are both pulling the same object in opposite directions. At first the object doesn't move. Then it does. What are we when the object moves?

________________ **9.** I am the force that keeps your feet on the ground. What am I?

________________ **10.** I am a way of measuring the effect of two forces on an object.

________________ **11.** I am a change in movement, caused by unbalanced forces. What am I?

Use with pages F4–F23.

Name ____________________ Date ____________________

Chapter 2 • Graphic Organizer for Chapter Concepts

Motion		
LESSON 1 WAYS TO DESCRIBE MOTION	LESSON 2 THE THREE LAWS OF MOTION	LESSON 3 WHY PLANETS STAY IN ORBIT
1. ____________ 2. ____________ 3. ____________	First Law: ____________ Second Law: ____________ Third Law: ____________	Law of Universal Gravitation: ____________

Name ____________________

Date ____________________

Changes in Motion

Materials

clear pastic bottle with cap

water

small piece of soap

Activity Procedure

1. Fill the bottle nearly to the top with water. Leave only enough space for a small air bubble. Add a small piece of soap to the water. This will keep the air bubble from sticking to the side of the bottle. Put the cap tightly on the bottle.
2. Lay the bottle on its side on a flat surface. You should see one small bubble in the bottle. Hold the bottle steady until the bubble moves to the center of the bottle and stays there.
3. **Predict** what will happen to the air bubble if you turn the bottle to the left or right. Turn the bottle and **observe** what happens. **Record** your observations.
4. Now **predict** what will happen to the air bubble if you move the bottle straight ahead at a steady speed. Move the bottle and **observe** what happens. **Record** your observations.
5. Repeat Step 4, but this time slowly increase the bottle's speed. **Observe** happens to the air bubble. **Record** your observations.

Name ______________________________

Draw Conclusions

1. **Compare** your predictions and your observations. What happened when you turned the bottle to the left or right, or moved it forward? ______________________________

2. From what you **observed**, how did a change in speed affect the bubble?

3. **Scientists at Work** Were you surprised by the way the air bubble moved? When scientists get surprising results, they often **hypothesize** about the cause of those results. Form a hypothesis about why the bubble moves the way it does. ______________________________

Investigate Further Predict what will happen to the air bubble if the bottle is moving at a steady speed and its direction changes. **Plan and conduct a simple investigation** to test your prediction. ______________________________

Name ______________________

Date ______________________

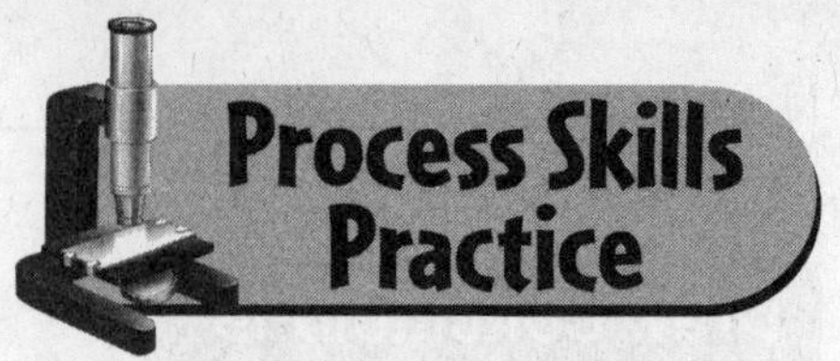

Hypothesize

When you hypothesize, you make an educated guess about the relationships between variables. A hypothesis must be something you can test in an experiment, and it may be proven wrong in an experiment. A hypothesis is based upon observation, prior knowledge, and prior experimental outcomes.

Think About Hypothesizing

Suppose you want to find out the effect of an inclined surface on an object's speed. In addition to a stopwatch, you have the following materials to work with:

a smooth board, 15 centimeters wide by 30 centimeters long
a cylindrical glass jar weighing 75 grams
a cylindrical glass jar weighing 150 grams
2 blocks of wood, 2 centimeters thick
2 blocks of wood, 4 centimeters thick

1. State a hypothesis about how the slope of an inclined surface might affect an object's speed. ______________________

____

2. Describe an experiment, using the materials listed above, that would test this hypothesis. ______________________

____

____

3. State a hypothesis about how the weight of a jar might affect its speed down the inclined board. ______________________

____

4. Describe an experiment that would test your hypothesis. ______________________

____

____

Use with page F33.

Name ____________________

Date ____________________

How Are Motion and Speed Related?

Lesson Concept

Motion is a change in an object's position. Speed is a measure of the distance an object moves in a given amount of time. Velocity is speed in a particular direction. Acceleration is a change in velocity, either in direction or in speed. Momentum, the product of an object's velocity and its mass, is a measure of how hard it is to slow down or stop an object.

Vocabulary

position (F34) **speed** (F35) **velocity** (F35)
acceleration (F35) **momentum** (F36)

Fill in each blank with a vocabulary term. Each term may be used more than once.

1. When track runners finish a race, they don't just suddenly stop at the finish line. The runners' ____________________ carries them well past the finish line, before they can slow down and then stop.
2. You can usually tell when an object is in motion because you can see its ____________________ changing.
3. Some people think that ____________________ just means speeding up, but it can also mean slowing down.
4. ____________________ isn't just an object's ____________________, it's also the object's direction of travel.
5. Earth is moving through space. One way we can tell Earth is moving is by observing how our ____________________ changes in relation to the stars.
6. If an object is traveling at a constant speed and then changes direction, we say its ____________________ has changed. We call this change ____________________.

Use with page F37.

Name ____________________

Date ____________________

How Mass and Velocity Affect Momentum

Materials

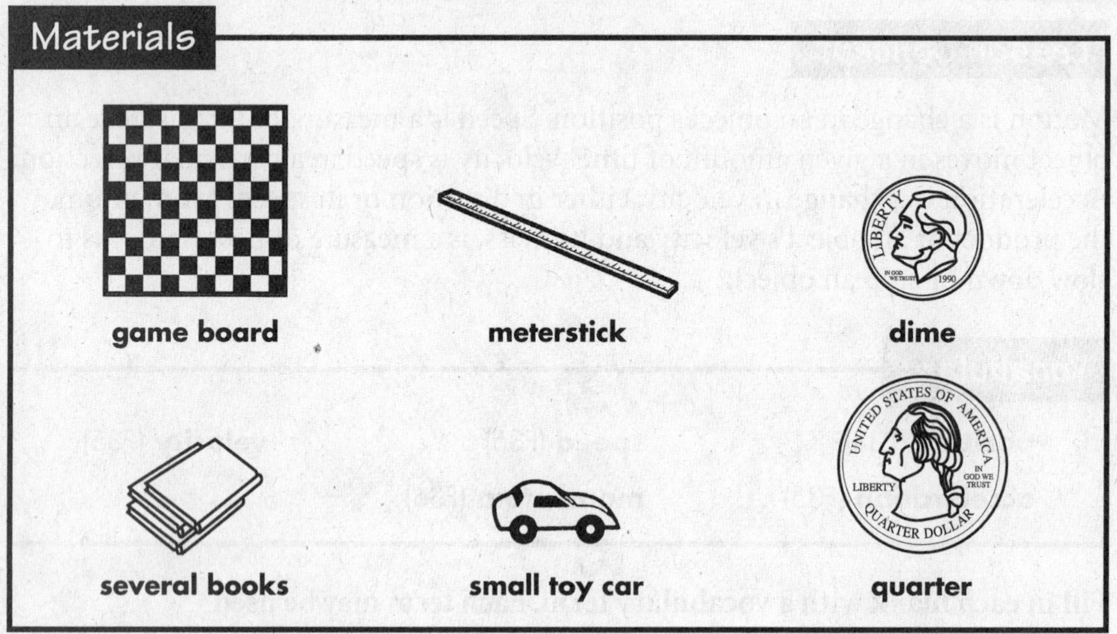

Activity Procedure

1. Make a ramp by setting one end of the game board on a stack of books about 15 cm high. Place another book as a barrier about 10–15 cm from the bottom of the ramp.
2. Position the car at the top of the ramp. Put the dime on one end of the car. Let the car roll down the ramp and strike the barrier. **Observe** what happens to the dime. **Measure** and **record** its distance from the barrier.
3. Repeat Step 2, this time placing the quarter on the car instead of the dime. **Observe** what happens to the quarter. **Measure** and **record** its distance from the barrier.
4. Repeat Steps 2 and 3 several times. **Measure** and **record** the distance for each trial.
5. **Predict** how the results would differ if the ramp were steeper. Add another book to the stack under the ramp, and repeat Steps 2 and 3 several times. **Measure** and **record** the distances for each trial.

Name ______________________

Draw Conclusions

1. Make a table to organize your data. **Compare** the results for the dime with the results for the quarter. **Infer** how the mass of the coin is related to the distance it travels. ______________________

____

____

2. What happened to the distances the coins traveled when you made the ramp steeper? Explain the results. ______________________

____

____

____

3. **Scientists at Work** While **gathering data**, scientists try to **identify and control variables**, or conditions, that may affect the results. In this investigation, what variables did you control in Steps 2 and 3? ______________________

____

____

What variable did you test? ______________________

____

Investigate Further **Plan and conduct a simple investigation** to test various methods of keeping the coin on the car when it strikes the barrier. Carefully select the equipment you will need, and conduct several trials for each method you test.

____

____

____

____

Name ______________________

Date ______________________

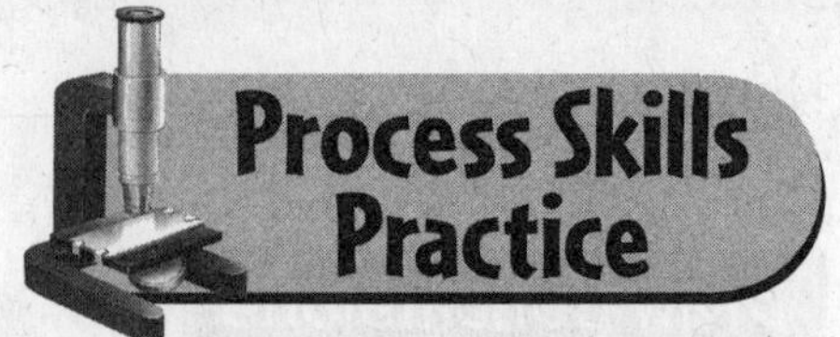

Identify and Control Variables

When you identify and control variables, you find out which conditions in an experiment make a difference in the outcome. Controlling variables means changing one condition while keeping all the other conditions the same.

Think About Identifying and Controlling Variables

Ann and Barbara decide to ride their bicycles from their houses to the park. Ann claims that her bicycle is faster than Barbara's, and that therefore, she will get to the park first. They both live the same distance from the park. The road from Ann's house is paved. The road from Barbara's house is dirt and gravel. Ann takes off her coat before she rides. Barbara likes the sound of her coat flapping in the wind, so she leaves her coat on. The two of them race from their separate houses, and Ann wins. Did she win because her bicycle is faster?

1. Was the race a fair test of which bicycle is faster? Explain. ______________________

____

____

2. What were some variables in the race? ______________________

____

3. Which condition was the same? In other words, which variable was controlled?

____

4. Which variables were not controlled? ______________________

____

5. What would be a good way of testing the hypothesis that Ann's bicycle is faster than Barbara's? ______________________

____

____

____

____

____

 Use with page F39.

Name ______________________

Date ______________________

What Are the Three Laws of Motion?

Lesson Concept

The first law of motion is that an object at rest tends to remain at rest and an object in motion tends to move in a straight line at a constant speed, unless an outside force acts on it. The second law is that an object's acceleration depends on the mass of the object and on the size and direction of the force acting on it. The third law is that for every action, there is an equal and opposite reaction.

Vocabulary

inertia (F41) **action force** (F43) **reaction force** (F43)

Write *true* in front of the true statements and *false* in front of the false statements. If the statement is false, write a correction in the space provided.

______ **1.** The same force that causes a pencil to fall to the floor also causes the moon to orbit Earth. ______________________

______ **2.** A moving object tends to continue moving in a straight line unless something pushes or pulls it out of its path. ______________________

____

______ **3.** The inertia of an object depends directly on its motion.

____

______ **4.** Newton's first law of motion explains why when you are riding in a car, you feel forced outward, away from the direction of turns.

____

______ **5.** An action force makes a rocket move. ______________________

____

______ **6.** Newton's second law of motion explains how an unbalanced force on an object causes it to accelerate. ______________________

____

Name ____________________

Date ____________________

Orbits and Inertia

Activity Procedure

1. Tie three or four metal washers securely to one end of the string.
2. CAUTION **Take the string with the washers outside to an open area. Be sure that you are far from any buildings or objects and that no one is standing close to you. Put on the safety goggles.** Hold the loose end of the string. Slowly swing the string and washers in a circle above your head. **Observe** the motion of the washers.
3. **Predict** what will happen if you let go of the string while swinging it in a circle.
4. CAUTION **Again, make sure that there are no people, buildings, or other objects near you.** Swing the string and washers in a circle again. Let the string slip through your fingers. **Observe** the motion of the washers. How does it **compare** with your prediction?
5. Using a drawing, **record** the motion of the washers in Steps 2 and 4. Be sure to show the forces acting in each situation. Now make a drawing of the moon orbiting Earth. **Compare** the two drawings.

Name ______________________

Draw Conclusions

1. **Compare** the path of the washers while you were swinging them with their path once you let go of the string. ______________________

2. The string and washers can be used to **model** the moon orbiting Earth. **Compare** the motion of the washers circling your head with the motion of the moon orbiting Earth. ______________________

3. **Scientists at Work** When scientists **experiment**, they must **communicate** their results to others. One way of doing this is with diagrams. Look at the drawing you made of the washers. What motions and forces does it show?

Investigate Further **Hypothesize** about the effect the length of the string has on the time the washers take to complete one revolution. Then **experiment** to test your hypothesis. ______________________

Name ______________________

Date ______________________

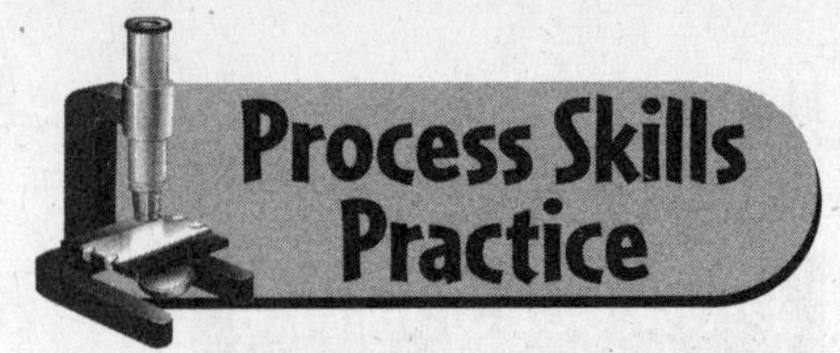

Communicate

When you communicate in science, you are showing the results of an activity, such as an experiment, in an organized fashion so that the results can be interpreted later. If you communicate well, you or someone else can repeat the experiment to demonstrate it to others, or you can build on the work to make further discoveries.

Think About Communicating

In the 1600s a mathematician named Johannes Kepler was given an assignment to analyze records of the motions of the planets to figure out the nature of their orbits. This was before telescopes, before Newton's laws of motion, and at a time when people knew very little about the planets. The records he studied had been kept very carefully by an astronomer named Tycho Brahe (TEE•koh BRAH•hee) and were considered very accurate. After studying the data, Kepler was able to describe the orbits of Mars and Earth as ellipses. He used this new information to figure out three laws of planetary motion, and he published his findings in two books. A few years afterward, a young scientist named Isaac Newton used the information communicated by Johannes Kepler to figure out the law of universal gravitation.

1. What kind of communication enabled Kepler to reach his conclusions?

____

2. How did Kepler communicate his own discoveries? ______________________

3. Kepler's books described the orbits of planets. If you were helping him write his books, how would you suggest he communicate his findings?

____

____

____

4. Part of effective scientific communication is making sure others will understand the information you are sharing. Do you think Brahe's scientific communication was effective? Was Kepler's? Explain. ______________________

____

____

____

Use with page F47.

Name ______________________

Date ______________________

Why Do the Planets Stay in Orbit?

Lesson Concept

The moon circles Earth in a path called an orbit. Gravitation between Earth and the moon keeps the moon from flying off into space because of its inertia. The balance between inertia and gravitation keeps Earth in orbit around the sun. It also keeps other planets and moons in their orbits.

Vocabulary

orbit (F48) **law of universal gravitation** (F49)

Answer each question with one or more complete sentences.

1. If Earth suddenly disappeared, the moon would no longer be under its gravitational influence. Would the moon then fly off in a straight line? Explain. ______________________

____

2. Newton's law of universal gravitation says that all objects in the universe are attracted to all other objects. You already know this means that the moon is attracted toward Earth. Does the law of universal gravitation also mean that Earth is attracted toward the moon? Explain. ______________________

____

3. Gravitational force decreases with distance. What does this mean for a space traveler who leaves Earth in a spaceship? ______________________

____

____

4. As you travel through space away from Earth, what does the universal law of gravitation say about objects you may encounter that have huge masses ?

____

____

Use with page F51.

Name ______________________

Date ______________________

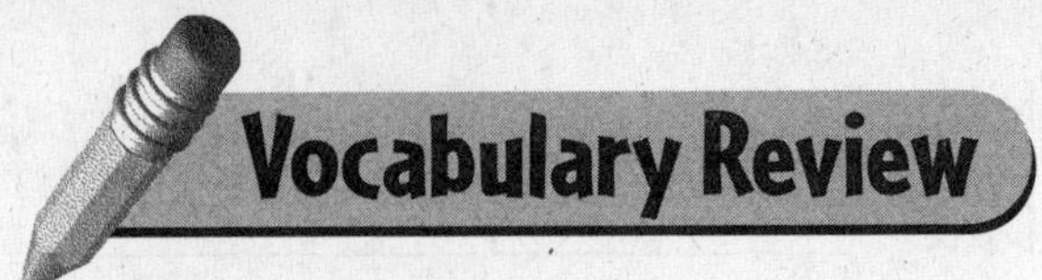

Recognize Vocabulary

Use the following terms to solve the crossword puzzle.

position	**speed**	**velocity**
acceleration	**momentum**	**inertia**
action force	**reaction force**	**orbit**
law of universal gravitation		

Across

2. a measure of the distance an object travels in a certain length of time

6. the force that pushes or pulls back in response to another force

7. an object's speed in a particular direction

8. any change in velocity

9. a force that acts on an object

10. the property that resists any change in an object's motion

Down

1. an object's place or location

3. a measure of how hard it is to slow down or stop an object

4. If you say that everything is attracted to everything else, you are stating the law of universal ____.

5. the path an object in space takes as it revolves around another object

1 2 3 4 5 6 7 8 9 10

Use with pages F30–F57.

Harcourt

Chapter 3 • Graphic Organizer for Chapter Concepts

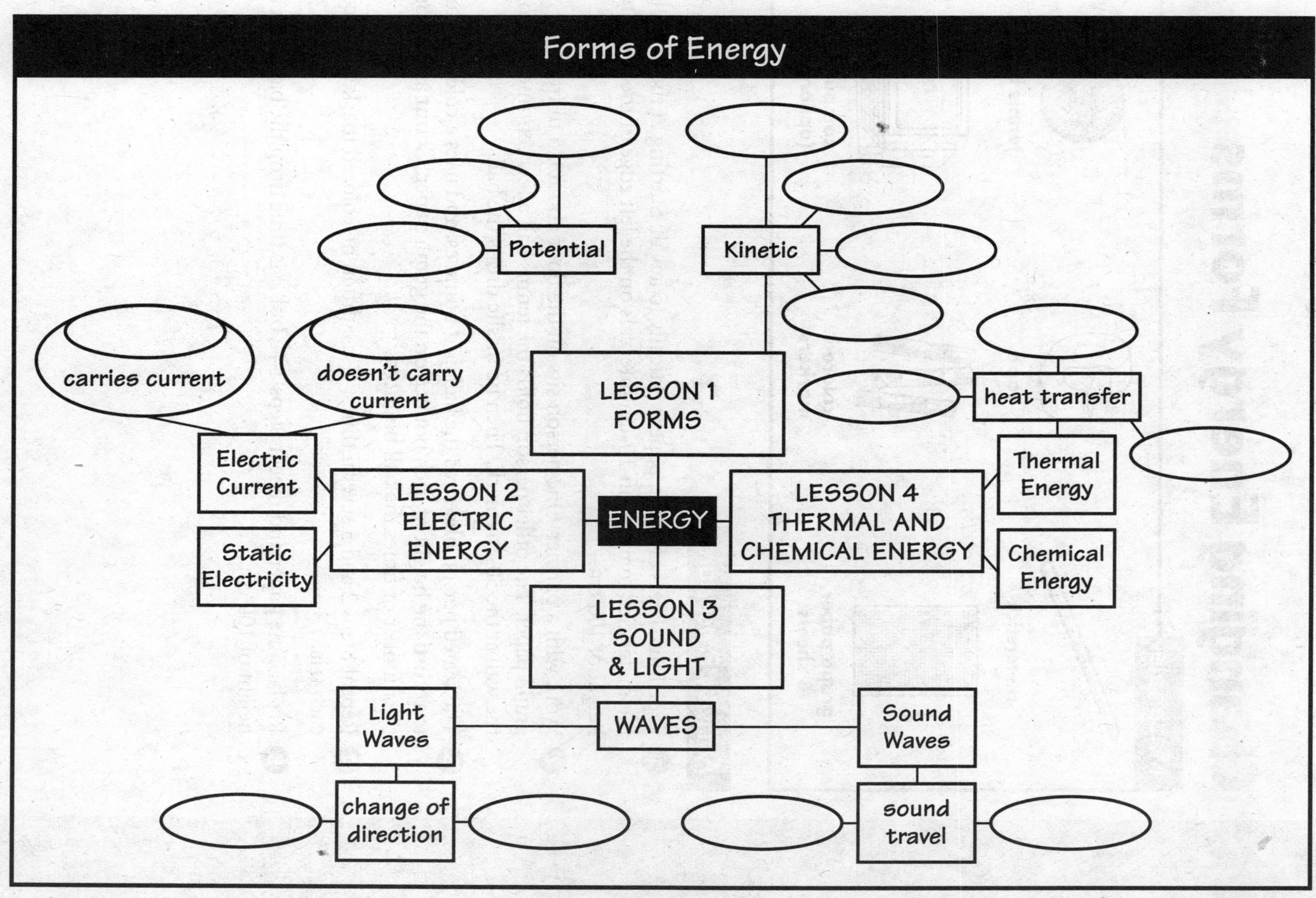

Name ______________________________ Date ____________________

Name ______________________

Date ______________________

Changing Energy Forms

Materials

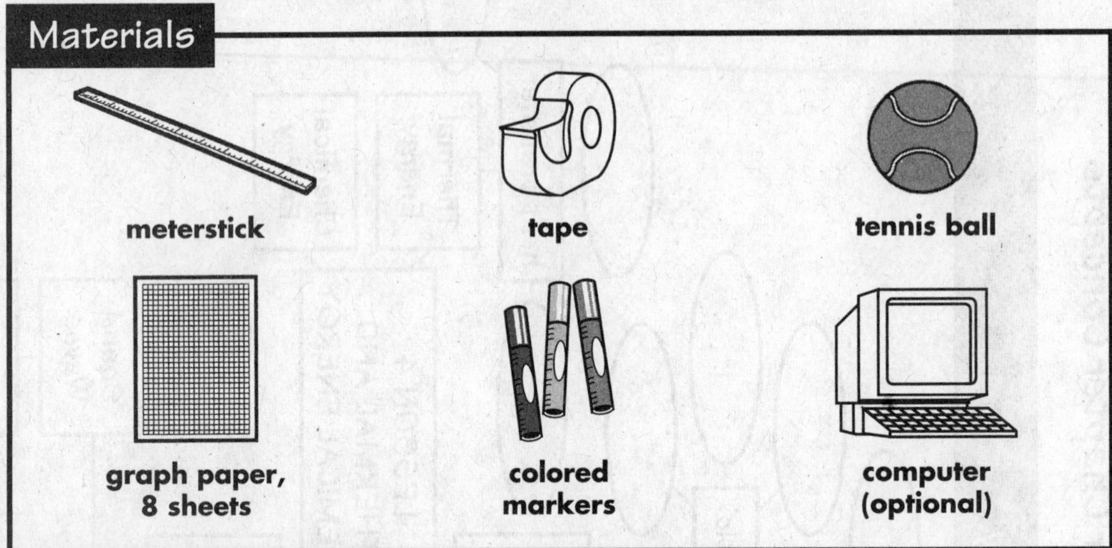

Activity Procedure

1. Tape four sheets of graph paper vertically to a wall. Starting at the floor, use the meterstick to mark off 10-cm intervals on the left edge of the paper to a height of 100 cm.
2. Work with a partner. One person sits on the floor about 0.5 m from the graph paper. The other person holds the tennis ball a few centimeters from the wall at the 50-cm mark. Then he or she drops the ball.
3. The seated person **observes** the ball as it bounces, and uses a colored marker to **record** the height of each bounce on the graph paper. **Count** and record the number of times the ball bounces.
4. Repeat Steps 2 and 3 several times. Use a different-colored marker to **record** each trial.
5. Replace the paper and repeat Steps 1–4, but this time drop the ball from a height of 100 cm.

Name ______________________

Draw Conclusions

1. **Compare** the drop height to the bounce height for each trial in the experiment. How are the heights related? ______________________

2. When you hold the ball in the air before dropping it, it has *potential energy* because of its position and because of gravitation. When you let go of the ball, it has *kinetic energy* because of its movement. **Infer** the point at which the ball has the most kinetic energy. ______________________

3. **Draw a conclusion** about how potential energy and kinetic energy are related in the bouncing ball. ______________________

4. **Scientists at Work** Scientists often use computers to help them **interpret data** and **communicate** the results of an experiment. Use a computer graphing program, such as *Graph Links*, to **compare** the height of each bounce and the number of bounces from one trial of the 50-cm drops and one trial of the 100-cm drops. Make a different-colored line graph for each trial.

Investigate Further Analyze the data you graphed in Step 4 and **predict** how high and how many times a ball dropped from a height of 200 cm will bounce. Then **experiment** and **compare** your results to your predictions.

Name ______________________

Date ______________________

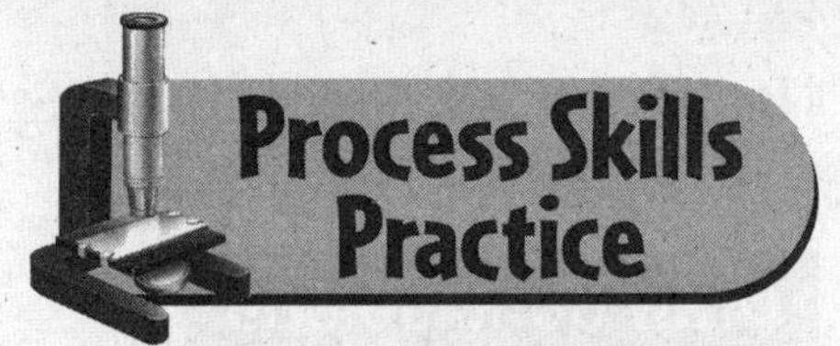

Communicate

When you communicate, you transmit data or information to others. You can use spoken or written words, graphs, drawings, diagrams, maps, and charts to communicate. Communicating in science means showing the results of an activity in an organized fashion so that the data can be interpreted or the activity repeated.

Think About Communicating

Here is some data from an experiment to observe the potential and kinetic energy of a basketball.

Dropped from 1 meter. Trial 1: Bounced 60 cm. Trial 2: Bounced 70 cm. Trial 3: Bounced 80 cm.

Dropped from 2 meters. Trial 1: Bounced 1 m 40 cm. Trial 2: Bounced 1 m 25 cm. Trial 3: Bounced 1 m 40 cm.

Communicate these results on the graphs.

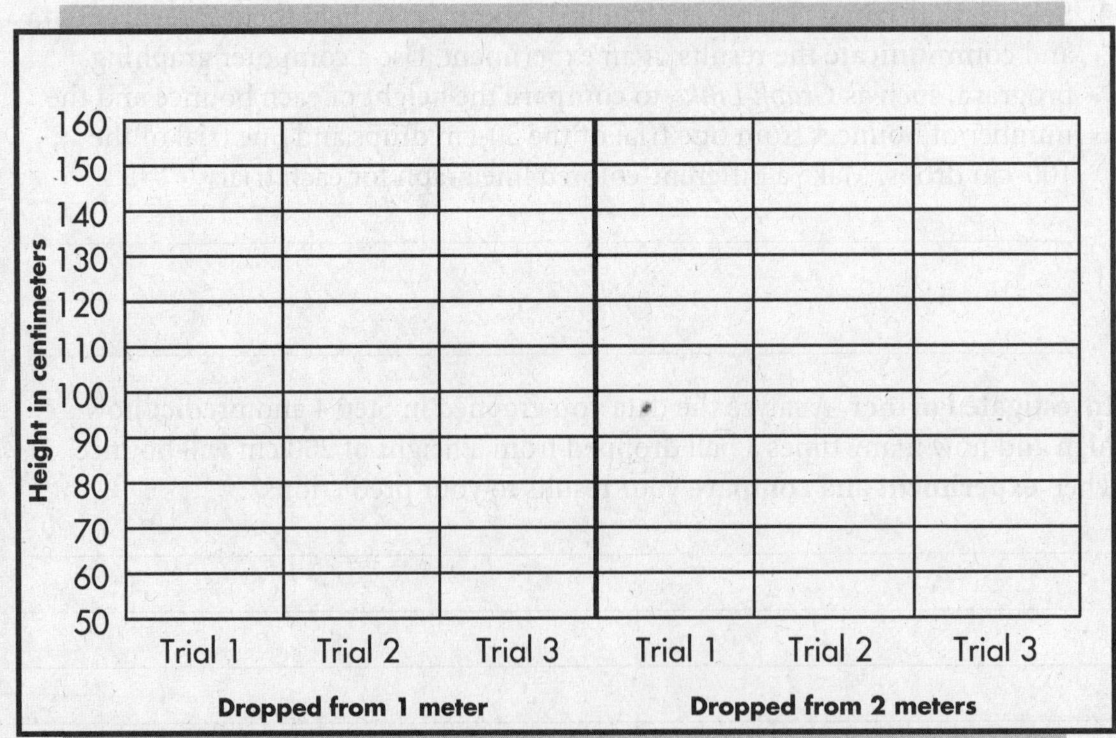

Use with page F61.

Name ______________________

Date ______________________

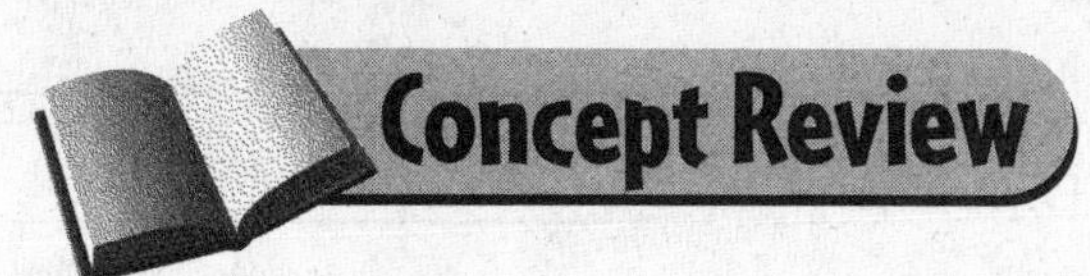

What Are Kinetic and Potential Energy?

Lesson Concept

Energy is the ability to cause changes in matter. There are two basic types of energy—kinetic energy and potential energy. Kinetic and potential energy can be found in many forms. Electric energy, thermal energy, mechanical energy, light, and sound are all forms of kinetic energy. Chemical potential energy, gravitational potential energy, and elastic potential energy are forms of potential energy. The law of conservation of energy says energy can change form but cannot be created or destroyed.

Vocabulary

energy (F62) **kinetic energy** (F62) **potential energy** (F62)

Decide whether the underlined term or phrase makes each statement true or false. If the statement is true, write the word *true* on the line. If the statement is false, write a word or phrase that makes the statement true.

_______________ **1.** Energy is the ability to do work.

_______________ **2.** The energy of motion is called kinetic energy.

_______________ **3.** The energy an object has because of where it is or because of its condition is called potential energy.

_______________ **4.** A boulder rolling down a hill has potential energy.

_______________ **5.** Mechanical energy is a form of potential energy.

_______________ **6.** Energy never changes from one form to another during any one activity.

_______________ **7.** Thermal energy and light energy are two forms of potential energy.

_______________ **8.** An apple that is ready to drop from the tree to the ground has gravitational potential energy.

_______________ **9.** The energy stored in a compressed spring is called elastic kinetic energy.

Name ______________________

Date ______________________

Electric Circuits

Materials

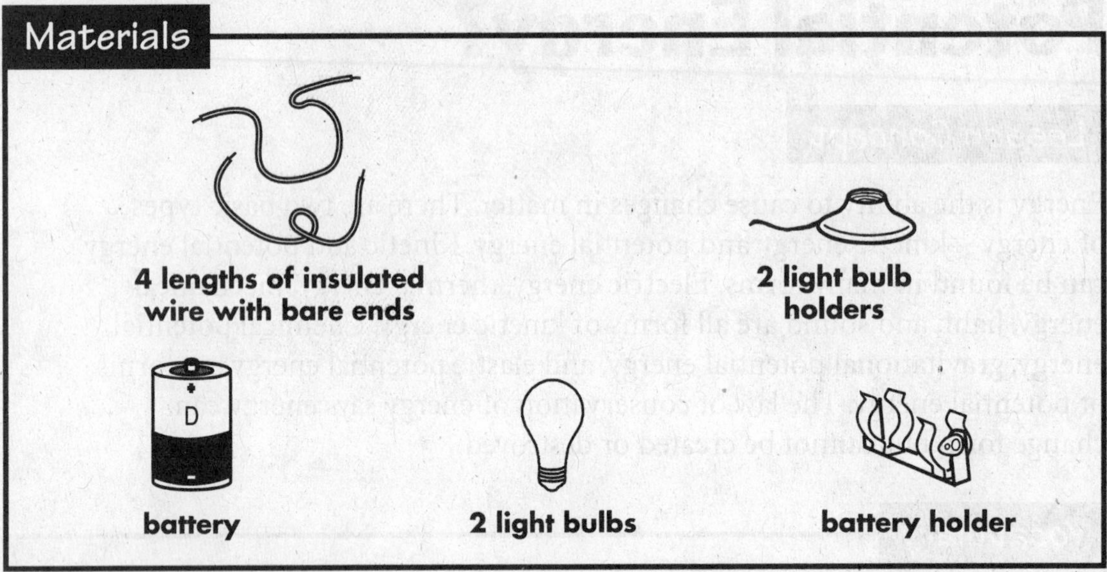

Activity Procedure

1. To make electricity flow between the terminals, or charged ends, of a dry cell or battery, you need to connect the terminals in some way, such as with a wire. Electricity will then flow through any device you put along this path. Connect the wires, bulb holders, and battery holder as shown in Picture A on page F67.
2. Insert the light bulbs and batteries. **Observe** what happens and **record** your observations.
3. Remove one of the bulbs from its holder. **Observe** and **record** what happens to the other bulb.
4. Now reconnect the wires, bulb holders, and battery holder as shown in Picture B on page F67. **Observe** what happens and **record** your observations.
5. Again remove one of the bulbs from its holder. **Observe** and **record** what happens to the other bulb.
6. Draw diagrams of both of the circuits you built. Use arrows to **compare** the path of the electric current in each circuit.

Name ______________________

Draw Conclusions

1. What happened to the other bulb when one bulb was removed from the first circuit? ______________________

2. What happened to the other bulb when one bulb was removed from the second circuit? ______________________

3. **Scientists at Work** Scientists often **compare** results before they **draw a conclusion**. Cross out one bulb in each of your drawings. Then diagram the path the electric current must take if it can't pass through the bulb you crossed out. Compare your diagrams, and then draw a conclusion about which type of circuit would be better to use for a string of lights. ______________________

Investigate Further In the investigation you demonstrated that electricity flowing through a circuit produces light and heat (the glowing bulbs were warm). Now **plan and conduct a simple investigation** to demonstrate that electricity flowing through a circuit can also produce sound and magnetism. Decide what equipment you will need to use in your investigation. ______________________

Name ______________________

Date ______________________

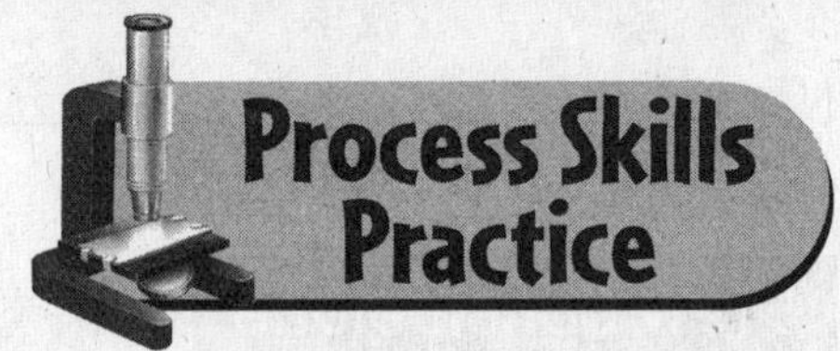

Compare and Draw Conclusions

When you compare, you identify common and distinguishing characteristics of objects or events. When you draw a conclusion, you pull together all that you have discovered in observing, researching, and investigating.

Think About Comparing and Drawing Conclusions

Comparing the characteristics of different things is a good way to learn those characteristics and draw conclusions about them. Look at the data in the chart below and then answer the questions that follow.

	Materials That Allow Electricity to Flow	Materials That Do Not Allow Electricity to Flow
Porous	watery substances, salt solutions, acid solutions	Leather, cotton, wool, parchment, ashes, chalk, hair, feathers, wood
Nonporous	iron, copper, silver, graphite, charcoal	rubber, porcelain, vinyl, plastics, precious stones, ceramic, glass, resin, amber

1. When you plug something into an electrical outlet, you don't want electricity to flow from the wires into your hand. The plug must therefore be made of material that does not allow electricity to flow. Compare the properties of the materials listed in the chart. Draw a conclusion about which materials would be good for making plugs. ______________________

____

2. Explain why you chose those materials. ______________________

____

____

3. List two materials that would be good to use for wires to carry electricity in a circuit and explain why. ______________________

____

Use with page F67.

Name ______________________

Date ______________________

What Is Electric Energy?

Lesson Concept

Electric energy is the movement of electrons between areas that have opposite charges. When objects with opposite charges are close enough together or when the charges are very large, electrons move between the objects. Electric current moves through an electric circuit. When electric current flows through a conductor, it produces a magnetic field, turning the conductor into an electromagnet.

Vocabulary

electric charge (F68) **electric force** (F69) **electric current** (F69)
conductor (F70) **electric circuit** (F71) **insulator** (F71)
resistor (F71) **electromagnet** (F72)

Match the term in the left column with its description in the right column.

_____ **1.** positive charge
_____ **2.** static electricity
_____ **3.** series circuit
_____ **4.** proton
_____ **5.** electric energy
_____ **6.** electric current
_____ **7.** conductor
_____ **8.** generator
_____ **9.** electron
_____ **10.** resistor
_____ **11.** electric force
_____ **12.** negative charge

A the energy produced by the movement of electrons
B an atomic particle with a negative charge
C the charge an object has when it has gained electrons
D the charge an object has when it has lost electrons
E the attraction or repulsion that unlike or like charges have
F the potential electric energy of a charged object
G an atomic particle with a positive charge
H the flow of electrons
I a circuit with only one path for the electrons
J a material that carries electrons easily
K a source of electrons
L a material that resists electric current

Use with page F73.

Name ______________________

Date ______________________

The Path of Reflected Light

Materials

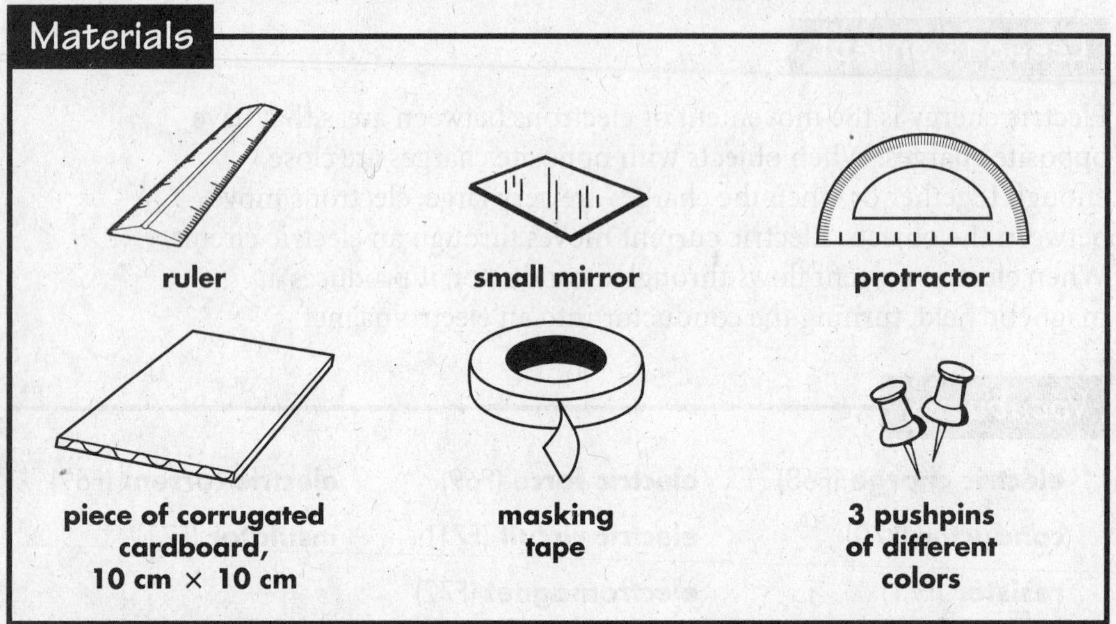

Activity Procedure

1. Lay the cardboard flat. Use the tape to attach the mirror vertically to one end of the cardboard. Push two of the pins into the cardboard, about 5 cm from the mirror.
2. Position yourself at eye level with the mirror. Align yourself so that your view of one pin lines up with the reflection of the other pin. Push a third pin into the cardboard at the edge of the mirror, right in front of where you see the reflection of the second pin. The first pin, the third pin, and the reflection of the second pin should appear to be in a straight line.
3. Draw lines on the cardboard to connect the three pins. These lines show how the reflected light from the first pin traveled to your eye.
4. Using the protractor, **measure** the angle between each line and the edge of the mirror. You will probably have to trace the edge of the mirror and then move it out of your way to make this measurement. **Record** your results.
5. Now remove the original pins and place two of them 10 cm from the mirror. Repeat Steps 2–4 with this new arrangement of pins. **Measure** the angles of the new lines, and **record** your results.

Name ______________________

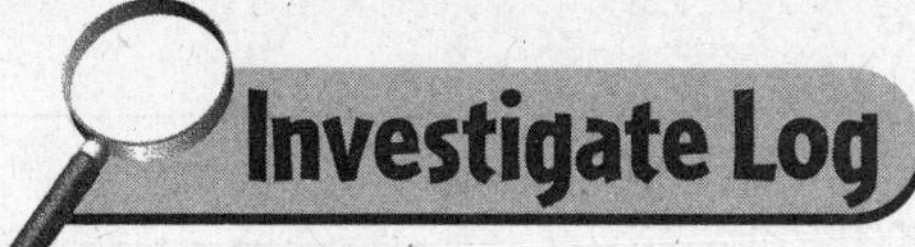

6 Now draw diagrams to **communicate** the results of the two experiments. Each diagram should show the locations of the pins and the mirror and the path of the reflected light.

Draw Conclusions

1. **Compare** the two angles you **measured** in each experiment.

____

____

2. The angle at which light strikes a mirror is the *angle of incidence.* The angle at which it reflects from the mirror is the *angle of reflection.* **Draw a conclusion** about the angle of incidence and the angle of reflection from a flat surface.

____

____

____

3. **Scientists at Work** When scientists **observe** a pattern that seems to always be true, they try to come up with a clear, simple rule. This helps them **predict** what will happen in the future. Predict what the angle of incidence and the angle of reflection would be if the pins were 20 cm from the mirror.

____

____

Investigate Further Hypothesize how light would be reflected from a mirror that was not flat. Then **plan and conduct a simple investigation** to test your hypothesis.

____

____

____

____

Name ______________________

Date ______________________

Process Skills Practice

Predict

When you predict, you anticipate outcomes of future events, basing your ideas on your prior experience, observations, or knowledge.

Think About Predicting

Louise was given a toy guitar for her birthday. She noticed that plucking on the thicker strings made a sound lower in pitch than the sound made by plucking on the thinner strings. She also noticed that if she tightened a string, the sound it produced would become higher in pitch. She also noticed that all the strings on her mother's guitar produced sounds lower in pitch than the strings on her toy guitar. She observed that all the strings on her mother's guitar were longer than the strings on her toy guitar.

Louise inferred from her observations that the thinner, the shorter, or the tighter the string, the higher the pitch of its sound. She thought she could use this inference to predict the sounds that other stringed instruments would make.

1. What is Louise trying to predict? ______________________

____

2. What information does she have that will help her predict? ______________________

____

3. A cello is a stringed instrument that looks like a very large violin. What could Louise predict about the sounds that a cello might make? Explain.

____

____

4. Louise knew that a piano is a stringed instrument. What could she predict about the strings that would be hammered when she played the keys that produce low-pitched sounds? ______________________

____

5. If you used Louise's observations, what could you predict about the sounds different-sized drums might make? Explain your answer by using Louise's inference. ______________________

____

____

Use with page F75.

Name ____________________

Date ____________________

What Are Light and Sound Energy?

Lesson Concept

Light energy is electromagnetic energy that travels through space and through certain materials. When light waves strike an obstacle, they are absorbed, reflected, or refracted. Lenses are curved pieces of transparent matter that refract light rays. Sound energy is vibrations that travel through matter. Solids and liquids conduct sound better than gases.

Vocabulary

reflection (F76) **refraction** (F76) **lens** (F77)

pitch (F79) **volume** (F79)

Choose the answer that best completes each statement.

1. A ____ lens is thicker in the middle than at the edges.
A concave **B** convex **C** reflection

2. The bending of light rays is called ____
A reflection **B** absorption **C** refraction

3. When light rays bounce off an object, the bouncing is called ____
A absorption **B** refraction **C** reflection

4. The colors of light that objects ____ are the colors we see.
A absorb **B** reflect **C** refract

5. Sound waves have two parts, compression and ____
A rarefaction **B** refraction **C** reflection

6. Light energy moves as waves called ____
A magnetic waves **B** vibrating waves **C** electromagnetic waves

7. The ____ is the colored part of the eye that narrows and widens to control the amount of light entering the eye.
A pupil **B** iris **C** cornea

Name ____________________

Date ____________________

Heat Flow

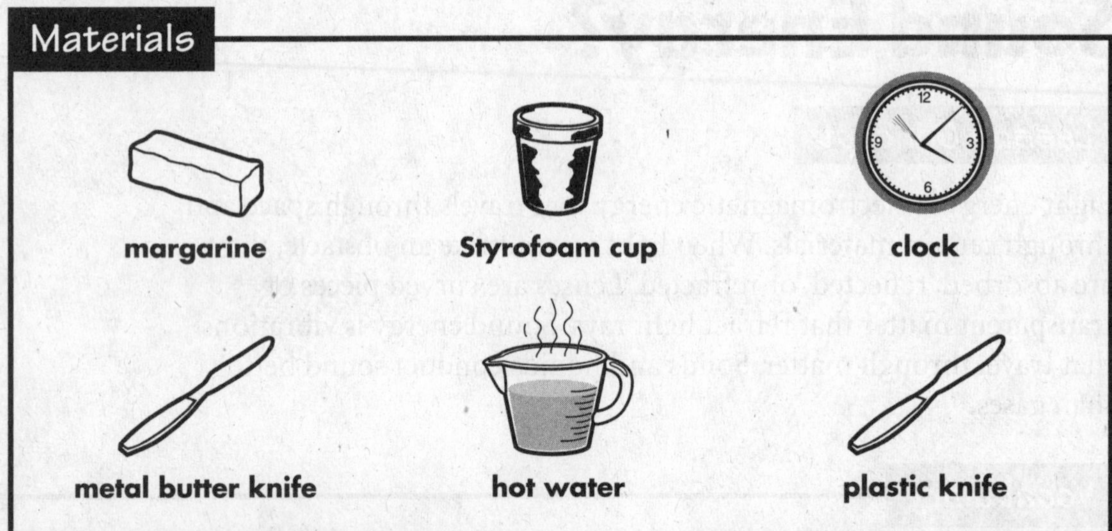

Activity Procedure

1. Place a dab of cold margarine near the middle of the metal knife. Place another dab of margarine the same size near the tip of the knife's blade.
2. **CAUTION** **Be careful when pouring the hot water.** Half-fill the cup with hot water. Put the metal knife's handle into the water. The dabs of margarine should be above the level of the water.
3. **Predict** which dab of margarine will melt first—the one near the middle of the knife or the one near the end of the knife.
4. **Observe** the metal knife for ten minutes and **record** your observations.
5. Repeat Steps 1–4 using the plastic knife.
6. **Experiment** to find out which material transfers heat faster—metal or plastic. Be sure to **identify and control variables** that might affect the results.

Name ______________________

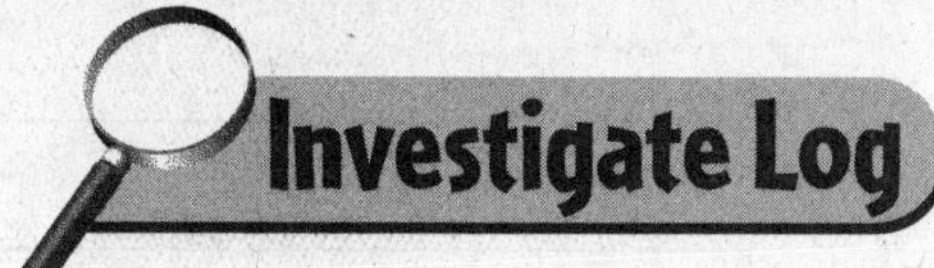

Draw Conclusions

1. **Draw conclusions** about how heat moves through the metal knife.

____

2. **Draw conclusions** about which material transfers heat faster.

____

3. **Scientists at Work** Scientists must **identify and control variables** in an experiment to see how changing one variable affects the results. What variables did you control in your experiment? What variable did you test?

____

Investigate Further **Experiment** to find out which knife cools faster. Decide what equipment you will need. ______________________

Name ______________________

Date ______________________

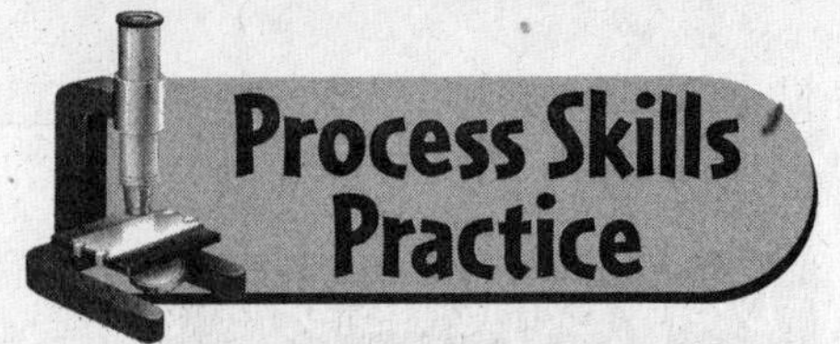

Identify and Control Variables

When you identify and control variables that affect the outcome of an experiment, you state which factors could affect the outcome of the experiment and you make sure that only one of those factors, or variables, is changed in any given test.

Think About Identifying and Controlling Variables

Suppose you are an architect trying to design an energy-efficient house. You want to know which wall and ceiling insulating materials work best so the house can be cooled and heated as inexpensively as possible. You also want lots of windows in the house so you can take advantage of natural light during the day. Windows, however, are where a house loses most of its warmed or cooled interior air. So you want windows that are good insulators but still allow light to pass through freely. You have a choice of three wall and ceiling insulating materials, and you have a choice of two window materials. You decide to build several small buildings the size and shape of doghouses for your test.

1. What are you testing? ______________________

____

2. What are some variables in your tests? ______________________

____

____

____

____

____

____

3. Which of the variables will you control? ______________________

____

____

4. Will using doghouse-sized models give you accurate results? Explain.

____

____

____

____

Use with page F83

Name ______________________

Date ______________________

What Are Thermal and Chemical Energy?

Lesson Concept

Thermal energy is the kinetic energy of molecules. The average kinetic energy of the molecules in an object is the object's temperature. Heat is the transfer of thermal energy from one object to another. Conduction is the direct transfer of heat between objects that touch. Convection is the transfer of heat through currents in a gas or a liquid. Radiation is the transfer of energy by electromagnetic waves. When atoms join to form molecules, thermal energy can be stored as chemical energy. Chemical energy can be released as kinetic energy.

Vocabulary

temperature (F84)	**heat** (F84)	**conduction** (F85)
convection (F85)	**radiation** (F85)	

Fill in each blank with a vocabulary term. You may use each term more than once.

1. When you add ______________ to an object, you increase the kinetic energy of the object's molecules, which increases its ______________.
2. If you leave a metal stirring spoon in a pot of soup while the soup is heating, the spoon will quickly get hot because of ______________.
3. When you sit near a campfire, the heat of the fire is transferred to you mostly by ______________.
4. If your house is heated by a furnace that blows hot air into the rooms, you are depending on the process of ______________ to stay warm.
5. A lizard sometimes stretches out on a rock to warm itself. The rock is warm because the sun has transferred thermal energy to it by ______________. The rock then transfers thermal energy to the lizard by ______________. The rock also transfers thermal energy to air above it and the lizard through a process called ______________.

Use with page F87.

Name ____________________

Date ____________________

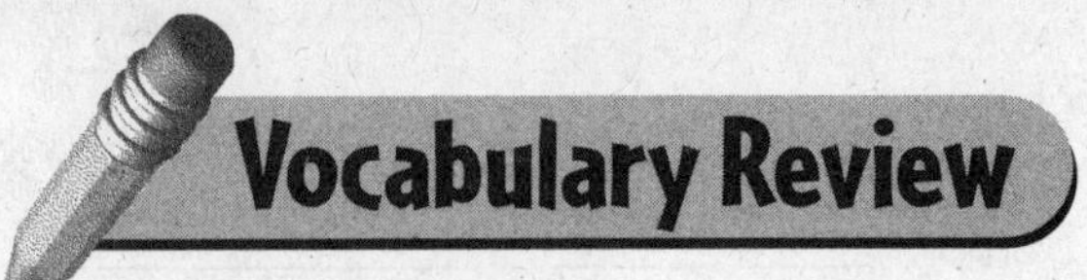

Recognize Vocabulary

Write the letter of the definition in the right column next to the term that it matches in the left column.

_____ **1.** conductor

_____ **2.** temperature

_____ **3.** electric circuit

_____ **4.** lens

_____ **5.** electric current

_____ **6.** convection

_____ **7.** potential energy

_____ **8.** heat

_____ **9.** insulator

_____ **10.** electric charge

_____ **11.** pitch

_____ **12.** electromagnet

_____ **13.** refraction

_____ **14.** energy

_____ **15.** electric force

_____ **16.** radiation

_____ **17.** conduction

_____ **18.** resistor

_____ **19.** volume

_____ **20.** reflection

_____ **21.** Kinetic energy

A a magnet formed by the flow of electric current

B energy of motion

C a material that doesn't carry electrons

D what an object gets when it gains or loses electrons

E the loudness of a sound

F the average kinetic energy of all the molecules in an object

G the transfer of thermal energy by electromagnetic waves

H energy an object has because of its condition

I a quality determined by the speed of vibration of sound waves

J a material that conducts electrons easily

K light that bounces off an object

L the attraction or repulsion between objects with a positive or negative charge

M the direct transfer of thermal energy between objects that touch

N the bending of light rays

O the ability to cause changes in matter

P the flow of electrons

Q the transfer of thermal energy from one substance to another

R a piece of clear material that bends light rays passing through it

S the transfer of thermal energy through currents in a liquid or a gas

T a material that resists the flow of electrons

U any path along which electrons can flow

Use with pages F60–F87.

Chapter 4 • *Graphic Organizer for Chapter Concepts*

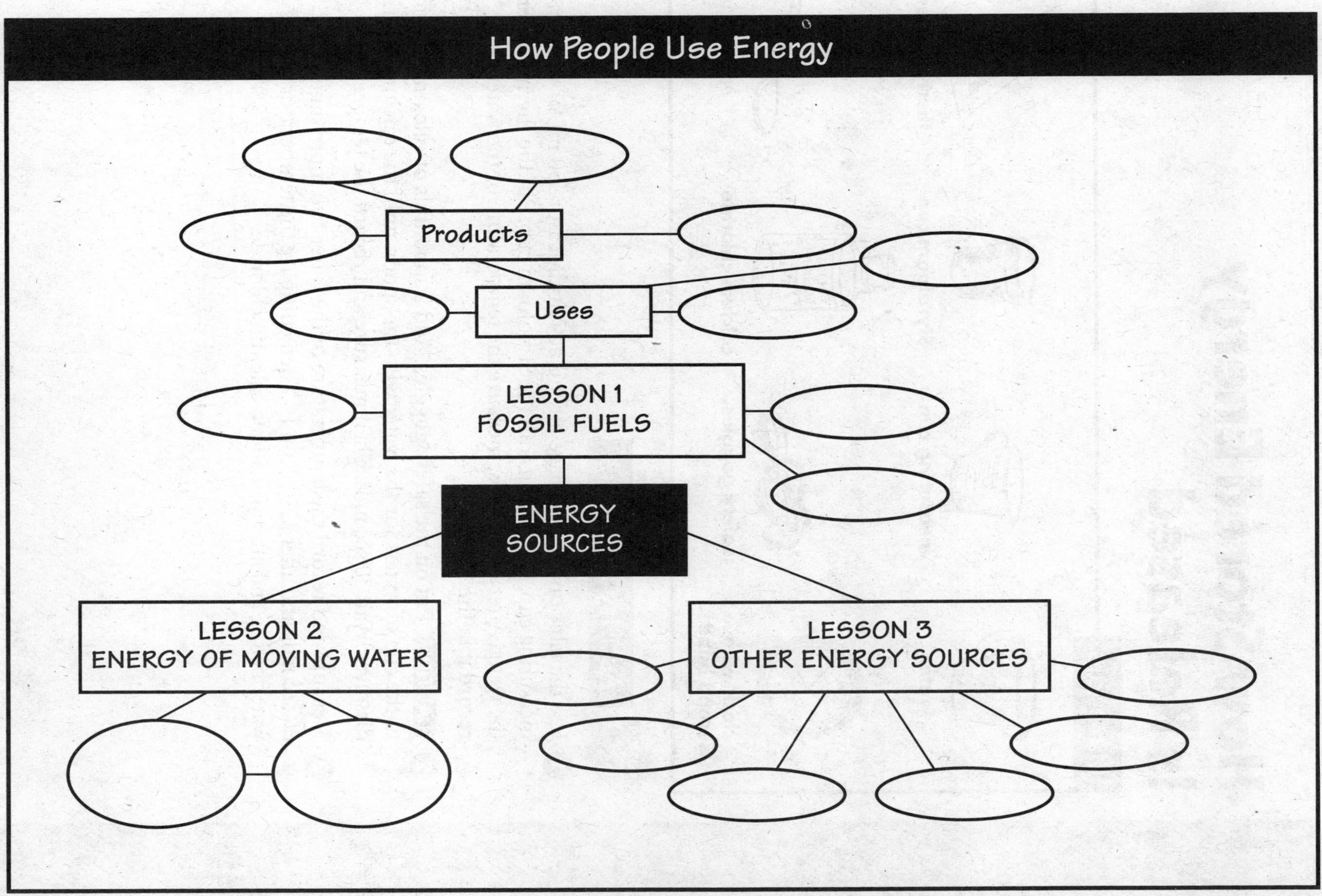

Name ______________________ Date ______________

Name ______________________

Date ______________________

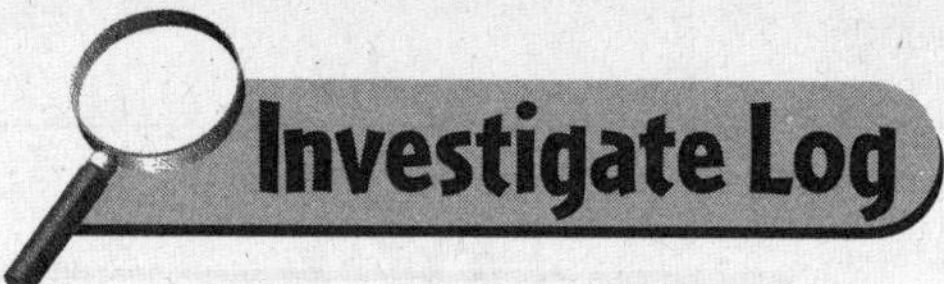

How Stored Energy Is Released

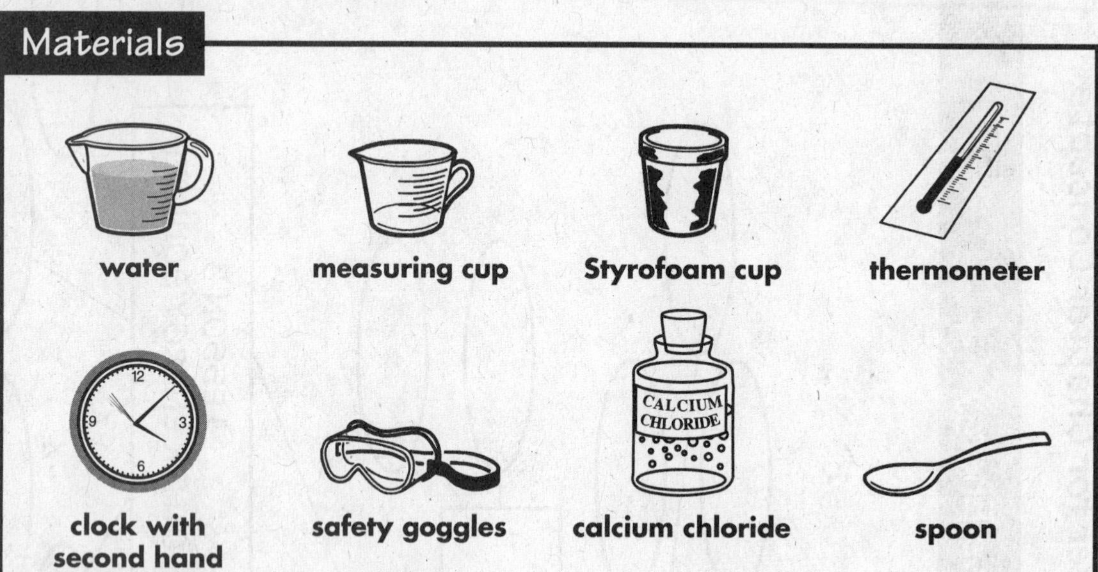

Activity Procedure

1. Use the table on the next page for this activity. Measure 50 mL of water in the measuring cup, and pour it into the Styrofoam cup. Put the thermometer in the water. After 30 seconds, **measure** the temperature of the water and **record** it in the table.
2. CAUTION **Put on the safety goggles.** Add 2 spoonfuls of calcium chloride to the cup of water. Stir the water with the spoon until the calcium chloride dissolves. Wait 30 seconds. Then **measure** and **record** the temperature.
3. **Measure** and **record** the temperature of the water two more times, after 60 seconds and after 120 seconds. Then **compare** the temperature of the water before and after you added calcium chloride.

 Use with pages F96–F97.

Name ______________________

Substance	Temperature
Water without chemical	
Water with chemical after 30 seconds	
Water with chemical after 60 seconds	
Water with chemical after 120 seconds	

Draw Conclusions

1. How did the temperature of the water change when you added calcium chloride? ______________________
2. **Infer** whether the calcium chloride gives off heat or absorbs heat as it dissolves in water. ______________________
3. What do you **infer** might have caused the water temperature to change?
____
____
4. **Scientists at Work** Scientists **observe** and **measure** to gather as much data as they can from an experiment. What did you learn from this experiment about how the chemical energy in some compounds can be released?
____
____

Investigate Further **Hypothesize** what will happen when a different chemical, such as magnesium sulfate (Epsom salts), is placed in water. Then **plan and conduct a simple investigation** to test your hypothesis. ______________________
____

Name ____________________

Date ____________________

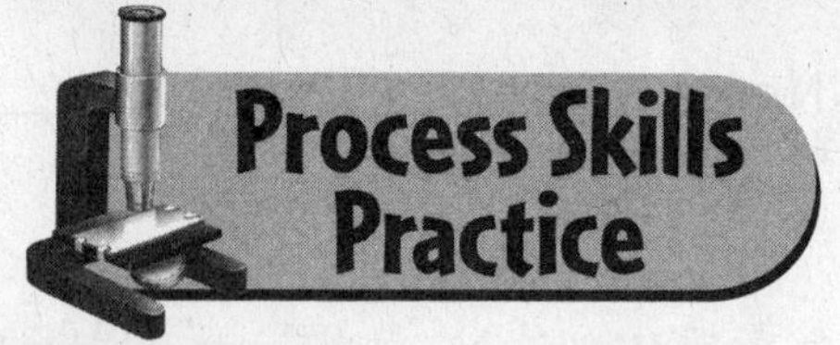

Observe and Measure

When you observe, you use one or more of your senses to perceive properties of objects and events. One type of observing is measuring. When you measure, you are making observations with the aid of instruments, such as stopwatches or thermometers.

Think About Observing and Measuring

Before you can effectively measure anything, you have to know what you will be measuring. Then you choose the appropriate instrument for the type of measuring you will be doing. In the following questions, you will be asked to make those decisions.

1. You are working for a veterinarian. It is your job to feed the dogs. Your instructions are to feed each dog twice a day, one-half cup at each feeding for every 15 pounds that the dog weighs. What observations will you be making, and what measuring instruments will you be using? ____________________

____

____

2. You are part of a mapping expedition that is going into unexplored territory. The expedition plans to take a boat up the river until it reaches the river's source. Your job is to map the course of the river for later expeditions. What observations will you make? What instruments and what units of measure will you use? ____________________

____

____

____

3. A local television station has asked you to be part of a weather watch. They expect you to call the station every day at 4:00 P.M. and tell them the temperature, sky conditions, the wind speed, and any other observation you think might be important. What will you be observing and what instruments will you use?

____

____

____

____

Use with page F97.

Name ____________________

Date ____________________

How Do People Use Fossil Fuels?

Lesson Concept

Coal, natural gas, and petroleum are fossil fuels formed from once-living matter that has been buried for millions of years. Fossil fuels are used to heat homes, move cars, and generate electricity. Because fossil fuels take millions of years to form, they are nonrenewable.

Vocabulary

chemical bonds (F98)

Answer each question with one or more complete sentences.

1. How did energy from sunlight become stored in fossil fuels?

____

____

2. How does burning fuel of any kind turn solar energy into thermal energy?

____

____

____

3. Why are fossil fuels the main source of energy for so many people?

____

4. Where is most of the chemical energy in living organisms stored?

____

____

5. What type of fossil fuel is the main source of energy for transportation?

____

6. Give at least two reasons other sources of energy besides fossil fuels should be used. ______________________________

____

____

Name ______________________

Date ______________________

Water Power

Materials

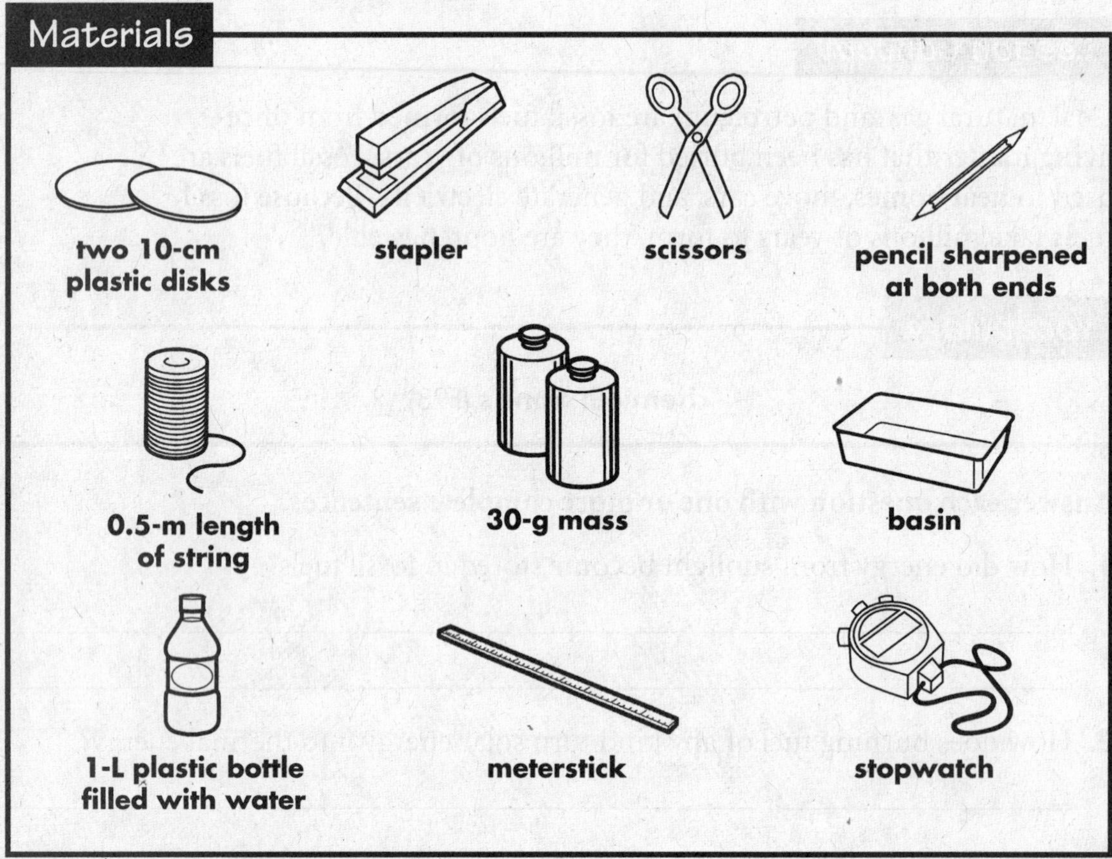

Activity Procedure

1. **CAUTION Be careful when using the scissors.** Staple the plastic disks together near their centers. Using the scissors, cut four 3-cm slits into the disks as shown on page F103. At each slit, fold the disks in opposite directions to form a vane.
2. Again using the scissors, punch a 0.5-cm hole at the center of the disks. Insert the pencil. It will serve as the axle on which the water wheel rotates.
3. Use the scissors to make a smaller hole next to the pencil hole. Insert one end of the string into the hole, and tie a knot in the string to keep it in place. Tie the mass to the other end of the string.
4. Place the basin near the edge of the desk. Hold your water wheel over the basin. Your fingertips should hold the pencil points so the pencil can turn. The mass on the string should hang over the edge of the desk.

Name ______________________

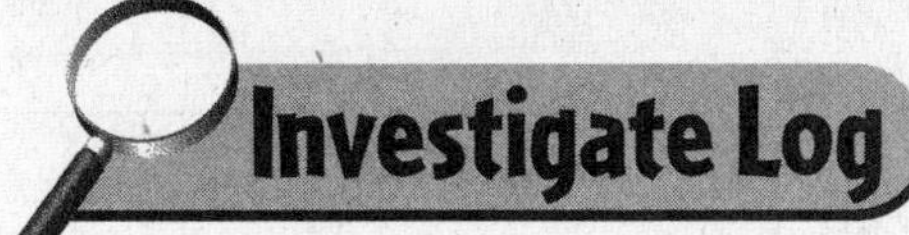

5 Have a partner slowly pour water over the wheel from a height of about 10 cm. Using the stopwatch, **measure** and **record** the time it takes for the mass to reach the level of the desk. Repeat this step several times.

6 Now repeat Steps 4 and 5, but have your partner pour the water from a height of about 20 cm. Again, **measure** and **record** the time it takes for the mass to reach the level of the desk.

Draw Conclusions

1. What **variables** did you **control** in your investigation? ______________________

   What variable did you change? ______________________

2. Recall that the greater the power, the more quickly work is done. Which of your trials produced more power? Why? ______________________

3. **Scientists at Work** Scientists often look beyond the results of an investigation. For example, how does the height from which the water is poured affect the speed at which the water wheel turns? **Plan and conduct a simple investigation** to find out. Be sure to **identify and control variables**, changing only the height from which the water falls. ______________________

Investigate Further **Hypothesize** about the rate of flow and the speed at which the water wheel turns. Then **plan and conduct a simple investigation** to test your hypothesis. Be sure to **identify and control variables**, changing only the rate of flow of the water. ______________________

Name ______________________

Date ______________________

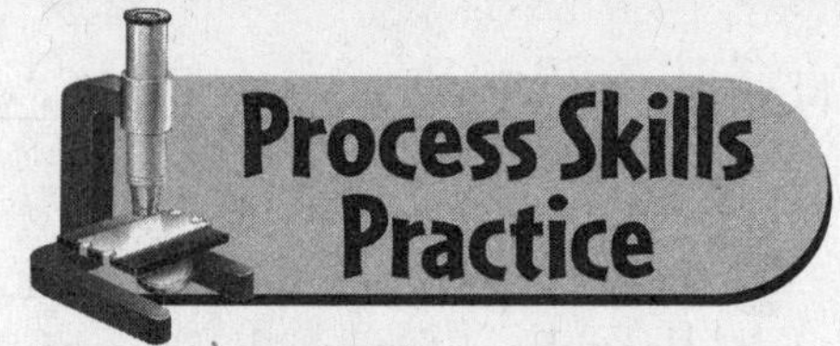

Identify and Control Variables

Identifying and controlling variables involves stating or controlling factors that affect the outcome of an experiment. It is important that only one variable be altered in any given test.

Think About Identifying and Controlling Variables

Read the descriptions of the experiments below. Then identify the variables that affect the outcome of each experiment.

1. People noticed that the number of a certain type of fish that live in a river seemed to have decreased since a dam was built on the river. Scientists who were concerned about the situation captured some of the fish and put them in giant tanks to study them. Both tanks were filled with river water. Plants, rocks, and insects from the river were also introduced into each tank. In one tank the water was 8 meters deep, the average depth of the undammed river. The water in the other tank was 30 meters deep, the depth of the river behind the dam. What is the variable in this experiment, and what could scientists learn by controlling it?

   ____

   ____

2. Many fish died in both tanks in the investigation in Question 1. Trying to determine the cause of the fish deaths, the scientists set up two tanks each with 8 meters of water in them. New fish were introduced, along with stones, insects, and plants from the river. One tank was lit by light that simulated sunshine. The other was kept dark. What is the variable in this experiment, and what could scientists learn by controlling it? ______________________

   ____

   ____

3. Patricia built two water wheels by placing a dozen plastic slats between two plastic coffee-can lids. On one water wheel, she placed the slats so they pointed straight to the center from the edge of the lids. On the other wheel, she placed the slats so they were tilted at a sharp angle from the edge of the coffee-can lids. Using a pencil as the axle, she suspended each wheel over a basin and asked an assistant to pour water over them at a steady rate from 10 centimeters above the wheel. What is the variable in Patricia's experiment, and what could she learn by controlling it? ______________________

   ____

Use with page F103.

Name ______________________

Date ______________________

How Can Moving Water Generate Electricity?

Lesson Concept

An electric generator changes mechanical energy to electric energy. One source of this mechanical energy is moving water. Hydroelectric energy stations use the energy of falling water to spin turbines that generate electricity. The mechanical energy present in ocean tides can also generate electric energy.

Vocabulary

hydroelectric energy (F104) **tidal energy** (F106)

Write a phrase from the chart to complete each sentence .

hydroelectric energy can be traced back to the sun
the potential energy of water under pressure
by holding back water at high tide and letting it fall through turbines at low tide
of falling water to spin turbines that generate electricity
to electric energy
the turbine spins the shaft of an electric generator
can also generate electric energy

1. An electric generator changes mechanical energy ______________.

2. The energy that spins a hydroelectric turbine comes from ______________ ______________________________.

3. Hydroelectric energy stations use the energy ______________ ______________________________.

4. The mechanical energy present in ocean tides ______________ ______________________________.

Name ______________________

Date ______________________

A Steam-Powered Turbine

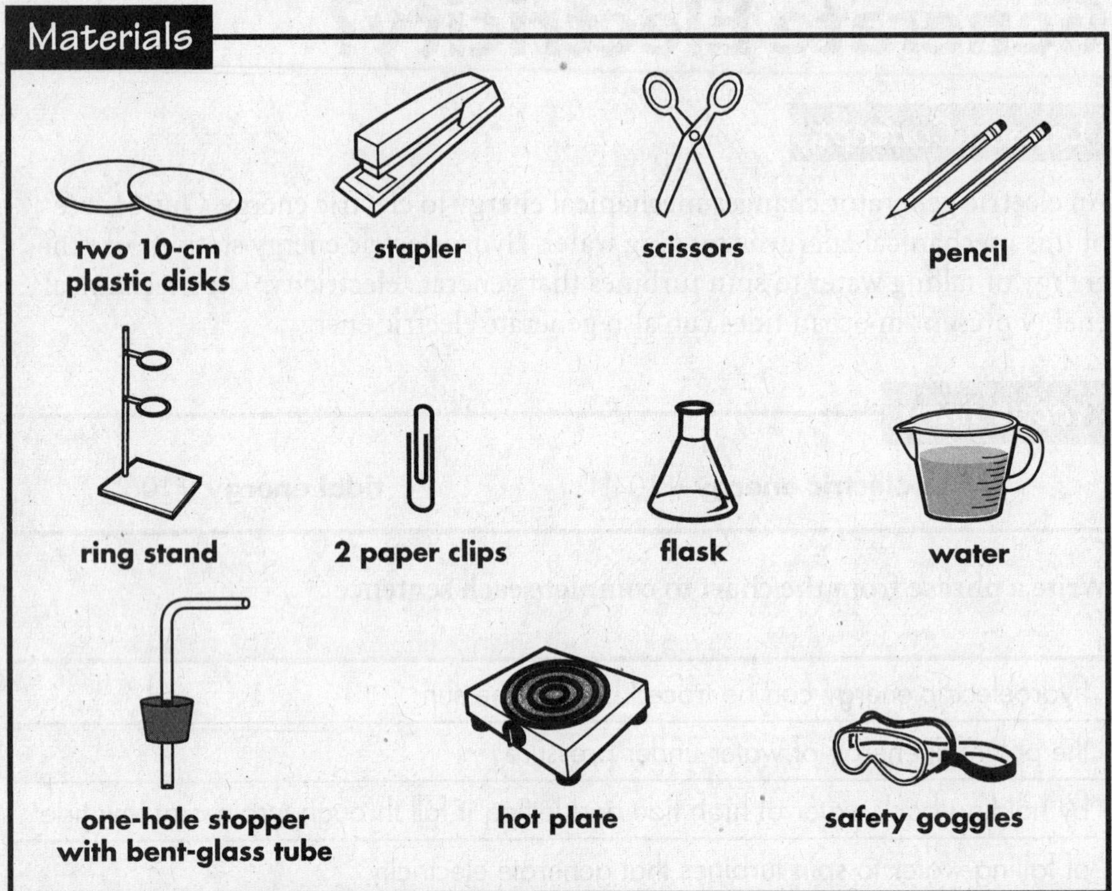

Activity Procedure

1. You can modify the water wheel you made in the last investigation by adding 12 more vanes to the wheel and enlarging the hole. Or you can follow Steps 2 and 3 to make your turbine.

2. CAUTION **Be careful when using the scissors.** Staple the plastic disks together near their centers. Using the scissors, cut sixteen 3-cm slits into the disks as shown on page F109. At each slit, fold the disks in opposite directions to form a vane.

3. Again using the scissors, cut a 0.5-cm round hole in the center of the disks. Make the hole as round as possible. Insert the pencil. It will serve as the axle on which the turbine rotates. The turbine should spin freely on its axle. Now suspend the axle and turbine from the ring stand arm with two bent paper clips.

Name ______________________

4. Fill the flask with water. Put the stopper with the bent glass tube in the flask. Set the flask on the hot plate. Point the open end of the glass tube toward the vanes on the bottom of the turbine.

5. CAUTION **Put on the safety goggles, and use caution around the steam.** Turn on the hot plate. **Observe** and **record** your observations of the turbine as the water begins to boil. Draw a diagram of your turbine to **communicate** your results. Be sure to include labels and arrows to show what happens.

Draw Conclusions

1. **Infer** the source of energy for turning the turbine. ______________________

____

2. **Communicate** in a short paragraph how the energy from the source was changed to turn the turbine. ______________________

____

____

____

3. **Scientists at Work** When scientists **communicate**, they try to show clearly or describe what is happening. In what two ways did you communicate the results of this investigation? Which way was clearer? ______________________

____

____

Investigate Further Plan and conduct a simple investigation to determine how much work your turbine can do. Decide what questions you will need to answer and what equipment you will need to use. ______________________

____

____

Name ______________________

Date ______________________

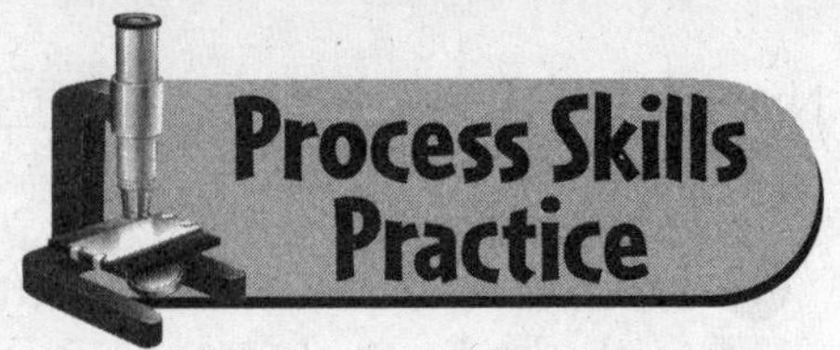

Communicate

Communicating involves the passing on of data. This may be done through spoken or written words, graphs, drawings, diagrams, maps, and charts. Communicating in science means showing the results of an activity in an organized fashion so the results can later be interpreted or the activity can be repeated.

Think About Communicating

In the questions below, you will find four types of information that a scientist might want to communicate. In the space provided, describe what you think would be the best way to communicate the information.

1. A laboratory was studying the nutritional requirements of a new breed of mouse they had developed for cancer research. They discovered that the healthiest mice were those fed a diet consisting of 15 percent protein, 75 percent carbohydrates, and 10 percent fats. What sort of graph, drawing, or chart would best communicate these results? ______________________

____

2. A group of scientists was surveying a large open area for the placement of windmills. They wanted to be sure each windmill would receive the greatest amount of wind possible, so they placed wind vanes in the area and kept track of the wind speed and direction over a period of six months. Then they took the average for each position. What would be the best way for them to communicate their results? ______________________

____

3. A fisher was keeping track of the height of the tides in a certain area as part of a study being done at a local university. He drove a long measuring stick into the ground at the water's edge at low tide. Then, every hour, he checked the water's depth on the measuring stick. What kind of graphic would best communicate what he discovered? ______________________

____

4. Scientists were studying the relative top running speeds of animals in East Africa. They clocked a cheetah at 100 kilometers per hour (km/hr), a gazelle at 72 km/hr, a wildebeest at 36 km/hr, a leopard at 65 km/hr, and a jackal at 40 km/hr. What would be the best way to communicate this information?

____

Use with page F109.

Name ______________________

Date ______________________

What Other Sources of Energy Do People Use?

Lesson Concept

In addition to fossil fuels and hydroelectric energy, the United States uses small amounts of energy from other sources. These sources include biomass, nuclear energy, wind, geothermal energy, and solar energy. Researchers continue to work on new sources of energy, such as fusion.

Vocabulary

nuclear energy (F110) **biomass** (F110) **solar energy** (F111)
fusion energy (F112) **geothermal energy** (F111)

List the advantages and disadvantages of each type of energy.

Type of Energy	Advantages	Disadvantages
Biomass		
Nuclear		
Solar		
Wind		
Geothermal		
Ocean Thermal		
Hydrogen		

Name ____________________

Date ____________________

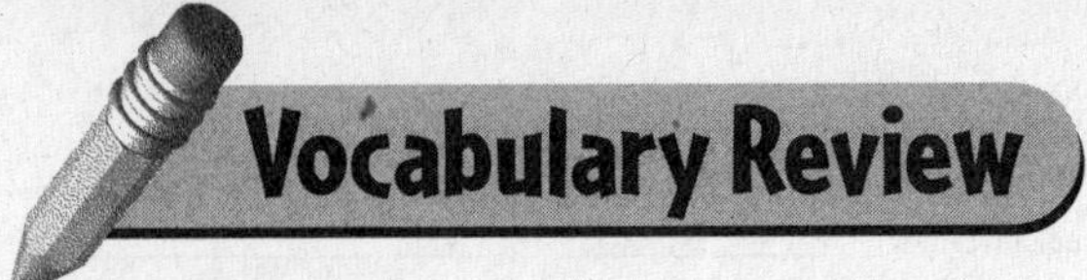

Recognize Vocabulary

Choose one of the words from the box to answer each riddle.

biomass	**nuclear energy**
hydroelectric energy	**solar energy**
geothermal energy	**chemical bonds**
fusion energy	**tidal energy**

1. I'm alive now, or I was fairly recently. Burning me doesn't release a lot of energy, but I'm free or very inexpensive, so a lot of people use me. What am I?

____

2. I'm not a wallet, and I'm not a purse or a backpack. I'm not a bank account, but I'm the thing that all living things keep their "saved-up" energy in. What am I?

____

3. Look for me at Niagara Falls or Glen Canyon Dam! I'm on the Missouri River and the Tennessee River, too. What am I? ____________________

4. Atoms are very tiny, but if you split them apart, you'll get me, the most powerful source of thermal energy on Earth. What am I? ____________________

5. If you want to get your energy directly from the source, you'll come to me. Too many cloudy days, however, could make it hard for you to get enough of me. What am I? ____________________

6. Dig deep to find me, preferably near a volcano or an earthquake zone. What am I? ____________________

7. I result from something that happens twice a day. See you at the beach! What am I? ____________________

8. I'm in the experimental stages. Scientists know how I work, but the heat needed to get me started is so high that it burns all known materials. What am I?

____

Use with pages F96–F113.